ELEGANT ENGLISH
The Charlotte Stout Hooker
Collection of British Porcelain
and Related Ceramics

ELEGANT ENGLISH

The Charlotte Stout Hooker Collection of British Porcelain and Related Ceramics

Letitia Roberts

DIXON GALLERY AND GARDENS, MEMPHIS

SPONSORS

ARMSTRONG RELOCATION & COMPANIES

OAKSEDGE *Office Campus*

Lucy M. Buchanan
Mary and John Dicken
Katherine and John Dobbs
Karen and Dr. Preston H. Dorsett
Liz and Thomas C. Farnsworth, Jr.
Allison and Thomas M. Garrott III and Family
Rose M. Johnston
Nell R. Levy
Mabel and Phillip H. McNeill, Sr.
Nancy and D. Stephen Morrow
Irene and Joseph Orgill III
Gwen and C. Penn Owen III
Ann and Stephen C. Reynolds
Linda W. Rhea
Christine and Daniel Richards
Susan and Charles F. Smith, Jr.
Marsha and Henri L. Wedell
Adele O. and J. Beasley Wellford
Barbara C. and Lewis C. Williamson, Jr.
Mary and Charles L. Wurtzburger
The Antiquarians

This publication was produced in conjunction with the exhibition *Everyday English: The Charlotte Stout Hooker Collection of British Porcelain*, on view at the Dixon Gallery and Gardens, Memphis, from July 31 through October 9, 2016.

© 2016 by Dixon Gallery and Gardens, Memphis

All rights reserved. No part of this publication may be reproduced or transmitted in any form or by any means, electronic or mechanical, including photocopy, recording, or any information storage and retrieval system, without permission in writing from the publisher.

Dixon Gallery and Gardens
4339 Park Avenue
Memphis, Tennessee 38117
(901) 761-5250
www.dixon.org

Library of Congress Control Number: 2016934503
ISBN: 978-0-9972445-0-2

Printed and bound in the U.S.A.

PAGE I: Minton porcelain saucer dish painted with a radiating guilloche pattern, 1800–1805 (cat. 240, detail)

PAGE II: Grainger, Lee & Co. Worcester porcelain blue-ground shell-shaped dessert dish, 1820–1830 (cat. 202, detail)

PAGE V: Derby porcelain white figure of Kitty Clive, 1750–1751 (cat. 74, detail)

PAGE VI: Derby porcelain pastoral group, 1771–1775 (cat. 85, detail)

PAGE XVIII: Worcester porcelain 'wet blue'–ground 'Fable' plate, ca. 1770 (cat. 159)

PAGE XIX: Worcester porcelain 'wet blue'–ground 'Fable' plate, ca. 1770 (cat. 160)

Unless otherwise indicated below, all photography is by Baxter Buck, courtesy of the Dixon Gallery and Gardens. All works of art in this publication have been reproduced with the permission of the owners.

Figs. 1, 2, 7, 14, and 19: Stout and Hooker Archives; Figs. 3 and 4: Courtesy of Martha H. Cummings; Fig. 9: © Ashmolean Museum, University of Oxford. Reference images accompanying catalogue entries: Cat. 13: Courtesy of The Philadelphia Print Shop, Ltd.; Cat. 41: The Royal Horticultural Society, Lindley Library; Cats. 49, 59, 79, 85: The Metropolitan Museum of Art, New York; Cats. 58, 88, 90, 91, 92: © The Trustees of the British Museum; Cat. 74: Private collection; Cat. 159: Courtesy of Errol Manners; Cat. 198: Courtesy of Baylor University, Crouch Fine Arts Library, Spencer Sheet Music Collection; Cat. 276: Mzilikazi1939, Wikimedia Commons, https://commons.wikimedia.org/wiki/File:Dayes_1799.l.jpg; Cat. 338: Courtesy of Dr. C.J.A. Jörg through the Groninger Museum, Groningen. Photographer: John Stoel, Haren.

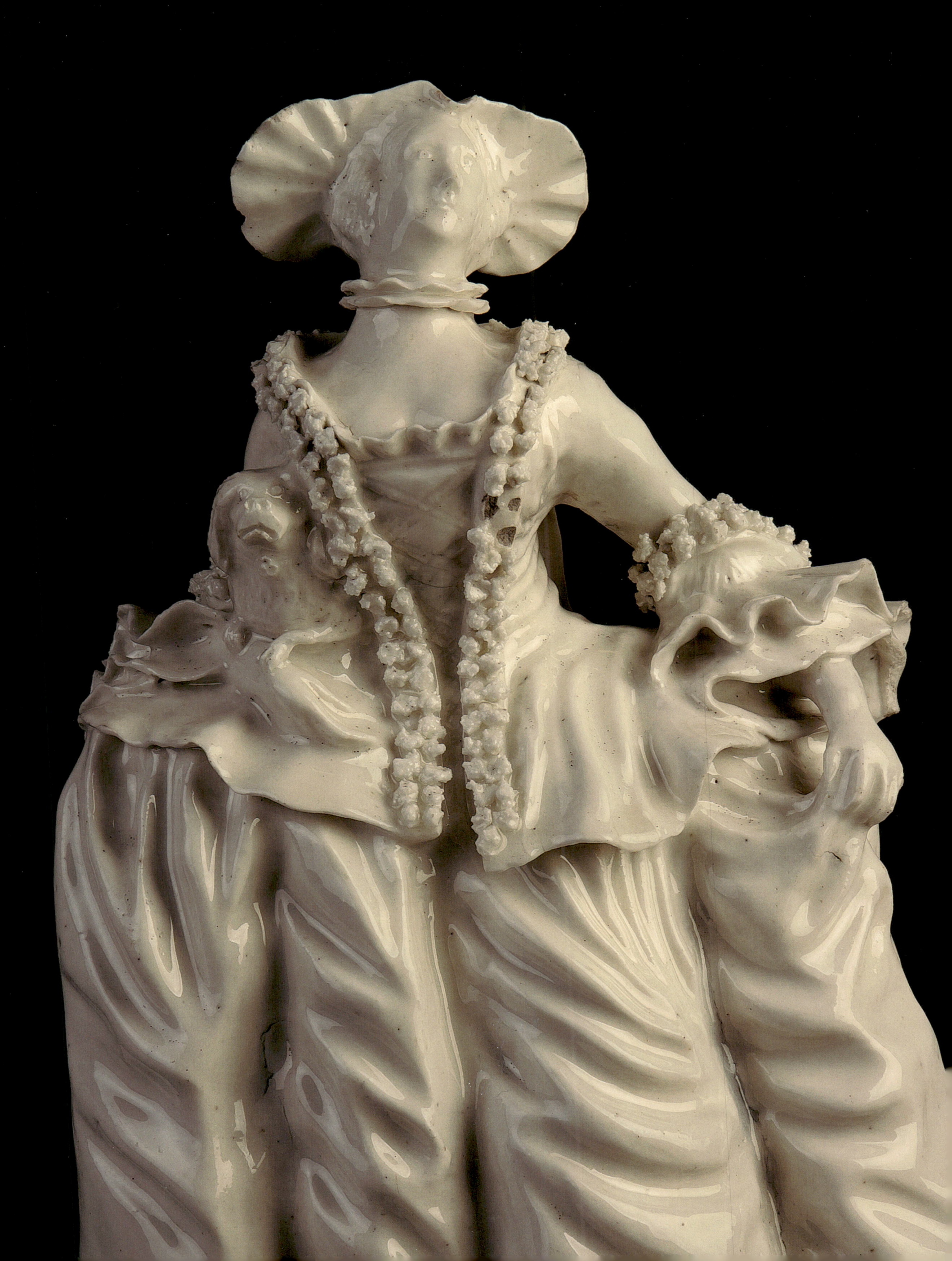

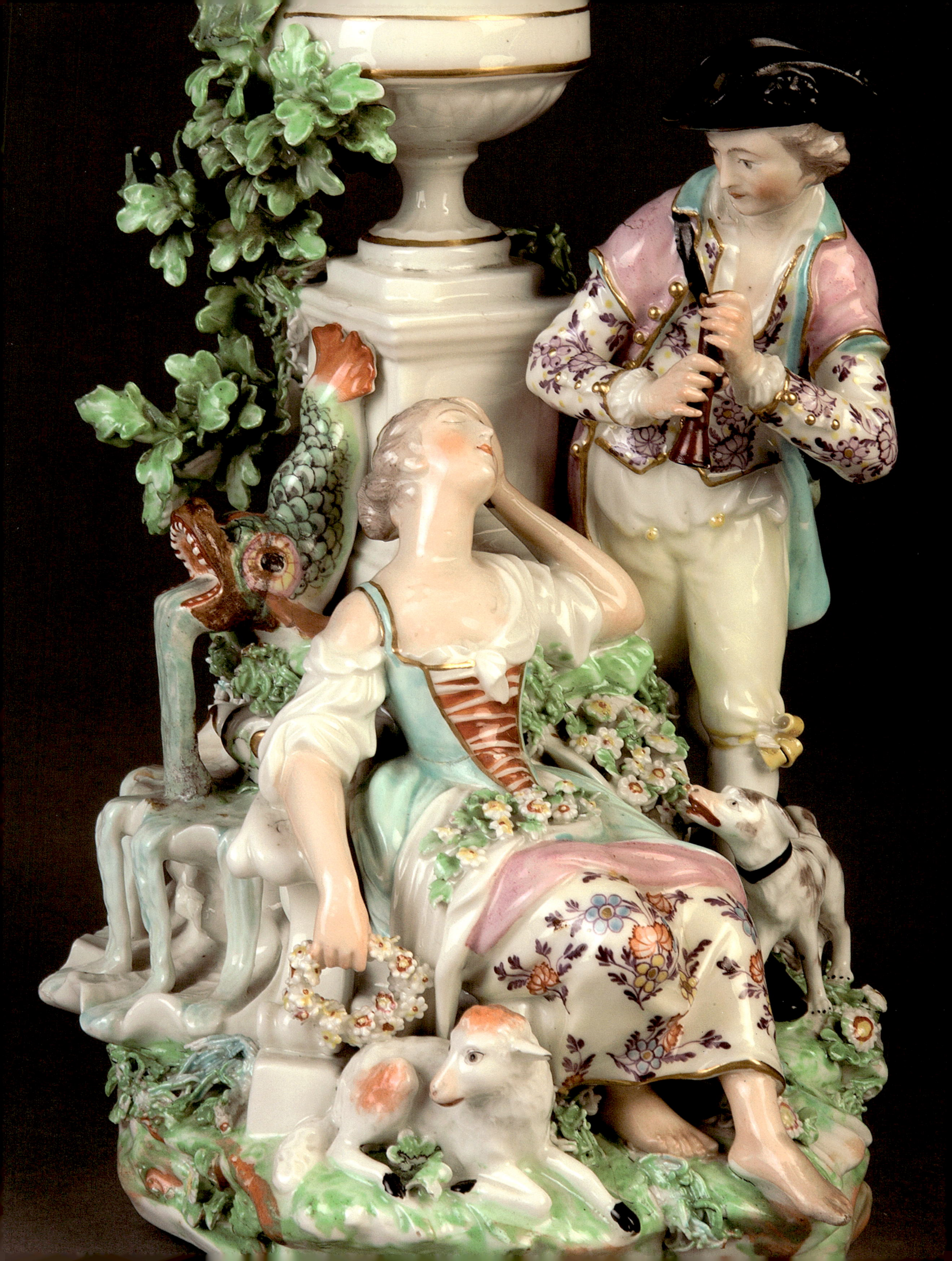

CONTENTS

Foreword *by Kevin Sharp*
ix

Preface
xi

Acknowledgments
xv

Annual Adventures,
Perennial Possibilities
The Story of the Charlotte
Stout Hooker Collection
1

Catalogue of the Collection
English Porcelain 31
Welsh Porcelain 108
Scottish Porcelain 111
English Pottery 111
Welsh Pottery 120
Chinese Ceramics 121
German Porcelain 125
Italian Porcelain 127
Other Continental Porcelain Factories 128
The Imitators 131

APPENDIX I
British Porcelain Factories Represented in
the Charlotte Stout Hooker Collection
133

APPENDIX II
Chronology of Acquisitions in the
Charlotte Stout Hooker Collection
135

Bibliography
143

Index
152

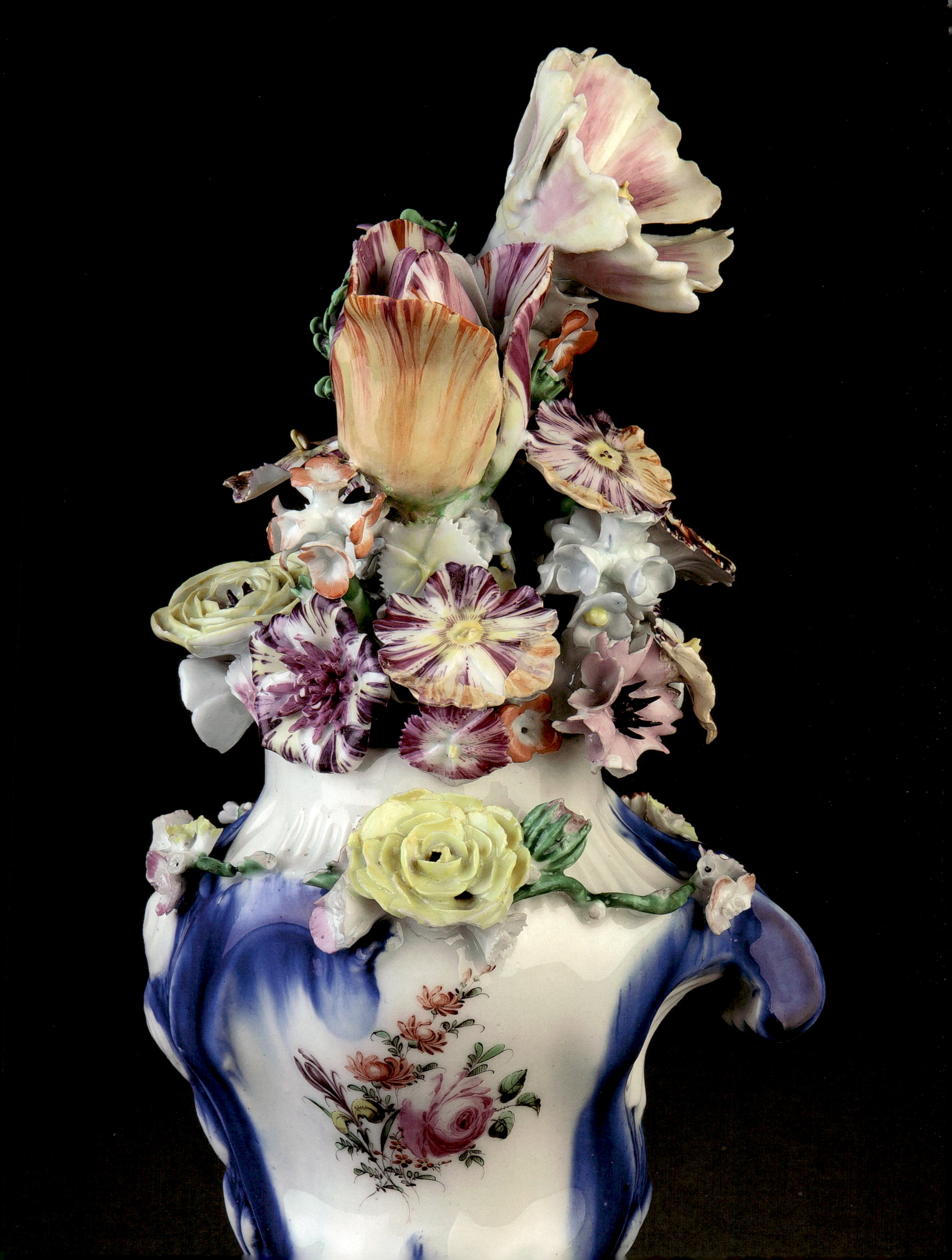

CATALOGUE OF
THE COLLECTION

NOTE

The catalogue has been arranged roughly chronologically, first by factory and then within the factory's production, but grouped by style and decoration, with wares generally preceding figures. Inscriptions and factory marks have been transcribed as closely as possible to their original appearance, using upper and lower case, italics for script, and so on. Any piece with an accession number between 2008.DA.2.1 and .209 or a purchase date prior to 1964 was initially in the collection of Warda Stevens Stout and was included in the gift of her British porcelain to her daughter Charlotte Stout Hooker in 1964. All references to Warda Stevens Stout and Charlotte Stout Hooker have been abbreviated to their initials: WSS and CSH. In 1989 Charlotte Stout Hooker lent 106 pieces from her collection to an exhibition at the Dixon Gallery and Gardens in Memphis, Tennessee: *British Treasures from Private Collections*, including "English Porcelain: The Hooker Collection," November 12–December 21, 1989. This exhibition is referred to under the "Exhibited" headings as "Dixon Gallery and Gardens, 1989."

PRECEDING PAGES Two Glamorgan Pottery pearlware small plates, 1825–1835 (cat. 330).

ABOVE Coalport porcelain coffee cup, 1820–1825 (cat. 233, detail of the interior).

ENGLISH PORCELAIN
Bow · *London, 1744–1776*

1

Bow White Prunus-Molded Baluster-Form Mug, ca. 1753
HEIGHT: 4¾ in. (12.1 cm)
MARK: None
PROVENANCE: Marshall Field & Company, Chicago, Illinois, 1946
ACCESSION NUMBER: 2008.DA.2.3

2

Bow White Prunus-Molded Teabowl, ca. 1753
DIAMETER: 3¼ in. (8.3 cm)
MARK: None
PROVENANCE: Malcolm Franklin, Inc., Chicago, Illinois, 1948 (purchased with its saucer, which in her Notebook WSS admitted to having broken)
ACCESSION NUMBER: 2008.DA.2.4

3

Bow Prunus-Molded Teabowl Enameled with 'Famille-Rose' Flowers, 1753–1758
DIAMETER: 2¹³⁄₁₆ in. (7.2 cm)
MARK: None
PROVENANCE: Mrs. Lilian B. Little, Oak Park, Illinois, 1947 (originally with a saucer, broken by WSS)
ACCESSION NUMBER: 2008.DA.2.5

4

Bow Prunus-Molded Plate Enameled with 'Famille-Rose' Flowers, 1755–1758
DIAMETER: 9⅛ in. (23.2 cm)
MARK: None
PROVENANCE: Mrs. Lilian B. Little, Oak Park, Illinois, 1948
ACCESSION NUMBER: 2008.DA.2.2

5

Bow Plate Painted with the 'Island House' Pattern, 1752–1756
Taken from a Chinese porcelain *famille-verte* original of the Kangxi Period (1661–1722)
DIAMETER: 8⅞ in. (22.6 cm)
MARK: None
PROVENANCE: Winifred Williams Antiques, Eastbourne, Sussex, England, 1954
ACCESSION NUMBER: 2008.DA.2.7

6

Bow Plate Enameled with 'Famille-Rose' Garden Vignettes, 1755–1760
DIAMETER: 9¼ in. (23.5 cm)
MARK: None
PROVENANCE: Taskey's Antiques, Chicago, Illinois, 1951
ACCESSION NUMBER: 2008.DA.2.1

7

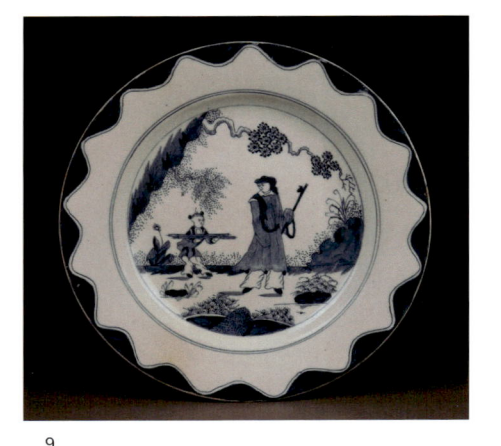

Bow Printed and 'Famille-Rose'-Enameled Chinoiserie Octagonal Plate, ca. 1765
WIDTH: 7½ in. (19.1 cm)
MARK: None
PROVENANCE: Winifred Williams Antiques, Eastbourne, Sussex, England, 1954
ACCESSION NUMBER: 2008.DA.2.16

8

Bow Lobed Sauceboat Painted in Underglaze Blue with the 'Desirable Residence' Pattern, 1755–1758
LENGTH: 6⅛ in. (15.6 cm)
MARK: None
PROVENANCE: Taskey's Antiques, Chicago, Illinois, 1948
ACCESSION NUMBER: 2008.DA.2.10

9

Bow Plate Painted in Underglaze Blue with the 'Image' Pattern, ca. 1760
DIAMETER: 8¹³⁄₁₆ in. (22.4 cm)
MARK: None
PROVENANCE: William H. Lautz, New York City, 1948
ACCESSION NUMBER: 2008.DA.2.11

This pattern has come to be known in the vernacular as the 'Golfer and Caddy' pattern; however, 'Image' was the name assigned to this pattern by the Bow factory, as evidenced by a reference in the 1756 Memorandum Book of John Bowcock, the clerk in Bow's Cornhill warehouse: "Apl. 28. Lord Southwell. Mr. Heylin has promised him to make an oval tureen, the image pattern, and to be done in 6 weeks without fail. Think of the Chinese head for Mr. Weatherby."[1] Edward Heylyn (1695–1765), a clothier from Bristol, was one of the Bow factory's five founding partners, along with Thomas Frye (1710–1762), an Irish painter and mezzotint engraver; George Arnold (1691–1751), a wealthy alderman of the City of London; and John Weatherby (d. 1762) and John Crowther (d. 1790), who were partners in a glassworks and also had a wholesale porcelain and pottery business. It has been suggested that "the Chinese head" in this Memorandum Book entry may refer to the model of the Mongolian bust, an example of which is cat. 16.

1. Cited in Adams and Redstone 1991, Appendix IV, p. 212; and Bradshaw 1992, pp. 56 and 245.

10

Bow Cylindrical Mug Painted in Underglaze Blue with Oriental Flowering Plants and Rockwork, ca. 1770
HEIGHT: 5⅝ in. (14.3 cm)
MARK: None
PROVENANCE: Henry Stern, New Orleans, Louisiana, 1946 (who had purchased it in England earlier that year as Lowestoft, with the advice and authentication of William B. Honey)
ACCESSION NUMBER: 2008.DA.2.12

While this mug is not a piece of Lowestoft porcelain, as supposedly affirmed in 1946 by William B. Honey (1889–1956), who was a prolific author and a knowledgeable and respected Keeper of Ceramics at the Victoria and Albert Museum (1938–1950), its certainty as a piece of Bow has also been questioned by the current authority on the Bow factory, Anton Gabszewicz. In correspondence dated September 8, 2015, he comments: "the grooved loop handle with a heart-shaped or triangular terminal is generally Bow, I cannot think of this at any other factory. The colour of the blue and the granular appearance of the paste together with the form all say Bow to me, but very late." With respect to the decoration, however, he mentions elements currently attributed to the factory at Isleworth: the leaves, but more especially the border. Two porcelain bowls with an interior border identical to that on this mug are illustrated by Roger Massey and colleagues in a section titled "Possible Isleworth Pieces," which includes pieces of various shapes, all decorated in underglaze blue, with "characteristics which suggest a possible Isleworth attribution but for which direct archaeological evidence is currently lacking."[1] There is still much to be discovered about the Isleworth factory, but if indeed the bowls are determined to be Isleworth (probably ca. 1770–1780), the most likely explanation for the identical borders is that either shortly before or after the Bow factory closed in 1776, the painter of the mug left Bow and gained employment at the Isleworth factory, taking with him a specific style and repertoire of motifs.

1. Massey, Pearce, and Howard 2003, p. 103; see the two bowls on p. 103 (DIAM. 6⁵⁄₁₆ in. [16 cm]) and p. 109 (DIAM. 7⅞ in. [20 cm]).

11

Bow Powdered-Blue Octagonal Small Plate, ca. 1760
WIDTH: 6⁹⁄₁₆ in. (16.7 cm)
MARK: Pseudo-Chinese four-character mark in underglaze blue
PROVENANCE: William H. Lautz, New York City, 1948
EXHIBITED: Dixon Gallery and Gardens, 1989
ACCESSION NUMBER: 2008.DA.2.13

10  11  12

12

Bow Oval Dish Molded and Painted in Underglaze Blue with Grapevines, 1765–1770

LENGTH: 10½ in. (26.6 cm)
MARK: Pseudo-Chinese six-character mark in underglaze blue
PROVENANCE: John's Antiques, Chicago, Illinois, 1948
ACCESSION NUMBER: 2008.DA.2.14

13

Bow Botanical Dish Painted with a 'Cotton Tree' Specimen, 1756–1760

Taken from an engraving in Maria Sibylla Merian, *De Metamorphosis insectorum Surinamensium of te verandering der Surinaamsche insecten*, pl. 10
DIAMETER: 8 5/16 in. (21.1 cm)
MARK: None, but the specimen name inscribed on the large leaf
PROVENANCE: William H. Lautz, New York City, 1952
LITERATURE: C.M. Scott and G.R. Scott 1961, p. 198 and pl. 159, no. 547
ACCESSION NUMBER: 2008.DA.2.6

According to Elizabeth Adams and David Redstone, "Botanical-style painting on plates was done at Bow to a greater extent than is generally realized. Three plate shapes were used, [however, the lobed circular dish, as in the present example] is unusual for Bow and ... may have been made as a replacement for a Chelsea one, but the number of surviving Bow botanical plates makes it virtually certain that it was a standard product. That type of decoration was done from the middle 1750s, but for how long is uncertain, [as] no dated examples are recorded."[1] Surely Bow was inspired to try its hand at botanical decoration on the success of the Chelsea 'Hans Sloane' botanical plates that appeared around 1753 (see cat. 41). While Sally Kevill-Davies has discussed the background and identified many of the print sources for the Chelsea plates (see cat. 41),[2] no such attention has been paid to the sources for the botanical decoration on Bow. However, the rare inscription on the large leaf of the specimen on the present dish, identifying it as a 'Cotton Tree,' led to the discovery of its source print in Maria Sibylla Merian's *De Metamorphosis insectorum Surinamensium of te verandering der Surinaamsche insecten*.[3]

Much has been written in recent years about Maria Sibylla Merian (1647–1717), whose talents remained almost unrecognized for well over two centuries, in part because she was a female artist, but perhaps also because she was more of an entomologist than a botanist, and "although she may have regarded plants firstly as sources of nourishment for her beloved insects, she drew them with the same care."[4] The daughter of a Swiss topographical artist and engraver, she grew up in the silk-manufacturing city of Frankfurt am Main, where she became fascinated with insects by observing the metamorphosis of silkworms from caterpillars into silken balls out of which emerged little moths. In 1665 she married one of her stepfather's former apprentices, Johann Andreas Graff (1636–1701), "perhaps more a marriage of convenience than a romantic attachment, [but] it at least offered [her] the prospect of working professionally with her spouse."[5] The couple moved to Nuremberg, Graff's native city, but his absence of professional success as an engraver and publisher forced (or perhaps enabled) Maria to utilize her own talents to help support them and eventually their two daughters. She taught embroidery and painting and actually published her own books of flower designs while continuing her studies of insects. In 1681, when her stepfather died, Maria returned to Frankfurt with her two daughters to help her then-impoverished mother, but the distance from her husband precipitated the gradual disintegration of her own marriage, and in 1685 Maria took her mother and daughters to West Friesland in the Netherlands to join her widowed brother in a colony of Labadists (followers of Jean de Labadie [1610–1674], a French Jesuit priest, who became a member of the Reformed Church in 1650 and founded his pious community in 1669). While living in the Labadist colony, Maria was introduced to a new panoply of exotic plants, animals, and insects brought back from an earlier Labadist mission to the Dutch colony of Suriname (Netherlands Guiana) in northern South America, and she was determined to explore them further. After her mother's death in 1690, Maria and her daughters moved to Amsterdam, where she continued to give painting lessons, deal in paints, and paint on commission, earning enough money to embark at age fifty-two in 1699, with her younger daughter Dorothea, on the perilous trip to Suriname. They remained there for two years before a case of malaria forced their return. But "her dream had been fulfilled, and she brought home a wealth of recorded observations, [finished drawings on vellum] and specimens. Encouraged to publish her findings, she spared no expense in preparing the original paintings,"[6] which resulted in her masterwork, *De Metamorphosis insectorum Surinamensium*, "the first work to illustrate the close association of certain tropical insects and plants"[7] while indistinguishably blending science and art.

But the story does not end there—for there is still the matter of the Bow connection. After publishing the Suriname volume in Latin and Dutch in Amsterdam, Maria attempted to publish it in English in London, and to that end contacted a London apothecary, James Petiver (1658/63–1718), whose own botanical publications included a book on the medicinal herbs of Peru. Petiver, presumably sensing competition, turned out to be less than helpful, and the Suriname book did not attract an English publisher. Maria's watercolors for the book, however, did attract the attention of the doctor and scientist Richard Mead (1673–1754), whose massive collections of books and manuscripts, drawings, gems, and coins were sold at auction at Samuel Baker's in London in 1754 and 1755. Lot 66 in the 1755 sale, described as: "Ditto [a capital collection] of exotics, flowers and insects by Merian, 95 in number, likewise elegantly bound in

ENGLISH PORCELAIN: BOW 33

13

14

Maria Sibylla Merian, *Cotton Plant*, 1726. Plate 10 from *Dissertatio de generatione et metamorphosibus insectorum Surinamensium*. Engraving by J. Mulder, P. Sluyter, and D. Stoopendaal.

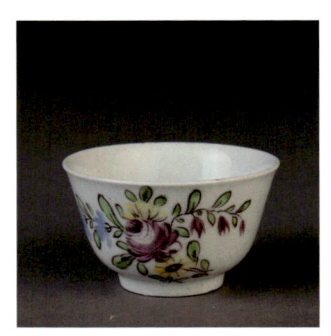

2 vol.,"[8] realized the then-enormous sum of £158 11s, and was acquired on behalf of King George II (1683–1760) for the Royal Library, now at Windsor Castle.

Richard Mead's interest in Merian's work can only be surmised: he had studied in Leiden and Utrecht while she was living in Holland, and he may have learned of her research and related artistic documentation at that time. Later in London, as both a doctor and a formidable collector, he encountered his singular rival, the aforementioned Sir Hans Sloane (1660–1753), and "curiously enough, both Mead and Sloane [were able to acquire] complete sets of watercolour originals for the plates in the Surinam book. Whether this was a mere coincidence, or due to an ambitious sense of rivalry between the two, [what is most] puzzling is the fact that there should be no fewer than two sets of the original watercolours by Maria Sibylla for the plates in the Surinam book in London, [although] the existence of multiple copies of the watercolours may be explained by her intention of selling them to raise money, but also as master copies for the colouring of the prints."[9]

Further research will be required to determine the connection between the Suriname book and the Bow factory. Given the identifying inscription "Cotton Tree" on this dish, it is probable that the painter was using a printed source rather than a watercolor. While Sir Hans Sloane's botanical volumes were available as sources for the Chelsea factory artists, it is unlikely that they would have been accessible to the rival Bow factory artists as well. It is tempting to speculate that, in the spirit of competition, Richard Mead permitted the Bow painters to use his own botanical books. However, he died in 1754 and his library was sold at precisely the time Bow initiated its botanical decoration. At Sir Hans Sloane's death in 1753, his library and collections (numbering 71,000 pieces) were bequeathed to King George II for the nation, and formed the foundation of the British Museum, which was opened to the public in January 1759. All of these events and dates preclude Bow's use of the Suriname book belonging to either of the two great London doctor-collectors. The remaining possibility is that, although the Suriname book was not published in London, copies or individual prints from it must have existed in other local collections, purchased either in London or more likely in Amsterdam, and Bow, detecting a source of decoration not used at Chelsea, seized the opportunity to offer to an eager public a different and probably less costly line of botanical wares.

1. Adams and Redstone 1981, p. 118.
2. Kevill-Davies 2015.
3. Initially published in Amsterdam in 1705 with sixty engraved plates and text in Latin and Dutch; an expanded edition was published in 1719 with twelve additional engravings.
4. Rücker and Stearn 1982, vol. 2, p. xi.
5. Jacob-Hanson 2000, p. 177.
6. Ibid., p. 181.
7. Rücker and Stearn 1982, vol. 2, p. xi.
8. Ibid., p. 41.
9. Ibid., pp. 42–43.

14
Bow Child's Toy Teabowl Enameled with Flowers, ca. 1765
DIAMETER: 2 in. (5.1 cm)
MARK: None
PROVENANCE: Collection of Sigmund John Katz, Covington, Louisiana: gift to WSS as "a typical example of the Longton Hall palette" (date of gift unknown)
ACCESSION NUMBER: 2008.DA.2.15

15
Bow Pine Cone–Molded Teacup and Saucer after a Worcester Porcelain Original, ca. 1770
DIAMETERS: 3½ and 5¹¹⁄₁₆ in. (8.8 and 14.4 cm)
MARKS: Anchor and dagger mark on the cup and numeral 85 on the saucer in iron-red
PROVENANCE: William H. Lautz, New York City, 1949
ACCESSION NUMBER: 2008.DA.2.17a, b

16
Bow White Bust of a Mongolian, ca. 1750
HEIGHT: 10¼ in. (26 cm)
MARK: None
PROVENANCE: Winifred Williams Antiques, Eastbourne, Sussex, England, 1953
EXHIBITED: Dixon Gallery and Gardens, 1989
ACCESSION NUMBER: 2008.DA.2.18

An entry in John Bowcock's 1756 Memorandum Book, discussed in cat. 9, may refer to the model of this chinoiserie bust, so uncharacteristic of the Bow figural repertoire. The inspiration for the bust and its pair, which in early literature were referred to occasionally as 'The Roumanian (or Hungarian) Minister and His Wife,' remains elusive. Dr. H. Bellamy Gardner mentions and illustrates a pair of busts of these models along with a pair of wood "reproduction rococo wall brackets in which Mongolian heads of the same general expression were used as finials, but [he had been] unable to trace originals in contemporary carvings or engravings."[1] A further source, suggested in the note to a pair of Bow Mongolian busts from the collection of Mrs. Sheffield,[2] was a pair of Meissen porcelain 'grotesque' Chinese busts modeled by Johann Joachim Kändler (1706–1775) in 1732,[3] but they are completely unrelated to the Bow busts in both style and spirit, and their rarity makes it highly unlikely that they would have been made available to the Bow factory in London. It is most probable that the inspiration for these busts came from one of the prolific chinoiserie prints or drawings of the period, still to be discovered.

1. Gardner 1929, p. 26 and pl. VII.
2. Sold at Sotheby's, London, April 1, 1952, lot 121.
3. Illustrated in Zimmermann 1926, pl. 24.

15

16

17

17

Bow Figure of an Actor, Probably David Garrick,
1750–1752
- Attributed to the 'Muses Modeller'
- HEIGHT: 8¼ in. (21 cm)
- MARK: None
- PROVENANCE: Collection of Mrs. Kenneth T. Knoblock, sold at Sotheby's, London, October 18, 1955, lot 117; James A. Lewis & Son, Inc., New York City, 1955; Collection of Sigmund John Katz, Covington, Louisiana, 1956
- EXHIBITED: Dixon Gallery and Gardens, 1989
- ACCESSION NUMBER: 2008.DA.2.20

It is now accepted that this figure depicts the celebrated English actor David Garrick (1717–1779), who was also a playwright, producer, and theater manager, and who arguably had the greatest influence over the British theater during the eighteenth century. Raymond Yarbrough discusses and illustrates the Bow figure's likeness to the actor beside a portrait of Garrick, ca. 1763, by Johan Zoffany (1733–1810).[1] As pointed out by Anton Gabszewicz, the Bow figure's costume

> is also quite similar to that worn by Garrick in the part of "Macbeth," which he first played [at Drury Lane] in 1744; see a picture in the catalogue *Pictures in the Garrick Club* by Geoffrey Ashton, plate 253. It had been suggested previously that this figure represents Garrick in the role of "Archer" in *The Beaux' Stratagem* [by George Farquhar (1677–1707)], but as he didn't play this part until 1757 and the porcelain is certainly not later than 1752, the supposition is incorrect.[2]

The identity of the Bow factory's talented sculptor referred to as the 'Muses Modeller' (named for a series of figures of the 'Nine Muses,' ca. 1750, of which 'Polyhymnia' seems to remain undiscovered)[3] has never been determined. But, based on similarities in the heads of a pair of Bow porcelain sphinxes to faces painted and engraved by Thomas Frye (1710–1762)—an accomplished portrait painter, miniaturist, and mezzotint-engraver, and the co-founder and longtime manager of the Bow factory—the collector-author Raymond Yarbrough speculates, "How far-fetched is it to wonder if the great Frye could have been the unidentified 'Muses Modeller at Bow'?"[4] The presence of an impressed T or T° under the base of some Bow figures as early as those by the 'Muses Modeller,' but as late as 1765, however, would tend to obviate the Yarbrough suggestion, given that this mark also appears on some figures and occasional wares made well after Frye's death, and at factories with no Frye associations: Worcester (until about 1770) and then Plymouth and Champion's Bristol. In those instances, the mark has been ascribed to the modeler John Toulouse (see cat. 150). Although no evidence has been found to suggest that John Toulouse worked at the Bow factory, Peter Bradshaw notes that Henry Sandon "has presented evidence to support the contention that there was a family of modelers named Toulouse who most probably came to England from France, which would explain the widespread use of the mark on models executed in different styles" and at different times and places.[5] This thought is furthered by Elizabeth Adams and David Redstone, who note that "the name Charles Toullous occurs in the Bow parish register in October 1750."[6] So the intriguing mystery and search for the identity of the 'Muses Modeller' continues.

1. Yarbrough 1996, pp. 38–41, color pl. 1, and p. 41, figs. 62 and 63. The portrait is in the National Portrait Gallery, London (NPG 1167).
2. Albert Amor 1999, p. 8. For the painting Gabszewicz mentions, see Ashton 1997, color pl. 16 and p. 141, no. 253: Zoffany's painting of "David Garrick as Macbeth and Hannah Pritchard as Lady Macbeth in *Macbeth* by William Shakespeare . . . at the point (Act II, scene 2) when Macbeth says 'Look out again, I dare not', and Lady Macbeth replies 'Infirm of purpose! / Give me the daggers'."
3. See Bimson 2007.
4. Yarbrough 1996, p. 55.
5. Bradshaw 1992, p. 29, commenting on H. Sandon 1978a, p. 208.
6. Adams and Redstone 1991, pp. 132 and 218.

18

Bow Figure of a Sailor, Known as 'Tom Bowling,'
1752–1753
- Attributed to the 'Muses Modeller'
- HEIGHT: 5⅞ in. (15 cm)
- MARK: None
- PROVENANCE: Collection of Mrs. Kenneth T. Knoblock, sold at Sotheby's, London, October 18, 1955, lot 110; James A. Lewis & Son, Inc., New York City, 1955; Collection of Sigmund John Katz, Covington, Louisiana, 1956
- LITERATURE: C.M. Scott and G.R. Scott 1961, p. 196 and pl. 146, no. 492
- ACCESSION NUMBER: 2008.DA.2.21

Traditionally, this figure of a jack-tar is known as 'Tom Bowling,' from the 1748 novel *The Adventures of Roderick Random*, by Tobias George Smollett (1721–1771). Peter Bradshaw, however, suggests that the name is anachronistic because it comes from "a sea shanty written by Charles Dibden (1754–1814) long after issue of the model: 'Faithful, below he did his duty, but now he's gone aloft.'"[1] The model forms a pair to the following model of the Sailor's Lass (see cat. 19), although in this instance the differences in their decoration indicate that the two figures are an "assembled pair."

1. Bradshaw 1992, p. 57.

ENGLISH PORCELAIN: BOW

18, 19   20   21   22, 23

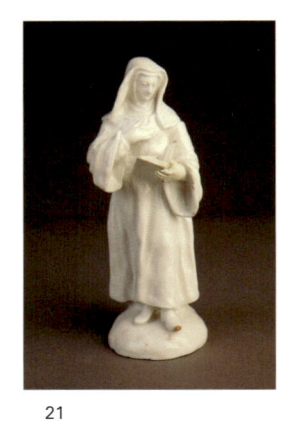

19
Bow Figure of a Sailor's Lass, 1752–1753
Attributed to the 'Muses Modeller'
HEIGHT: 5 9/16 in. (14.2 cm)
MARK: None
PROVENANCE: Collection of Mrs. Kenneth T. Knoblock, sold at Sotheby's, London, October 18, 1955, lot 111; James A. Lewis & Son, Inc., New York City, 1955; Collection of Sigmund John Katz, Covington, Louisiana, 1956
LITERATURE: C.M. Scott and G.R. Scott 1961, p. 196 and pl. 146, no. 493
ACCESSION NUMBER: 2008.DA.2.22

20
Bow Allegorical Group of 'Charity,' 1752–1753
Attributed to the 'Muses Modeller'
HEIGHT: 9 7/8 in. (25.1 cm)
MARK: None
PROVENANCE: Collection of Mrs. Radford, Lested Lodge, Hampstead, London, sold at Sotheby's, London, November 3, 1943, lot 80; Arthur Filkins, London; Collection of Mrs. Kenneth T. Knoblock, sold at Sotheby's, London, October 18, 1955, lot 114; James A. Lewis & Son, Inc., New York City, 1955; Collection of Sigmund John Katz, Covington, Louisiana, 1956
EXHIBITED: London, The Royal Northern Hospital, 25 Park Lane, *Porcelain through the Ages*, February 13–March 27, 1934, cat. no. 131; Dixon Gallery and Gardens, 1989
LITERATURE: King 1924, fig. 5
ACCESSION NUMBER: 2008.DA.2.19

21
Bow White Figure of a Nun, ca. 1755
HEIGHT: 6 9/16 in. (16.7 cm)
MARK: None
PROVENANCE: Albert Amor, Ltd., London, 1954
ACCESSION NUMBER: 2008.DA.2.25

22
Bow Figure of a Monk, 1758–1760
HEIGHT: 5 9/16 in. (14.1 cm)
MARK: None
PROVENANCE: William H. Lautz, New York City, 1952
ACCESSION NUMBER: 2008.DA.2.23

23
Bow Figure of a Priest Reading His Breviary, 1762–1765
HEIGHT: 5 15/16 in. (15.1 cm)
MARK: None
PROVENANCE: Winifred Williams Antiques, Eastbourne, Sussex, England, 1953
ACCESSION NUMBER: 2008.DA.2.24

24
Bow Allegorical Figure of 'Asia' from a Set of 'The Four Quarters of the Globe' ('The Four Continents'), 1765–1770
HEIGHT: 8 3/16 in. (20.8 cm)
MARK: None
PROVENANCE: Purportedly sold at Christie's, London (unidentified sale); Letitia Lundeen, Richmond, Virginia, 1991
ACCESSION NUMBER: 2008.DA.2.303

25
Bow Figure of Ceres, Allegory of 'Earth' from a Set of 'The Four Elements,' 1765–1770
HEIGHT: 9 5/16 in. (23.7 cm)
MARK: None
PROVENANCE: Collection of Mrs. Adrienne Long, sold at Parke-Bernet Galleries, Inc., New York City, December 5, 1946, lot 124, with Neptune (cat. 26)
EXHIBITED: Dixon Gallery and Gardens, 1989
ACCESSION NUMBER: 2008.DA.2.26

26
Bow Figure of Neptune, Allegory of 'Water' from a Set of 'The Four Elements,' 1765–1770
HEIGHT: 9 1/16 in. (23 cm)
MARK: None
PROVENANCE: Collection of Mrs. Adrienne Long, sold at Parke-Bernet Galleries, Inc., New York City, December 5, 1946, lot 124, with Ceres (cat. 25)
EXHIBITED: Dixon Gallery and Gardens, 1989
ACCESSION NUMBER: 2008.DA.2.27

24 　　　　　　　25, 26 　　　　　　　　27 　　　　　　　　28

Charles Gouyn
St. James's, London, ca. 1748–1759/60

27
Charles Gouyn's St. James's Factory ('Girl-in-a-Swing')
White Figure of a Bird, ca. 1759
   Modeled after the Chelsea pair of birds, ca. 1750
   HEIGHT: 5⅛ in. (13 cm)
   MARK: None
   PROVENANCE: Collection of Alfred E. Hutton, Esq., Kensington, London, and Aldwick, West Sussex (a pair); Collection of Mrs. Harrison Williams, New York City, sold at Parke-Bernet Galleries, Inc., New York City, May 22, 1952, lot 62 (a pair); Collection of Mrs. Kenneth T. Knoblock, sold at Sotheby's, London, October 18, 1955, lot 120 (a pair); Albert Amor, Ltd., London, 1955
   EXHIBITED: London, England, Chelsea Town Hall, *The Cheyne Exhibition*, June 1924, no. 222; Dixon Gallery and Gardens, 1989
   LITERATURE: Blunt 1924, p. 61, pl. 2, no. 222 (the pair), right; Gardner 1942, pp. 37–38, pl. VIII (the pair), right; King and Glendenning 1942, p. 154, no. 13, and pl. LVII, b (the pair to this bird) and d (this bird); Honey 1946, p. 51 and pl. 2A; Lane 1961a, p. 79, n. 8; C. M. Scott and G. R. Scott 1961, p. 197 and pl. 151, no. 512
   ACCESSION NUMBER: 2008.DA.2.35

It has long been accepted that Charles Gouyn (d. 1785), a Huguenot jeweler from Dieppe, was a senior partner with Nicholas Sprimont (1713/15–1771) in the early years of the Chelsea factory (see cat. 28), but after a disagreement, Gouyn left Chelsea around 1748 to work independently. The factory that produced this bird and its pair, a number of other figures and groups, and many small *objets de vertu* or "toys" (scent bottles, snuffboxes, bonbonnières, étuis or needle cases, and seals) was mysterious in its absence of documentation, and its work was thus initially credited to Chelsea; but it was eventually reclassified as the 'Girl-in-a-Swing' factory, named after its best-known figure: a white porcelain girl seated on a swing between two trees surmounted by now-missing candle nozzles.[1] In fact, it was the business, if not the factory itself, established by Charles Gouyn in St. James's, London, presumably ca. 1748/49. "In 1751 Gouyn described himself in a newspaper advertisement as 'late Proprietor and Chief Manager of the Chelsea-House,'"[2] but it was a chance discovery by Bernard Dragesco in the City Library in Caen, France, that served to clarify Gouyn's connection to Chelsea and then to his own operations in St. James's.[3] "Although Gouyn's porcelain manufactory may have ceased operation some time after 1760, it was probably not as late as 1777 when he ceased paying rates on the premises at Brick Street,"[4] where it is thought that the actual production occurred.

A Chelsea white figure of a finch, ca. 1748–1749, the model that probably served as the prototype for this figure of a bird, is in the collection of the Colonial Williamsburg Foundation (no. 1963-64).[5]

1. See Adams 2001, p. 57, fig. 5.19; and the Victoria and Albert Museum, London, no. C.587-1922.
2. Oxford 2004, vol. 51, p. 993, entry by Tessa Murdoch.
3. Dragesco 1993.
4. Adams 2001, p. 48.
5. Illustrated in Austin 1977, p. 111, no. 103; another is illustrated in Crane 2015a, p. 98, pl. 10; and Crane 2015b, p. 96, fig. 5.

Chelsea
London, ca. 1744–1769

28
Chelsea White 'Goat and Bee' Jug, 1745–1749
   HEIGHT: 4½ in. (11.4 cm)
   MARK: Incised triangle mark (the alchemical sign for fire)
   PROVENANCE: James A. Lewis & Son, Inc., New York City, 1952
   EXHIBITED: Dixon Gallery and Gardens, 1989
   ACCESSION NUMBER: 2008.DA.2.36

An enameled 'Goat and Bee' jug is illustrated by Simon Spero with the comment,

> This most iconic model in early English porcelain was probably intended as a promotional novelty with which to launch the Chelsea factory in the mid 1740s. In the intricacy of its design, its associations with silver and the sheer detailing of its modeling, it conveys an imaginative sense of both originality and luxury, ideal for the introduction of an ambitious enterprise to a sophisticated metropolitan market. This notion of a promotional device is perhaps borne out by the absence of any comparable models in the subsequent production at Chelsea.[1]

The inspiration for the model remains elusive, and, while it is presumed to have been designed by the factory's proprietor, the trained silversmith Nicholas Sprimont (1713/15–1771—his actual date of birth is unknown, but he was baptized on January 23, 1715), there have been many theories about Sprimont's design source. Surprisingly, it almost certainly was not copied from a silver original, as all of the known silver 'Goat and Bee' jugs have nineteenth-century marks, although O. Glendenning and Mrs. Donald MacAllister comment that the design "is supposed to be taken from a silver model by Edward Wood made in 1737,"[2] a statement occasionally referred to,[3] but never elaborated upon, nor can the location or an illustration of the Wood jug be found (Edward Wood [d. 1752] actually specialized in the making of silver salt cellars). The "Flemish whimsicality"[4] of the opposing goats motif, however, does reappear in silver on Sprimont's masterful 'Ashburnham' centerpiece of 1747.[5]

Further inspirations have been proposed: the first by Zorka Hodgson, who supplied an interesting but unpersuasive argument for a Venetian woodcut by Domenico Campagnola (1500–1564), titled *Two Goats at the Foot of a Tree* (1530), which seems to have been indulged but politely forgotten over the years.[6] Another inspiration was suggested by Paul Crane, with an illustration of a jug identical to this example along with the print of an urn with goat's-head handles from a design by François Boucher (1703–1770) in his *Livre de Vases*.[7] In her discussion of these *Livre de Vases* designs, Alicia Priore mentions Boucher's friendship and professional association with Juste-Aurèle Meissonnier (1695–1750), "*architecte-dessinateur de la chamber et du cabinet du roi*" and a renowned silversmith, some of whose drawings Boucher owned and may have found influential in his vase designs.[8] It is highly likely that Nicholas Sprimont was acquainted with Meissonnier's work, which is said to have influenced his design for his "crayfish salt" in both silver, ca. 1742–1743, and Chelsea porcelain, ca. 1745 and 1752–1756,[9] and which probably was based on a print after a drawing by Meissonnier.[10]

It is difficult, however, to ignore the nearly life-size figures of a pair of recumbent goats modeled by Johann Joachim Kändler (1706–1775) in 1732 for the Japanese Palace of Augustus II (1670–1733), elector of Saxony and king of Poland. By 1736 the palace's porcelain menagerie numbered 159 mammals and 319 birds, but "when work on the palace came to an end in about 1740, . . . a number of animal figures were removed from the palace and found their way elsewhere."[11] Could one of the goats, or perhaps a drawing of it, have reached London at that time?[12]

Nicholas Sprimont was from a Walloon family of silversmiths in Liège. He emigrated to London in 1742 as a young but already accomplished silversmith and registered his mark, *NS* below a star, "in the records of the Worshipful Company of Goldsmiths on 25 January 1742/3."[13] Little is known about the origins of the Chelsea factory or how the unlikely Sprimont became its proprietor and active director from its inception ca. 1744/45 throughout its existence until 1768, when his long-declining health finally forced him to close the business. In August 1769 Sprimont sold the factory lease and business to James Cox, a "jeweler and exporter of musical boxes, clocks and automata,"[14] who resumed the operation for a short time before reselling the manufactory to William Duesbury (1725–1786), the proprietor of the rival Derby porcelain factory, "for want of sufficient skill in the Nature of the said Business and from his want of Time to Attend the same and from the loss of assistance of . . . Francis Thomas" (the recently deceased factory manager, whose own private business dealings and potential embezzlement of porcelain had precipitated a lawsuit by Duesbury).[15] The advertised sale of the Chelsea porcelain factory, its building leases, equipment, and remaining stock began in May 1769 and was not concluded until February 14–17, 1770, with the sale by "Mr. Christie at his Great Room, Pall Mall," for which the catalogue stated, "*N.B.* The Public may be assured that this will positively be the last SALE of the Produce of that DISTINGUISHED MANUFACTORY, the Molds, Kilns, Models, &c. being sold to Mr. DUESBURY of Derby."[16] The final bill for the purchase by William Duesbury "was not settled until 1771";[17] and the court case continued through November 1776, when the judge ordered David Burnsall, the hapless executor of Francis Thomas's estate, "to deliver the unfinished china, Dresden patterns, implements and books to the Plaintiff, together with the sum of any items sold," thus concluding Duesbury's absorption of all aspects of the Chelsea factory into his prospering manufactory in Derby.[18]

From 1770 until 1784, when the Chelsea factory buildings were finally demolished, Duesbury operated both factories concurrently in what is referred to as the "Chelsea-Derby" period, since it has not been determined with certainty what each factory was producing during this time, and only a limited number of pieces are marked with the gold conjoined anchor and D mark of the period, during which Chelsea's gold anchor mark also continued to be used, probably for upper-echelon marketing purposes. So firm attributions remain arguable, although it is assumed that the figure production was carried out at Derby, and it has been suggested that much of the initial decoration was accomplished at Chelsea to accommodate the orders and tastes of the important London clientele. Hints of the production during the early years of the Chelsea-Derby period appear in the catalogues for the sales by "Mr. Christie at his Great Room in Pall-Mall"; their titles were "The Last Year's Produce (Being the first Public Sale) of the Chelsea and Derby Porcelaine Manufactories," April 17–20, 1771;[19] "Part of the Remaining Stock of the Chelsea Porcelane Manufactory" in 1778 and 1779; "Derby and Chelsea" in 1780, 1781, 1782, 1783, and 1784; "All the Remaining Finished and Unfinished Stock of the Chelsea Porcelain Manufactory in Lawrence Street, near the Church, Chelsea, with All the Buildings and Fixtures thereto belonging . . . sold by Auction By Mess. Christie and Ansell, on the Premises," December 11–13, 1783; and at last, a six-day sale of "Derby Porcelain," May 17–22, 1785.[20]

1. Spero 2011, p. 13, no. 1.
2. Glendenning and MacAllister 1935, p. 30.
3. See Adams 2001, p. 29; and Spero 2003a, p. 7, no. 1; both citing the year of the Wood jug as "1735."
4. Clarke 1959, p. 49.
5. Victoria and Albert Museum, London, no. M.46: 1,2-1971; illustrated in Schroder 2015, p. 18, pl. 29.
6. Hodgson 1990, pp. 40 and 41, pls. 21 and 22.
7. Haughton Gallery 2015, p. 10. The Boucher design is from pl. 4 of 12 in his *Livre de Vases*, engraved by Gabriel Huquier (1695–1772), Paris, ca. 1738.
8. Priore 1996, pp. 9–11. She illustrates the title page of the book (in the Department of Drawings and Prints at the Metropolitan Museum of Art, New York, no. 33.57.16) on p. 6, fig. 1, and the aforementioned vase on p. 9, fig. 4.
9. For silver-gilt and porcelain examples, see Schroder 2015, p. 19, pls. 31 and 32; for the Chelsea salts, see also Adams 2001, p. 26, fig. 3.2; and Victoria and Albert Museum, London, no. C.73-1938.
10. See Mallet 1984, p. 235; and Victoria and Albert Museum, London, no. 29564:121, for an 1801 version of the print by Jean-Baptiste-Claude Chatelain (1710–1758) after a book of Meissonnier's designs titled *Livre de Légumes*, published in 1734.
11. Wittwer 2000, pp. 36–39 and pls. 28 and 29.
12. A Kändler billy goat of the 1732 model is in the Victoria and Albert Museum, London, no. C.111-1932; illustrated in Schroder 2015, p. 22, pl. 38 (right). A pair of Kändler billy and nanny goats is in the Philadelphia Museum of Art, bequest of John T. Dorrance, Jr., 1989, nos. 1989-22-1 and 2.
13. Schroder 2015, p. 16.
14. Ibid., p. 175.
15. See Pemberton 2015, p. 31.
16. See Nightingale 1881, Appendix, p. 1.
17. Ibid., p. 182.
18. Pemberton 2015, p. 35.
19. Reproduced in Nightingale 1881, Appendix, pp. 15–36, along with extracts from further sales of "Derby and Chelsea" in 1773.
20. Ibid., Appendix, pp. 37–92.

29

Chelsea Scolopendrium-Molded Cinquefoil Beaker and Saucer, ca. 1752

Modeled after a Chantilly porcelain original of ca. 1735
Beaker: H. 2 7/16 in. (6.2 cm); Saucer: DIAM. 5 3/16 in. (13.2 cm)
MARK: Raised anchor mark on each piece
PROVENANCE: William H. Lautz, New York City, 1948
EXHIBITED: Dixon Gallery and Gardens, 1989
ACCESSION NUMBER: 2008.DA.2.37a, b

In his discussion of "French Influences at Chelsea," T. H. Clarke illustrates a Chantilly porcelain scolopendrium teabowl, ca. 1735, and its Chelsea counterpart among a number of pieces of French porcelain from the Saint-Cloud, Mennecy, Chantilly, and Vincennes factories, which served as prototypes and inspirations for early Chelsea.[1] Following some correspondence between Philip Dormer

29

30

31

32

33

34

Stanhope, Earl of Chesterfield (1694–1773) and the Marquise de Monconseil in Paris, Clarke quotes a letter of June 30, 1752, in which "Lord Chesterfield thanks the Marquise for the porcelain she has sent him which is 'charming, perfect and will make our manufacture here blush. I showed it to the manager ("*intendant*") who was very struck with it and asked me as a favour to lend it to him for a few days so that he could copy it ("*pour lui server de modèle*") which I could not refuse him—particularly as I ordered two or three of the same for use, since yours will be quite useless.'"[2] Citing this letter among other evidence "that French porcelain was being copied in England at this time," and often quite plagiaristically, Clarke found it tempting to speculate that perhaps this Chantilly teabowl is "the piece which Lord Chesterfield lent to the Chelsea manager for a few days" to serve as a model.[3]

1. Clarke 1959, pl. 21a and b.
2. Ibid., pp. 48–49. Clarke quotes from the Bradshaw edition of *Lord Chesterfield's Letters*, vol. 3, pp. 962, 999, 1018, and 1067, of which the originals are in French.
3. Ibid., pp. 49 and 50–51.

30
Chelsea Kakiemon-Style 'Lady in a Pavilion' Pattern Peach-Shaped Dish, 1750–1752

Also referred to contemporarily by the factory as the 'Lady' pattern and the 'Old Japan Lady' pattern
LENGTH: 6 1/16 in. (15.4 cm)
MARK: None, but with eight stilt marks on the base
PROVENANCE: William H. Lautz, New York City, 1949
EXHIBITED: Dixon Gallery and Gardens, 1989
ACCESSION NUMBER: 2008.DA.2.38

31
Chelsea Kakiemon-Style 'Phoenix and Banded Hedges' Pattern Octagonal Plate, 1752–1755

WIDTH: 9 3/4 in. (24.7 cm)
MARK: Red anchor mark
PROVENANCE: Winifred Williams Antiques, Eastbourne, Sussex, England; William H. Lautz, New York City, 1948
ACCESSION NUMBER: 2008.DA.2.39

32
Chelsea Kakiemon-Style 'Yellow Tiger' Pattern Octagonal Soup Plate, 1752–1755

WIDTH: 9 1/4 in. (23.5 cm)
MARK: None, but with three stilt marks on the base
PROVENANCE: Winifred Williams Antiques, Eastbourne, Sussex, England, 1953
EXHIBITED: Dixon Gallery and Gardens, 1989
ACCESSION NUMBER: 2008.DA.2.40

33
Chelsea 'Famille-Rose' Octagonal Soup Plate with a Bird Perched on a Tree Peony, 1752–1754

WIDTH: 9 1/4 in. (23.5 cm)
MARK: None, but with three stilt marks on the base
PROVENANCE: Albert Amor, Ltd., London, 1956 (who commented that the "exact pattern [is] unrecorded")
LITERATURE: Adams 1987, p. 103, pl. 86
ACCESSION NUMBER: 2008.DA.2.42

35

36

37

38

39

40

34
Chelsea Kakiemon-Style Quatrefoil Oval Platter with a Garden Scene, ca. 1755
LENGTH: 15 9/16 in. (39.5 cm)
MARK: Red anchor mark
PROVENANCE: Wilson Galleries, Chicago, Illinois, 1948
ACCESSION NUMBER: 2008.DA.2.41

35
Chelsea Japanese-Style 'Brocade Imari' Pattern Scalloped Plate, 1754–1756
DIAMETER: 9 5/8 in. (24.5 cm)
MARK: None
PROVENANCE: Purportedly from the collection of Hugh Cecil Lowther, 5th Earl of Lonsdale (1857–1944), Lowther Castle, Cumbria, England; Wilson Galleries, Chicago, Illinois, 1948
EXHIBITED: Dixon Gallery and Gardens, 1989
ACCESSION NUMBER: 2008.DA.2.43

36
Chelsea Plate of 'Warren Hastings' Type, 1754–1755
Painted probably by Jefferyes Hamett O'Neale (ca. 1734–1801) with cartouches of birds and animals
DIAMETER: 9½ in. (24.1 cm)
MARK: Red anchor mark
PROVENANCE: Mrs. Lilian B. Little, Oak Park, Illinois, 1948
ACCESSION NUMBER: 2008.DA.2.44

See cat. 159 for a brief biography of Jefferyes Hamett O'Neale. The attribution of fable and related animal subjects, a decorative idiom that originated on Chelsea porcelain, is still somewhat controversial. Traditionally the cartouches on Chelsea plates and platters of this pattern have been attributed to O'Neale. The molded design, possibly inspired by Meissen, but equally the product of Nicholas Sprimont's ingenuity as a silversmith, was identified in the Chelsea sale catalogues of 1755 and 1756 as the 'wrought' pattern, but came to be known as the 'Warren Hastings' pattern after the large Chelsea service belonging to Hastings (1732–1818), the British statesman who spent much of his career in India and became governor of Bengal (1773–1785).[1] Elizabeth Adams illustrates a small platter with this 'Warren Hastings'–type decoration,[2] and suggests that if "O'Neale was working for the decorating establishment of Thomas Hughes in Clerkenwell from 1754 to 1756," as suggested by William Tapp,[3] then "with fable decoration so closely identified with the Chelsea factory," there might have been two fable painters employed there, O'Neale being the later of the two.[4] Recently, however, this two-fable-painter theory seems to have lost its earlier following; Stephen Hanscombe, who believes that O'Neale was the singular painter of this imaginative ilk of decoration on Chelsea, notes that his opinion is shared by John Mallet, Errol Manners, and Simon Spero, currently the three leading Chelsea authorities.[5] In support of his theory, Hanscombe identifies O'Neale's hand with an illustrated list of the features in his painting, including the stylistic characteristics of his landscapes, skies, trees, buildings, animals and birds, people, and classical scenes.[6] While certain of those features (rocks in the foreground, distant mountains, old and gnarled trees, a streaky blue sky, sometimes with purple added and often with flocks of birds) can be seen in the three cartouches on this plate, others are absent, which, along with their unidentifiable fable subjects, is characteristic of 'Warren Hastings'–type pieces, and plates of this type are attributed firmly by Hanscombe to the artist,[7] whose "subjects largely derive from Francis Barlow, *Aesop's Fables, with his Life*, published in London in 1687, as well as the following sources: illustrations after Barlow, engraved by James Kirk; in a drawing book published by Robert Sayer, 1749; John Guy, *Fables*, London, 1727 and 1738; and Dr. Samuel Croxall's translation, *Fables of Aesop's and others*, published in

40 ENGLISH PORCELAIN: CHELSEA

Philip Miller, *Norway Spruce*, 1755–1760. Print from *Figures of the Most Beautiful, Useful and Uncommon Plants described in the Gardeners Dictionary*, vol. 1, pl. 1. The Royal Horticultural Society, Lindley Library.

41

London in 1722."[8] Nevertheless, the painting of the flowers and insects in the center of these pieces is not attributed to O'Neale, but would have been the work of another anonymous Chelsea factory artist.

1. See Ferguson 2013, pp. 15–25.
2. Adams 2001, p. 111, fig. 8.21.
3. Tapp 1938, p. 36. Tapp's reliability is not absolute, and, in fact, was refuted in Massey 2005c, p. 191.
4. Adams 2001, p. 111.
5. Hanscombe 2010, p. 23.
6. Ibid., pp. 14–21.
7. Ibid., pp. 53–55, pls. 34–37.
8. Ferguson 2013, p. 24.

37
Chelsea 'Warren Hastings'–Type Molded Plate Painted with Floral Sprays, 1754–1756
DIAMETER: 9⅜ in. (23.8 cm)
MARK: Red anchor mark
PROVENANCE: Waldhorn Company, Inc., New Orleans, Louisiana, 1946
ACCESSION NUMBER: 2008.DA.2.45

38
Chelsea Acanthus-Molded and Spirally Writhen Octofoil Saucer, 1752–1755
DIAMETER: 4⅞ in. (12.4 cm)
MARK: Red anchor mark
PROVENANCE: Winifred Williams, London, 1974
ACCESSION NUMBER: 2008.DA.2.306

39
Chelsea Circular Écuelle and Cover Painted with Floral Bouquets and Sprigs, ca. 1756
DIAM. 5⅜ in. (13.6 cm); w. across handles 7¼ in. (18.4 cm)
MARK: Red anchor mark
PROVENANCE: Wilson Galleries, Chicago, Illinois, 1951
EXHIBITED: Dixon Gallery and Gardens, 1989
ACCESSION NUMBER: 2008.DA.2.46a, b

40
Chelsea Silver-Shape Dish Painted with Floral Sprays and Sprigs, ca. 1756
Based on the silver original of 1746–1747 by Nicholas Sprimont (1713/15–1771)
LENGTH: 9¹³⁄₁₆ in. (24.9 cm)
MARK: Red anchor mark

PROVENANCE: Purportedly from the Collection of Field Marshal Paul Sanford Methuen, 3rd Baron Methuen (1845–1932) of Corsham Court, Corsham, near Chippenham, Wiltshire; Wilson Galleries, Chicago, Illinois, 1948
ACCESSION NUMBER: 2008.DA.2.47

This dish is one of several Chelsea porcelain models based closely on silver prototypes created by Nicholas Sprimont, the factory's proprietor. In silver, the model served as a stand for a sauceboat (an example with the stand marked for 1746/47 is in the Museum of Fine Arts, Boston).[1] In porcelain, the model, unique to Chelsea, was made from about 1750 in four sizes and with a variety of decorations. For more information on Sprimont and the Chelsea factory, see cat. 28.

1. See Adams 2001, p. 19, fig. 2.3.

41
*Chelsea 'Hans Sloane' Botanical Plate Painted with a Branch of Norway Spruce (*Picae Abies*)*, 1756–1757
Taken from an engraving in Philip Miller, *Figures of Plants*, vol. 1, pl. 1
DIAMETER: 8¼ in. (21 cm)
MARK: Red anchor mark
PROVENANCE: Dorothy G. Hale and Company, Chicago, Illinois, 1951
EXHIBITED: Dixon Gallery and Gardens, 1989
LITERATURE: C. M. Scott and G. R. Scott 1961, p. 198 and pl. 159, no. 546
ACCESSION NUMBER: 2008.DA.2.48

The specimen branch of Norway spruce, also called the silver or yew-leaved fir, was taken directly from the hand-colored engraving titled "*Abies piceæ foliis brevioribus, glaucis conis biuncialibus laxis*" in Philip Miller's *Figures of the Most Beautiful, Useful and Uncommon Plants described in The Gardeners Dictionary . . .*, of which three hundred single prints (available colored for 5 shillings or plain for 2 shillings, sixpence) were issued in fifty monthly installments from 1755, and subsequently published in two folio volumes in 1760. Philip Miller (1691–1771), a nurseryman by heritage and education, was appointed in 1722 to be the Curator of the Chelsea Physic Garden, the property of Sir Hans Sloane, Bart. (1660–1753), a renowned physician and naturalist with a vast collection of botanical and natural history specimens, who had acquired the garden in 1713 with his purchase of the Manor of Chelsea from William, Lord Cheyne. Sir Hans's appointment of Miller coincided with his deed of the garden to the Society of Apothecaries in perpetuity on their payment of £5 per annum and their supplying the Royal Society (of which he became president in 1727) with fifty dried and identified plants for their herbarium. Under Miller and his circle of botanically

ENGLISH PORCELAIN: CHELSEA   41

42

43

44

45

46

47

knowledgeable colleagues, the garden thrived, and in 1731 he published the first folio edition of *The Gardeners Dictionary*, dedicated to his patron, Sir Hans Sloane. Its success generated seven subsequent editions during Miller's lifetime; translations appeared in French, German, and Dutch; and it was even available in the American colonies. On the strength of the *Gardeners Dictionary*, the *Figures of Plants* emerged, with its engravings based on drawings of live plants by R. Lancake, John Miller, and Georg Dionysius Ehret (1708–1770), Philip Miller's talented brother-in-law.

For the above and further information about the Enlightenment —the age in which naturalism and intellectual curiosity flourished internationally—Sir Hans Sloane, Bart., the Chelsea Physic Garden, Philip Miller and his colleagues, and the Chelsea porcelain 'Hans Sloane' wares and their various design sources, see Sally Kevill-Davies, who illustrates a similarly decorated Chelsea plate and its source engraving and cites Miller's comment "that this tree 'grows naturally in many parts of Germany, but the finest of this sort are growing upon Mount Olympus, from whence I have received some of the cones, which were of an extraordinary size.'"[1]

1. Kevill-Davies 2015, p. 58, no. 1 (illustration); p. 59 (quotation).

42

Chelsea Botanical Plate Painted with Fruit and Vegetables, ca. 1758
  DIAMETER: 8 9/16 in. (21.8 cm)
  MARK: Red anchor mark
  PROVENANCE: William H. Lautz, New York City, 1949
  ACCESSION NUMBER: 2008.DA.2.49

43

Chelsea Kidney-Shaped Dish Painted with Exotic Birds, 1758–1760
  LENGTH: 11 in. (28 cm)
  MARK: Brown anchor mark
  PROVENANCE: Wilson Galleries, Chicago, Illinois, 1948
  EXHIBITED: Dixon Gallery and Gardens, 1989
  ACCESSION NUMBER: 2008.DA.2.50

44

Chelsea Plate Painted with Exotic Birds, 1758–1760
  DIAMETER: 8 5/8 in. (21.9 cm)
  MARK: Brown anchor mark
  PROVENANCE: Mrs. Lilian B. Little, Oak Park, Illinois, 1948
  ACCESSION NUMBER: 2008.DA.2.51

45

Chelsea Rocaillerie-Molded Plate Painted with Birds and Fruit, 1760–1765
  DIAMETER: 8 5/8 in. (21.9 cm)
  MARK: Gold anchor mark
  PROVENANCE: Taskey's Antiques, Chicago, Illinois, 1948
  ACCESSION NUMBER: 2008.DA.2.52

46

Chelsea Scalloped Plate Painted with Green Camaïeu Birds, 1760–1765
  DIAMETER: 8 5/8 in. (21.9 cm)
  MARK: Gold anchor mark
  PROVENANCE: William H. Lautz, New York City, 1948
  ACCESSION NUMBER: 2008.DA.2.53

42 ENGLISH PORCELAIN: CHELSEA

48 49

Luigi Riccoboni, *Narcisin (Habit de Narcisin de Malalbergo)*, 1728. Print from *Histoire du Théâtre Italien*. The Metropolitan Museum of Art, New York, Thomas J. Watson Library (Jacob S. Rogers Fund, 1935).

47
Chelsea Pine Cone–Molded Coffee Cup and Saucer with Claret-Ground Panels and Floral Sprigs, 1759–1760
  Cup: H. 2⅝ in. (6.7 cm); Saucer: DIAM. 5 in. (12.7 cm)
  MARK: Gold anchor mark on each piece
  PROVENANCE: Winifred Williams Antiques, Eastbourne, Sussex, England; T. Leonard Crow, Tewkesbury, Gloucestershire, England, 1949
  LITERATURE: Savage 1952, pl. 35 (b): the cup with a different saucer from the same service
  ACCESSION NUMBER: 2008.DA.2.54a, b

48
Chelsea Figure of a Carpenter, 1754–1755
  Modeled by Joseph Willems (ca. 1710–1766)
  HEIGHT: 7¾ in. (19.7 cm)
  MARK: None
  PROVENANCE: "Property of a Nobleman," sold at Sotheby's, London, February 5, 1952, lot 119; James A. Lewis & Son, Inc., London and New York City; Collection of Sigmund John Katz, Covington, Louisiana, 1956
  EXHIBITED: Dixon Gallery and Gardens, 1989
  LITERATURE: C.M. Scott and G.R. Scott 1961, p. 196 and pl. 146, no. 495
  ACCESSION NUMBER: 2008.DA.2.56

Pierre-Joseph Willems is the only modeler whose name has been associated with the early years of the Chelsea factory. His year of birth is generally thought to have been 1710, but according to Arthur Lane, "1715 Willems born at Brussels (retrospective date given in register-entry of his burial at Tournay, March 19, 1767);"[1] likewise, Elizabeth Adams states that he was "born at Brussels in 1715 [and] was very slightly older than [Nicholas] Sprimont [whose year of birth is unknown, but he was baptized in January 1715, so presumably he was born between 1713 and January 1715, lending greater credence to Willems's birth year as 1710]. By the age of twenty-four he was at Tournai [which was then in France, now in Belgium], where he [was] married . . . [in] November 1739. He may have continued to work at Tournai in the faïence factory of François Joseph Carpentier for the next few years, leaving it to go to England, where he is recorded in the rate books for Chelsea from 1748."[2] In addition to his prolific and elegant sculptural output at Chelsea from about 1749 onward, as a fine draughtsman Willems also taught drawing and modeling. Eventually he returned to Tournai and in 1766 was lured back to the porcelain factory there by its proprietor, François-Joseph Peterinck (1719–1799), but not before he had created a rich repertoire of figure models for the Chelsea factory, which were often inspired by Meissen porcelain prototypes as well as prints and other graphic and sculptural sources.

One of Willems's best-known series of figures is the *'Cris de Paris*,' depicting the Paris street criers or vendors after Meissen's two series of these figures modeled by Peter Reinicke (1715–1768) and Johann Joachim Kändler (1706–1775). The earlier, larger models were created ca. 1744 from among the sixty engravings by Anne Claude Philippe de Tubières-Grimoard de Pestels Levieux de Lévis, comte de Caylus (1692–1765), of drawings by the sculptor and painter Edmé Bouchardon (1698–1762).[3] The second series of smaller models was based on watercolor drawings by the Parisian artist Christophe Huet (1692–1765), made specifically for this purpose in 1753.[4] Willems derived his Chelsea figures from both series, although their interpretation is closer to the earlier series, and, according to Lane, the March 5, 1767, "second Inventory of effects of Joseph Willems included: '. . . [a quantity of prints and books] . . . vingt quatre dessins à la plume représantans les cris de paris, vingt quatre dessins idem. . . .' The forty-eight pen-drawings of 'cris de paris' might conceivably have been copied from the famous set of engravings by the comte de Caylus after Bouchardon. On the other hand, some Chelsea red-anchor figures [ca. 1752–1758] in the same vein appear to be original inventions."[5] The figure of the 'Carpenter' appears to be among Willems's original models for the Chelsea *'Cris de Paris*,' as no Bouchardon print, Huet drawing, or Meissen counterpart has been discovered as a prototype.[6] Adams adds an interesting note that "the names of some of the eighteenth-century inhabitants of Chelsea have been preserved to us, and it is pleasant to think that this [figure of a carpenter] might be a portrait in his younger days of Robert Ranson, who in September 1770 tendered a bill totalling £1 0s. 3d, for various bits of carpentry work he had done on the Chelsea factory premises."[7]

1. Lane 1961a, p. 133.
2. Adams 2001, p. 68.
3. The comte de Caylus's engravings of Bouchardon's drawings were published between 1737 and 1746; Eberle 2001, pp. 24–25.
4. Ibid., p. 26.
5. Lane 1961a, pp. 135 and 136.
6. See Manners 2013, p. 40.
7. Adams 2001, p. 129.

49
Chelsea Italian Comedy Figure of 'Narcisin,' also called 'The Captain,' ca. 1755
  Modeled after the Meissen porcelain original by Peter Reinicke (1715–1768) in September 1744 (model number 576) for the 'Duke of Weissenfels Series,' from the engraving "*Habit de Narcisin de Malalbergo*" by François Joullain (1697–1778) after Charles-Antoine Coypel, in Luigi Riccoboni's *Histoire du Théâtre Italien* (Paris: Pierre Delormel, 1728)
  HEIGHT: 6³⁄₁₆ in. (15.7 cm)
  MARK: Red anchor mark

ENGLISH PORCELAIN: CHELSEA

50　　　　　51　　　　　52　　　　　53

PROVENANCE: Collection of Sigmund John Katz, Covington, Louisiana, 1956
EXHIBITED: Dixon Gallery and Gardens, 1989
ACCESSION NUMBER: 2008.DA.2.55

Meredith Chilton, who provides details about the Meissen porcelain 'Duke of Weissenfels Series' of Italian Comedy figures, illustrates a Bow porcelain figure of the model, called 'Narcisin,' ca. 1760–1765, and mentions that both the Bow and the Chelsea versions of the figure are "also known as 'The Captain'."[1] However, this is a persistent misidentification of 'The Captain,' which is an altogether different Italian Comedy figure, also represented in the 'Duke of Weissenfels Series' and based on the Joullain print of "*Habit de Capitan Italien*."[2] It is worth noting that this figure's name has a variety of spellings: Narcisin, Narcizin (German), Narcissino, and Narcisso—perhaps an appropriate reflection of his multifarious stage character, which Birte Abraham describes as "roguish; he is a cowardly villain who would do anything for money. He is cunning, witty and often makes jokes at the expense of one and all. Yet he has a very good singing voice and [in the original Meissen model, he is] portrayed . . . in mid-song,"[3] a feature that seems to have escaped the figure's translation into Chelsea porcelain.

1. Chilton 2001, pp. xvi and 308, no. 101 ('Duke of Weissenfels Series'), and p. 277, no. 23 ('Narcisin').
2. For Meissen figures of 'Narcisin' and 'The Captain,' see Abraham 2010, pp. 67 (right) and 69 (left), along with the Joullain prints, pp. 66 (right) and 68 (left), respectively; Rückert 1966, who also illustrates both of the Meissen figures and prints, pl. 234, nos. 963 and 962, respectively; and Ducret 1973, who illustrates the same figure of 'Narcisin' and print, p. 182, figs. 314 and 316, respectively.
3. Abraham 2010, p. 66.

50
Chelsea Group of a Pastoral Musician: The Bagpiper and His Dog, ca. 1756
From a Meissen porcelain model of 1750–1755
HEIGHT: 9⅛ in. (23.2 cm)
MARK: None
PROVENANCE: Stoner & Evans, London; Collection of Sigmund John Katz, Covington, Louisiana, 1956
EXHIBITED: Dixon Gallery and Gardens, 1989
LITERATURE: Stoner 1955, p. 25 and pl. 22 (right); C.M. Scott and G.R. Scott 1961, p. 196 and pl. 146, no. 494
ACCESSION NUMBER: 2008.DA.2.57

51
Chelsea Sweetmeat Figure of a Lady, 1758–1765
Modeled by Joseph Willems (ca. 1710–1766)
HEIGHT: 6 9/16 in. (16.7 cm)
MARK: Gold anchor mark
PROVENANCE: Albert Amor, Ltd., London, 1956
EXHIBITED: Dixon Gallery and Gardens, 1989
ACCESSION NUMBER: 2008.DA.2.58

This figure and her male companion were modeled by Willems (see cat. 48) as a pair of gardeners, intended to decorate the dining table at the dessert course, their open baskets serving as sweetmeat dishes for dried fruits, nuts, or small candies. A pair of figures of this model and her companion is in the collection of the Victoria and Albert Museum, London (nos. C.166-1931 and C.156-1931, respectively).

Chelsea-Derby *London and Derby, 1770–1784*

52
Chelsea-Derby Neoclassical Plate Painted with a Fruit Roundel, 1775–1780
DIAMETER: 9⅛ in. (23.2 cm)
MARK: Gold conjoined anchor and D mark
PROVENANCE: William H. Lautz, New York City, 1949
ACCESSION NUMBER: 2008.DA.2.62

53
Chelsea-Derby Neoclassical Teabowl and Saucer, 1775–1780
DIAMETERS: 3 and 4 15/16 in. (7.6 and 12.5 cm)
MARK: Gold conjoined anchor and D mark on each piece
PROVENANCE: Margo (Authentic Antiques), St. Louis, Missouri, 1946 (sold as "Salopian")
ACCESSION NUMBER: 2008.DA.2.60a, b

A service in this pattern belonged at one time to Arthur Wellesley, 1st Duke of Wellington (1769–1852) at Apsley House, London, as indicated by a drawing of elements of this cup and saucer's decoration with the notation "Duke of Wellington's cup and teabowl," which appears in "The Wallis Papers," a personally annotated copy of *The Pottery and Porcelain of Derbyshire* by Alfred Wallis and William Bemrose, Jr.[1] Alfred Wallis was the great-grandson of the Derby gilder John Yates (d. 1821), and was also related to Thomas Soar, who used the numeral 1 as his identifying mark while employed as the chief gilder at the Derby factory between 1785 and 1795.

1. Published to accompany the 1870 Midland Counties Exhibition in Derby, and reproduced partially in Twitchett 2002, pp. 28–29 and 36, pl. 7.

54

55

56

57

58

Gérard Jean-Baptiste Scotin II, after Antoine Watteau, *La Cascade—Aqua Saliens*, 1729. Etching. The British Museum, 1838,0526.1.28.

54
Chelsea-Derby Pine Cone–Molded Double-Handled Caudle Cup, Cover, and Stand, ca. 1780
 Cup and Cover: H. 4¾ in. (12.1 cm); Stand: DIAM. 6³⁄₁₆ in. (15.7 cm)
 MARK: Gold conjoined anchor and D mark on the cup and stand
 PROVENANCE: Wilson Galleries, Chicago, Illinois, 1948
 EXHIBITED: Dixon Gallery and Gardens, 1989
 ACCESSION NUMBER: 2008.DA.2.61a–c

Derby *Derbyshire, ca. 1748 onward*

55
Derby Six-Shell Sweetmeat or Pickle Stand Encrusted with Shells and 'Seaweed' and Painted with Insects, ca. 1760
 HEIGHT: 10¹³⁄₁₆ in. (27.5 cm)
 MARK: None
 PROVENANCE: D.M. & P. Manheim, New York City, 1953; Collection of Warda Stevens Stout, Memphis, Tennessee, 1964; Collection of Alice Stout Edwards, Point Lookout, Missouri, 1998
 ACCESSION NUMBER: 2008.DA.2.316

56
Derby Scroll-, Shell-, and Mask-Molded Wall Pocket Painted with Flowers and Insects, 1760–1765
 HEIGHT: 9¾ in. (24.8 cm)
 MARK: None
 PROVENANCE: Taskey's Antiques, Chicago, Illinois, 1948
 EXHIBITED: Dixon Gallery and Gardens, 1989
 ACCESSION NUMBER: 2008.DA.2.66

57
Derby Rococo Vase Applied with Flowers and Painted with Birds, 1760–1765
 Modeled after a Longton Hall original of ca. 1755
 HEIGHT: 8¹³⁄₁₆ in. (22.4 cm)
 MARK: None
 PROVENANCE: T. Leonard Crow, Tewkesbury, Gloucestershire, England, 1949 (sold as Longton Hall, 1752–1756)
 ACCESSION NUMBER: 2008.DA.2.64

58
Derby Underglaze Blue-Ground Rococo Vase and Cover Painted with Watteau-Type Figures and Birds, 1760–1765
 HEIGHT: 10⅛ in. (25.7 cm)
 MARK: None
 PROVENANCE: Marshall Field & Company, Chicago, Illinois, 1948
 ACCESSION NUMBER: 2008.DA.2.63a, b

In spite of considerable research and speculation by scholars of the mid-twentieth century, including the enthusiastic but not always reliable Major W. H. Tapp,[1] the painter or painters of the figures and birds on this vase and other pieces with decoration of this ilk have not been identified, nor have the specific sources of the decoration. However, it is possible that the figures were adapted from an engraving by Gérard Jean-Baptiste Scotin II (1698–after 1755) after the painting *La Cascade* (The Fountain) by Jean-Antoine Watteau (1684–1721), a copy of which (1725–1750) is in the Wallace Collection, London.[2] A more precise rendering of the print appears on Worcester porcelain of ca. 1754–1760;[3] and it appears in reverse

ENGLISH PORCELAIN: CHELSEA-DERBY | DERBY   45

59

Pierre Alexandre Aveline, after François Boucher, *Trois Amours dont un tient une flèche* (Three Cupids of which one holds an arrow), from *Premier Livre de Groupes d'Enfans* (First Book of Groups of Children). Etching and engraving. The Metropolitan Museum of Art, New York, The Elisha Whittelsey Collection, The Elisha Whittelsey Fund, 1957, 57.559.40.

60

on John (or late James) Pennington's Liverpool porcelain of ca. 1770–1778.[4]

1. See Tapp 1939 and Godden 1985a, pp. 99–103, on the "china painter" Thomas Hughes.
2. Dacier and Vuaflart 1921, vol. 2, pp. 18–19, and vol. 4, no. 28.
3. Cook 1948, item 19.
4. See Hillis 2011, p. 325, pl. 8.14 (left); and Handley 1991, p. 52, no. 2.12 and color pls. I and III, and p. 230, no. 8.28.

59

Derby Flower-Encrusted Rococo Potpourri 'Frill' Vase and Cover Painted in Puce Camaïeu with Cherubs on Clouds, 1765–1770

HEIGHT: 11 5/16 in. (28.7 cm)
MARK: Incised cross mark
PROVENANCE: Marshall Field & Company, Chicago, Illinois, 1948
EXHIBITED: Dixon Gallery and Gardens, 1989
ACCESSION NUMBER: 2008.DA.2.65a, b

By the mid-1750s at the Vincennes factory in France, "*enfants de Boucher*" ("Boucher babies," or cavorting cherubs) were a popular form of decoration based on the hundreds of prints by numerous artists engraving the works of François Boucher (1703–1770). The cherubs appeared in polychrome and in both blue and puce *camaïeu* (monochrome) on all manner of Vincennes porcelain wares, including pieces recorded as having been sold as early as 1755 and 1756 by the Parisian *marchand mercier* Lazare Duvaux to members of the English aristocracy, such as the pair of blue-ground "*pot pourris Pompadour*" bought by Frederick St. John, 3rd Viscount St. John, 2nd Viscount Bolingbroke (1732–1787) in 1756.[1] Through French prints, porcelain, and other decorative arts, the taste for cherubic innocence, completely rococo in spirit, quickly crossed the English Channel to be translated onto the porcelain of Chelsea and Derby, generally painted in puce *camaïeu*, and traditionally attributed, though largely without substantiation, to Richard Askew (ca. 1730–1798). While no specific prints after Boucher have been identified as the source of the cherub decoration on this vase, one image titled *Trois Amours dont un tient une flèche* [Three Cupids of which one holds an arrow] from the *Premier Livre de Groupes d'Enfans* [sic], a suite of six prints engraved by Pierre Alexandre Aveline (1702–1760) and published in Paris chez Huquier (1695–1772), shows two of the three cherubs in very similar poses to the present examples.[2]

It is always tempting for ceramics scholars to attribute the painting on various factory products to specific artists, particularly when the subjects and the hand fall into a recognized idiom, as do the cherubs or cupids among clouds painted on this potpourri vase and on various other Chelsea, Chelsea-Derby, and Derby wares predominantly in the 1765–1785 period, but continuing on through ca. 1795. By seldom-questioned tradition, this decoration was attributed to Richard Askew; like so many painters associated with English porcelain factories, he was a peripatetic artist, whose biography has been patched together from various local records, correspondence, and accounts.[3] But Andrew Ledger has seriously challenged the Askew attribution through research correcting prior biographical details proving that

1. There is no evidence that Askew lived in Chelsea in the 1760s and therefore little reason for saying he ever worked for [Nicholas] Sprimont. 2. Askew worked at Chelsea for [William] Duesbury for only a very short time in April and May 1771. 3. Askew would not have worked for Duesbury senior at either Chelsea or Derby after his incriminating letter written on 21st April 1772 to his son [Robert Askew, requesting him to steal pigments (?) from the Derby factory, where Robert had been employed that year as an apprentice] was discovered by Duesbury. 4. He worked as some form of an enamel painter from mid-1772 to mid-1794, including but not exclusively in central London (1772–1784), Dublin (1786) and then probably in Birmingham. 5. His only certain time working at Derby was for [William] Duesbury II from about mid-1794 to about end-1795 or perhaps early 1796, which is the only period for which secure attributions can be made.[4]

These "secure attributions" to Askew are largely for piecework, on which John Twitchett comments that "it has been said that [Askew's] figures, and particularly Cupids, have heavy limbs and jowls, and this may help in differentiating between Askew's work and that of [other painters], whose figures do not show these characteristics."[5]

One such "other painter" is Fidelle Duvivier (1740–after 1796), another peripatetic porcelain painter from a Catholic (rather than Huguenot) family of talented artists from Tournai.[6] Duvivier may be best recognized for his later painting on New Hall porcelain, but he painted at Derby from October 1769 until presumably 1773, when his four-year agreement with William Duesbury would have expired. So in at least 1771 his tenure at Derby coincided with that of Richard Askew and Zachariah Boreman (see next paragraph), but it is impossible to know whether the three accomplished artists influenced one another in their styles or subjects. As a Frenchman, Duvivier possibly had the greatest access to the Boucher-inspired prints, from which he painted puce or rose *camaïeu* cherubs in France at Sceaux, both on faïence and on Mennecy porcelain, ca. 1766–1768, before he emigrated to England, and also when he returned to the Continent to work again at Sceaux and in the Netherlands, where they are seen on Oude Loosdrecht porcelain and on a few Ansbach porcelain pieces that he decorated for The Hague.[7] In comparing Duvivier's cherubs to those formerly attributed to Askew, Charlotte Jacob-Hanson comments that on the Duvivier faces, "the eyes [are] simple lines with solid vertical ovals below them, [the hands have] pointing index fingers, [and the pose often shows] one

46 ENGLISH PORCELAIN: DERBY

61   62   63

leg cocked or bent with the foot pointing inward."[8] But most particularly, the Duvivier painting appears to have been executed with a lighter touch than that attributed to the hand of Askew. Given these characteristics, the present vase cannot be the work of Fidelle Duvivier.

So the question as to whom these pieces of the early 1770s can be attributed remains alive, and it is possible that there is not yet an answer. However, Ledger suggests one more possibility, proposing Zachariah Boreman (1738–1810; see cat. 66) as a "strong candidate.... He is much admired as the leading landscape painter on porcelain [and a talented painter of other subjects as well, particularly flowers. But] there is a much weightier logistical argument for considering Boreman. There were very few lots in the 1771 and 1773 auctions [at Christie's in London] decorated with landscapes and not many more with flowers, the largest number having cupids or figures."[9] Boreman is known to have been working for Duesbury during this period, so it is fair to speculate that cherubs were among his various subjects. Clearly more research is necessary, and we can only hope that a compelling attribution will emerge from yet undiscovered documents.

1. J. Paul Getty Museum, Los Angeles, no. 84.DE.3.1–2; see Sassoon 1991, pp. 12–19, no. 3; and Manners 2007, pp. 458–460, pl. 71, and also p. 462, pl. 76 for the now-famous portrait by an anonymous artist, ca. 1759, depicting Nicholas Sprimont with his wife and sister-in-law amid Chelsea vases, including a Chelsea "*pot pourri Pompadour.*" The painting is further illustrated in Gallagher 2015, p. 184, fig. 7.
2. See Jean-Richard 1978, pp. 86–88, no. 238.
3. In this instance, information about Askew is largely from Jewitt 1878, vol. 2, pp. 98–100.
4. Ledger 2011, p. 44.
5. Twitchett 1980, p. 183.
6. Duvivier is the subject of much recent research by Charlotte Jacob-Hanson, whose counsel and generously shared scholarship is gratefully acknowledged.
7. As discovered by Jacob-Hanson for her forthcoming publication, *In the Footsteps of Fidelle Duvivier: A Career Summary with New Discoveries of His Work for the Sceaux Manufactory in France.*
8. Charlotte Jacob-Hanson, correspondence of August 30, 2015.
9. Ledger 2011, pp. 44–45.

60
Derby Teabowl and Saucer Painted with Flowers, 1775–1780

DIAMETERS: 3 1/16 and 5 1/16 in. (7.8 and 12.8 cm)
MARKS: Crowned D mark in blue on each, and the cup with an incised script N.
PROVENANCE: Mrs. Lilian B. Little, Oak Park, Illinois, 1948
ACCESSION NUMBER: 2008.DA.2.67a, b

61
Derby Coffee Cup and Saucer with a Gilt-Striped Ground, 1780–1782

Cup: H. 2½ in. (6.4 cm); Saucer: DIAM. 5 1/16 in. (12.9 cm)
MARK: Gold anchor mark on each piece
PROVENANCE: Marshall Field & Company, Chicago, Illinois, 1948
ACCESSION NUMBER: 2008.DA.2.59a, b

The gold anchor marks on this cup and saucer would suggest that they either were manufactured at Chelsea or could be referred to as Chelsea-Derby. However, Alasdair Morrison posits that

> It was in [William] Duesbury's interest to keep customers reasonably confused about where exactly his wares were made, . . . and having paid good money for the valuable Chelsea brand, he would have felt fairly free in his use of it—so long as it could be used to commercial advantage. . . . I am by no means so sure that all pieces with the gold Anchor/D mark (or gold anchor mark) were made at Chelsea. Some may have been only decorated there; some, I suspect, not even that. We know he sometimes pirated the Meissen and Sèvres marks: so why not pirate his own prestige mark, perhaps especially on wares that were of good quality?[1]

He goes on to say that "William Duesbury held sales of porcelain at Christie's [in London] 1771 and 1773 and annually from 1778 to 1785."[2] Among the wares included in the latter sales, some are identifiable through the pattern books, but the tea wares often are not. However, the present cup and saucer with their gold-striped decoration, "used on more luxury items, . . . turn up in these sales in a few tea sets," for which Morrison cites a description from the sale in 1782, Day Four, lot 69, and another from the sale in 1783, Day One, lot 58;[3] he also illustrates a "sugar-box" (covered sugar bowl) identically decorated to the present cup and saucer and also marked with a gold anchor.[4] On this basis and on the paste and glaze of the "sugar-box," he attributes it fully to Derby.

1. Morrison 2004, pp. 53–54.
2. Ibid., p. 56.
3. Ibid., p. 64.
4. Ibid., p. 58, pl. 28.

62
Derby Plate Painted with 'Chantilly' Sprigs, ca. 1785

DIAMETER: 8 5/8 in. (21.8 cm)
MARKS: Crowned crossed batons and D mark and pattern number 34 in puce
PROVENANCE: B. Manheim, New Orleans, Louisiana, 1946
ACCESSION NUMBER: 2008.DA.2.68

63
Derby Scalloped Plate in an 'Angoulême Sprig' Pattern, ca. 1785
DIAMETER: 8⅝ in. (21.8 cm)
MARKS: Crowned crossed batons and D mark and pattern number 84 in purple
PROVENANCE: Antiques on the Corner, Inc., Lookout Mountain, Tennessee, 1986
ACCESSION NUMBER: 2008.DA.2.317

According to John Twitchett, "We know from research that the [Derby] patterns started in the 1780s" and were recorded in various books, among them the Plate Book, which lists and describes pattern number 84, noting that the cost of its decoration was "marked '5d Gilding 6d. Painting.'"[1]

1. Twitchett 2002, pp. 290 and 306.

64
Derby 'Smith's Blue'–Bordered Jug Monogrammed EL *between Floral Bouquets*, ca. 1785
HEIGHT: 6¹³⁄₁₆ in. (17.3 cm)
MARK: Crowned crossed batons and D mark in purple
PROVENANCE: Collection of Mr. A. Green, Bushey Heath, Hertfordshire, England; Winifred Williams Antiques, Eastbourne, Sussex, England, 1956
EXHIBITED: Dixon Gallery and Gardens, 1989
ACCESSION NUMBER: 2008.DA.2.69

65
Derby 'Smith's Blue'–Bordered and Festoon-Molded Coffee Cup and Saucer, ca. 1785
Cup: H. 2⁷⁄₁₆ in. (6.2 cm); Saucer: DIAM. 4⅞ in. (12.3 cm)
MARKS: Crowned crossed batons and D mark and pattern number N54 in purple on each piece
PROVENANCE: Marshall Field & Company, Chicago, Illinois, 1946
ACCESSION NUMBER: 2008.DA.2.70a, b

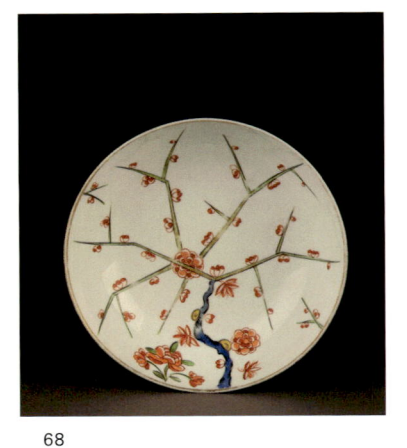

66
Derby Topographical Coffee Cup and Saucer, ca. 1785
The cup painted probably by Zachariah Boreman (1738–1810) *en grisaille* with a *View of Breadsall, Derbyshire*
Cup: H. 2⅝ in. (6.7 cm); Saucer: DIAM. 5¹⁄₁₆ in. (12.9 cm)
MARKS: Crowned crossed batons and D mark and pattern number 172 in blue on the cup and purple on the saucer, and the cup with the view identification in blue script
PROVENANCE: T. Leonard Crow, Tewkesbury, Gloucestershire, England, 1950
ACCESSION NUMBER: 2008.DA.2.71a, b

According to John Twitchett, Zachariah Boreman is thought to have apprenticed at the Chelsea factory, working there under William Duesbury.[1] This would appear to be confirmed by Andrew Ledger, who states that Boreman's name appears "continuously in the surviving wage bills from October 1770 to June 1773, and on 26th August 1783 [he] signed a three-year agreement with Duesbury senior to transfer to Derby within thirty days."[2] He promptly proceeded north to the Derby factory and worked there for eleven years before returning in 1794 to London, where, according to John Haslem, "he took employment with some of the local china enamellers,

48 ENGLISH PORCELAIN: DERBY

70   71   72

but chiefly in the decorating establishment of the former Derby painter [John] Sims in Pimlico"[3] (see cat. 289), "where he continued painting until his death in 1810."[4]

1. Twitchett 2002, p. 53.
2. Ledger 2011, pp. 44–45.
3. Haslem 1876, p. 67.
4. Twitchett 2002, p. 56.

67
Derby Yellow-Ground Spirally Fluted Plate Reserved with a Floral Roundel, ca. 1790

Painted by William Cooper Junior (dates unknown) in the manner of William Billingsley (1758–1828) with a central flower spray
DIAMETER: 9 3/8 in. (23.8 cm)
MARKS: Crowned crossed batons and D mark, numeral 134 and numeral 3 for William Cooper Junior (as painter and/or gilder) on the footrim, all in purple
PROVENANCE: Marshall Field & Company, Chicago, Illinois, probably 1947; Mrs. Lilian B. Little, Oak Park, Illinois, 1947
EXHIBITED: Dixon Gallery and Gardens, 1989
ACCESSION NUMBER: 2008.DA.2.72

Other than from the writings of William Jewitt, little is known about either William Cooper Senior, "a clever flower painter," at Derby from "about 1770, to his death, in 1776"; or his son William Cooper Junior, who "was apprenticed for seven years on the 1st of January 1777, to learn the 'Art of Painting upon China or Porcelain Ware.'"[1] John Twitchett quotes Jewitt and adds that the younger Cooper "used the numeral 3 on the footrim of his pieces between 1785 and 1798."[2]

Considerably more is known of William Billingsley, about whom much has been written. He was born in Derby, the son of a flower painter who had worked at the Chelsea factory and later probably independently in Derby. William was apprenticed to William Duesbury in 1774, where, in his two decades at Derby, he became one of the factory's most adept, imitated, and celebrated flower painters. However, as a result, and as pointed out by Twitchett, "he is possibly the most wrongly attributed painter in the history of ceramics."[3] In 1795 Billingsley left Derby for the Pinxton factory, where he worked until 1799 before moving on to Mansfield, working there for three years. After forty-four years in Derbyshire, Billingsley moved to Torksey in Lincolnshire, where he seems to have stayed until his short foray to Wales in 1808, followed later that year by his move to Worcester. He was employed there, along with his son-in-law Samuel Walker, by Martin Barr, where the two "are reported to have been largely responsible for the improvement in the Worcester body."[4] In 1813 Billingsley and Walker established the Nantgarw Porcelain Works in Wales, which was not entirely successful; and in 1820 the molds and other equipment were purchased by John Rose of Coalport, for whom Billingsley himself spent his last years working, until his death in 1828.

1. Jewitt 1878, vol. 2, pp. 108–109.
2. Twitchett 2002, p. 67.
3. Ibid., p. 50.
4. Ibid., p. 52.

68
Derby Kakiemon-Style Saucer Painted with a Prunus Tree, ca. 1820

DIAMETER: 5 11/16 in. (14.5 cm)
MARKS: Crowned crossed batons and D mark and numeral 28 in iron-red
PROVENANCE: Jean Sewell Antiques, London; Antiques on the Corner, Inc., Lookout Mountain, Tennessee, 1988
ACCESSION NUMBER: 2008.DA.2.318

69
Derby Kakiemon-Style 'Partridge' Pattern Shell-Shaped Dish, ca. 1820

WIDTH: 10 in. (25.4 cm)
MARKS: Crowned crossed batons and D mark and numeral 11 in iron-red, and numeral 1 or / in underglaze blue on the footrim
PROVENANCE: C.R. Fenton & Co., Ltd., Old Ford, England; Atlanta Antiques Exchange, Atlanta, Georgia, 1982
ACCESSION NUMBER: 2008.DA.2.320

70
Derby Imari 'King's' or 'Old Japan' Pattern Plate, 1820–1825

DIAMETER: 8 7/8 in. (22.6 cm)
MARKS: Crowned crossed batons and D mark and numeral 6 in iron-red
PROVENANCE: Sarah Burrell, Lookout Mountain Antiques, Lookout Mountain, Tennessee, 1974
ACCESSION NUMBER: 2008.DA.2.321

71
Derby 'Brocade Imari' Pattern Plate, ca. 1830

DIAMETER: 10 1/8 in. (25.7 cm)
MARK: BLOOR DERBY and crown "thumbprint" mark printed in red
PROVENANCE: Sarah Burrell, Lookout Mountain Antiques, Lookout Mountain, Tennessee, 1974
ACCESSION NUMBER: 2008.DA.2.322

73   74

Charles Mosley after Thomas Worlidge, *Mrs. Clive in the Character of the Fine Lady in Lethe*, ca. 1750. Mezzotint engraving. Private collection.

72
Derby Imari Circular Inkstand in the 'Witches' Pattern [Number 2451], 1820–1825
LENGTH: 5¹¹⁄₁₆ in. (14.4 cm)
MARKS: Crowned crossed batons and D mark and numeral 23 in iron-red
PROVENANCE: Geoffrey Godden Chinaman, Worthing, Sussex, England; Antiques on the Corner, Inc., Lookout Mountain, Tennessee, 1988
EXHIBITED: Dixon Gallery and Gardens, 1989
ACCESSION NUMBER: 2008.DA.2.319

73
Derby Circular Pastille Burner with Floral and Neoclassical Decoration, ca. 1825
HEIGHT: 4⅛ in. (10.5 cm)
MARKS: Crowned crossed batons and D mark and numeral 23 in iron-red
PROVENANCE: Antiques on the Corner, Inc., Lookout Mountain, Tennessee, 1989
ACCESSION NUMBER: 2008.DA.2.323

74
Derby White Figure of Kitty Clive, 1750–1751
Modeled possibly by Andrew Planché (1728–1805) from an engraving by Charles Mosley (1718–1756), ca. 1750, after a watercolor by Thomas Worlidge (1700–1766), depicting the actress in the role of Mrs. Riot in David Garrick's play *Lethe, or Aesop in the Shades*
HEIGHT: 9½ in. (24.2 cm)
MARK: None
PROVENANCE: Albert Amor, Ltd., London, 1954 (sold as Bow)
EXHIBITED: Dixon Gallery and Gardens, 1989
ACCESSION NUMBER: 2008.DA.2.73

Andrew Planché is the first of only two modelers who have been identified as having worked at the Derby factory in its earliest years (the other is Agostino Carlini [1718–1790]; see cat. 75). Of Huguenot origin, from 1740 Planché served his apprenticeship to The Worshipful Company of Goldsmiths in London, which would have been completed in 1747, after which he may have made a trip to France, probably visiting the Chantilly factory, where he could have learned how to make soft-paste porcelain. He then settled in Derby, and it is thought that he established a small porcelain works there as early as 1748. William Duesbury most likely learned the secrets of porcelain-making from him before Planché's departure around 1756–1758. Although his movements during the ensuing quarter century are not well known, by 1765 Planché had anglicized his name to Andrew Planche Floor (*le plancher* being the French word for "floor") and was living in Woodthorpe in York, having joined a troupe of players.[1] In 1780 Planché and his wife, Catherine, were recorded in the city of Bath, he working as an actor, prompter, and occasional playwright with the Orchard Street Theatre Company, again largely under his anglicized name. He died in somewhat distressed circumstances in 1805 and was buried at St. James's Church in Bath.[2]

Hilary Young illustrates the figure of this model in the collection of Lady Charlotte Schreiber as "possibly Derby, about 1750–3";[3] the uncertainty perhaps arising because at one point it was suggested—incorrectly, as chemical analysis has proved—that the figure had been produced at Charles Gouyn's St. James's factory.[4] Young further mentions what serves as the irony of WSS's ownership of this figure:

> [I]t was during [the late seventeenth and early eighteenth centuries] that the appreciation of china—like the twin passions for expenditure on luxury goods and luxurious living—became established as a female trait in the rhetoric of eighteenth-century English satirical writing and art. For instance, in Garrick's farce *Lethe*, Mrs. Riot is censured for buying china . . . ; and in his *Marriage à la Mode*, [the artist William] Hogarth shows a taste for porcelain contributing to the downfall of Countess Squanderfield.[5]

Catherine ("Kitty") Raftor Clive (1711–1785) was a popular and talented British actress, who in 1747 became a founding member of David Garrick's theatrical company and one of his leading ladies. In 1769 she retired to a villa called Little Strawberry Hill in Twickenham, Richmond-upon-Thames, which had been bought and given to her ca. 1754 by her friend Horace Walpole (1717–1797)—the art historian, man of letters, and Whig politician, who lived nearby at Strawberry Hill—and she died there in 1785. The watercolor from which the Mosley mezzotint engraving was made was described by Walpole in the 1781 Appendix to his inventory of the contents of Strawberry Hill, which he compiled originally before or in 1774: "Mrs. Catharine [*sic*] Clive, the excellent comedian, in the character of the fine lady in Lethe; in water-colours by Worlidge."[6] Hugh Tait adds a historical note that

> the first production of [Garrick's] *Lethe* was in April 1740 . . . [a shorter version, which appeared in print] in 1745, . . . containing neither the character, Mrs. Riot (The Fine Lady), nor the famous lines about "the Fine Lady's life which Mrs. Kitty Clive, the actress, spoke so well." This character, Mrs. Riot, and her splendid scenes do appear in the next and fuller edition, published in 1749, in which year Garrick presented the revised version at Drury Lane.[7]

Kitty Clive acted brilliantly in the new role. The watercolor and the Mosley engraving would have been made shortly thereafter, in the flush of her theatrical success, as would the Bow porcelain figure

50   ENGLISH PORCELAIN: DERBY

75 76 77 78

of the actress, ca. 1750, which, based on the identical graphic source, was most likely the direct inspiration for the Derby model.

For a brief comment on David Garrick, see cat. 17.

1. See Massey 2005a, p. 71.
2. See Twitchett 2002, pp. 95 and 98; and Barkla and Barkla 1995 and 1996.
3. See Victoria and Albert Museum, London, no. 414:135/A-1885; and Young 1999, p. vii. Lady Charlotte Schreiber, who bought this figure as Chelsea, also purchased a figure of Henry Woodward as the pair to Kitty Clive, which turned out to be Bow; see the Victoria and Albert Museum, London, no. 414:135-1885.
4. White 2014, p. 167.
5. Young 1999, p. 190.
6. Walpole 1774 [1786], Appendix, p. 130. See also Yarbrough 1996, pp. 26 and 21, where the print is illustrated, fig. 31.
7. Tait 1960b, p. 98.

75

Derby 'Dry-Edge' Group of a Shepherd Bagpiper and His Dog, ca. 1755

Modeled possibly by Agostino Carlini (1718–1790)
HEIGHT: 6⅞ in. (17.5 cm)
MARK: None
PROVENANCE: Albert Amor, Ltd., London, 1956
EXHIBITED: Dixon Gallery and Gardens, 1989
ACCESSION NUMBER: 2008.DA.2.74

It has been suggested by Peter White that the modeler of a small group of Derby figures of the "Dry-Edge Group B" type, dating from ca. 1753, to which the present figure belongs, was possibly Agostino Carlini, one of the two identified sculptors working in the early years of the factory,[1] the other being Andrew Planché (1728–1805; see cat. 74). Carlini's purportedly Genoese origins are obscure, and he is first identified as working in The Hague between 1749 and 1751, when, according to John Mallet, he "was the only sculptor regularly paid for work at the Huis ten Bosch [House in the Woods],"[2] the summer residence of William IV, Prince of Orange and Nassau (1711–1751), who became Stadtholder of Holland in 1747. Probably shortly after William IV's death Carlini left the Netherlands for London, and it is "just possible [that he arrived] in England in time to have modeled some of the 'Dry-Edge' figures recorded in the Duesbury London 'Account Book' [of 1751–1753].... There is a gap in Carlini's curriculum vitae from about 1752, when we lose sight of him in Holland, to 1760, in which year the sculptor exhibited at the Society of Artists a design for a monument to General [James] Wolfe [1727–1759], who had died the previous year at Quebec."[3] He continued as a sculptor in London and became a founding member of the Royal Academy in 1768. To what degree he contributed models to Duesbury at Derby can only be a matter of speculation based on the similarity of certain Derby figures, animals, and possibly a pair of rococo wall brackets to the exuberant Italian spirit of Carlini's sculpture in other mediums, particularly wood. But in that regard, Carlini's acknowledged artistry was inevitably the victim of the skill of the modelers at the factory itself, who were responsible for transforming his originals into their porcelain counterparts.

1. White 2014, p. 171.
2. Mallet 2003, p. 44.
3. Ibid., p. 49.

76

Derby Mythological Group of Venus and Cupid, 1758–1760
HEIGHT: 7⅝ in. (19.4 cm)
MARK: None
PROVENANCE: Collection of Mrs. Adrienne Long, sold at Parke-Bernet Galleries, Inc., New York City, December 6, 1946, lot 303 (as "Kloster Veilsdorf porcelain... circa 1775")
EXHIBITED: Dixon Gallery and Gardens, 1989
ACCESSION NUMBER: 2008.DA.2.75

77

Pair of Derby Groups of Seated Pastoral Musicians: A Bagpiper with a Dog and a Lutanist with a Sheep, ca. 1765

The bagpiper probably based on the Meissen porcelain figure of Harlequin playing the bagpipes, modeled originally by Johann Joachim Kändler, ca. 1738, and remodeled ca. 1745, each paired with Columbine playing a hurdy-gurdy
HEIGHT: 7½ in. (19 cm)
MARKS: Each with three patch marks, otherwise unmarked
PROVENANCE: Collection of Hermann Emden, Hamburg, Germany, sold at Rudolph Lepke's Kunst-Auctions-Haus, Berlin, November 6, 1908, lots 810 and 811, illustrated in the catalogue, pl. 67; Collection of Mrs. John Russell Pope, New York City, sold at Parke-Bernet Galleries, Inc., New York City, January 31, 1948, lot 535
EXHIBITED: Dixon Gallery and Gardens, 1989
ACCESSION NUMBER: 2008.DA.2.76.1 and .2

78

Pair of Derby Figures of the 'Ranelagh Dancers,' ca. 1765
HEIGHT: 10¹³⁄₁₆ and 10⅜ in. (27.5 and 26.4 cm)
MARKS: Each with three faint patch marks, otherwise unmarked
PROVENANCE: The Cuthbertson Collection, sold at Parke-Bernet Galleries, Inc., New York City, May 26, 1949, lot 26
EXHIBITED: Dixon Gallery and Gardens, 1989
ACCESSION NUMBER: 2008.DA.2.78.1 and .2

A series of figures of 'Ranelagh Masqueraders' was first produced by the Chelsea factory, ca. 1759–1763, as models commemorating the

ENGLISH PORCELAIN: DERBY

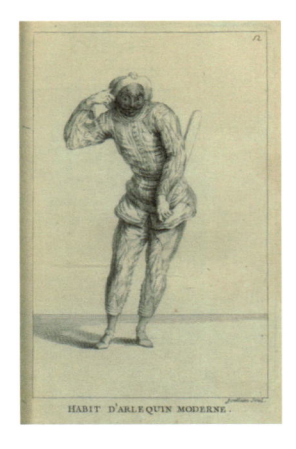

François Joullain, *"Habit d'Arlequin Moderne,"* 1728. Print from Luigi Riccoboni, *Histoire du Théâtre Italien.* The Metropolitan Museum of Art, New York, Thomas J. Watson Library (Jacob S. Rogers Fund, 1935).

79

80, 81

Jubilee Ball on May 24, 1759—the first masquerade ball ever held in the Ranelagh Gardens (a fashionable public pleasure garden in Chelsea, located just east of what is today the Chelsea Royal Hospital)—in this instance to celebrate the twenty-first birthday of George William Frederick, Prince of Wales (1738–1820), a year before he became King George III.[1] The Derby figures of the 'Ranelagh Dancers,' which were issued in several sizes, were inspired not by the Chelsea models themselves, but rather by the occasion and the popularity of masked balls to which a ticket was required. In Derby's pair, the lady wears the ticket in the form of an oval medallion suspended on a sash across her right shoulder,[2] and it has been suggested that the model was based on a mezzotint by James McArdell (1728/29–1765), published in 1757 after the portrait by Thomas Hudson (1701–1779) of Mary, Duchess of Ancaster and Kesteven (d. 1793), who in 1761 was appointed Mistress of the Robes to Queen Charlotte (1744–1818). In the original Derby model, the gentleman holds a letter (here missing) inscribed "Domini Lucretiae."[3]

As a historical note, the molds for the 'Ranelagh Dancers,' as well as for Milton (cat. 86), among many others, managed to survive the closure of the old Derby factory in 1848. As John Haslem records, in 1849

> Mr. Samuel Boyle, having purchased the whole of the plant, had it transferred to the Staffordshire Potteries. . . . Boyle's manufactory was at Fenton, and had formerly been Messrs. Mason's ironstone works. . . . In the course of a few years, however, Boyle fell into difficulties, the things were again sold, and were dispersed among different purchasers.[4]

Peter Bradshaw continues the story, noting that in 1852

> the material was purchased by Alderman William Taylor Copeland [(1797–1868), who had acquired the Spode factory in 1833]. During transportation in barges or while off-loading, many items fell into the canal and were lost, but the remainder is stored to this day [1990] in a room in the manufactory known as "the morgue." The author saw the contents of the "morgue" in 1984. It was then thick with black dust and included many thousands of arms, legs and torsos as clay squeezes, lead and terracotta master models and mould sections all mingled pell-mell.[5]

Miraculously, out of the maelstrom of body parts, in 1933 the Spode factory was able to recover and reproduce a number of the most popular early Derby models, which they revived again in the 1950s, among them the 'Ranelagh Dancers' (see cat. 250). In 2009 the Portmeirion Group purchased Spode and Royal Worcester from the administrators, and the Spode factory in Stoke was threatened with demolition, but not before a valiant rescue mission was performed by the American craftsman Donald G. Carpentier (1951–2014), who, with a small team of tireless workers, managed to save and export to the United States more than 60,000 of the old Spode molds (by then, even thicker with black dust) as well as some of the original wooden shelving on which they had been stored for as long as two centuries. With its historic buildings deteriorating, the Spode site, which was acquired in 2010 by the Stoke-on-Trent City Council, is still in danger, but it is hoped that the proposed redevelopment of the least historic areas of the site will enable the conservation and preservation of the factory that was for so many years the heartbeat of the town of Stoke.

1. For eleven Chelsea 'Ranelagh Masqueraders,' see Austin 1977, pp. 140–147, nos. 130–139.
2. Toppin 1951, p. 70, notes that "Admission tickets for Vauxhall Gardens, in gold and silver were designed by [William] Hogarth [(1697–1764), the famous British painter, best known for what he called his 'modern moral subjects']. Two [tickets] are illustrated in [Warwick] Wroth's *The London Pleasure Gardens [of the Eighteenth Century*, London: Macmillan] (1896), pp. 292 and 294."
3. See Bradshaw 1981, p. 196, who credits the suggested print source to Toppin 1951, p. 70; and likewise, Bradshaw 1990, pp. 86, 97, and 98, pl. 75, no. E17.
4. Haslem 1876, p. 30.
5. Bradshaw 1990, pp. 31 and 32.

79

Derby Italian Comedy Figure of Harlequin, 1770–1775
Model number 199 (the pair to a figure of Columbine)
HEIGHT: 6½ in. (16.5 cm)
MARK: None
PROVENANCE: Marshall Field & Company, Chicago, Illinois, 1951
EXHIBITED: Dixon Gallery and Gardens, 1989
ACCESSION NUMBER: 2008.DA.2.79

This figure was taken from the Chelsea model of ca. 1755,[1] which in turn may have been based on the engraving of *"Habit d'Arlequin Moderne"* by François Joullain (1697–1778) in Luigi Riccoboni's *Histoire du Théâtre Italien*, published by Pierre Delormel in Paris, 1728.[2] In the "Price List of Groups and Single Figures Enamelled and Gilt, and in Biscuit" published by John Haslem, in which the author includes the assigned factory number for the models made between about 1772 and 1795, number 199 is listed on p. 174 as "Ditto [Pair] Harlequin and Columbine, height 5½ inches [(13.9 cm) with a price of] 10s. 6d. enamelled and gilt, and 12s. in biscuit."[3] The size indicated is smaller than the Stout-Hooker example because of the figures' lower, plain mound bases, and also because they may be later versions of slightly earlier Derby models from which subsequent molds were made, and the resulting figures would undergo the usual 7 to 10 percent shrinkage during the cooling process after firing. This model, also made in mirror image at Bow, ca. 1760–1770, is unusual in that, as Meredith Chilton points out, no English porcelain version of this figure corresponds to any in

52 ENGLISH PORCELAIN: DERBY

82    83    84

the Meissen 'Duke of Weissenfels Series' of 1744, on which most of the other English porcelain Italian Comedy figures were based (see cat. 49).[4]

1. See Chilton 2001, p. 277, no. 26, and p. 279, no. 32.
2. See ibid., p. 111, fig. 176; and Bradshaw 1990, pp. 300–302, no. 199 and pl. 248.
3. See the price list in Haslem 1876, pp. 170–178; see also Twitchett 1980, p. 67.
4. Chilton 2001, p. 277, no. 26.

80

Derby Allegorical Figure of Britannia with Her Lion and Symbols of Puissance, 1765–1770

Model number 259, 1st of three sizes (a larger version of the earlier model issued as number 121), adapted probably from a lead statue by John Cheere (1709–1787)
HEIGHT: 14⅛ in. (35.9 cm)
MARKS: Four faint patch marks, otherwise unmarked
PROVENANCE: Collection of Mrs. Henry D. Burnham, Boston, Massachusetts, sold at Parke-Bernet Galleries, Inc., New York City, March 15, 1946, lot 320
EXHIBITED: Dixon Gallery and Gardens, 1989
ACCESSION NUMBER: 2008.DA.2.80

Understandably, the figure of Britannia was an enduring model, which seems to have appeared as early as 1763, when "models of *Britannia* were included in a large consignment of Derby porcelain dispatched for sale to London in 1763, some of which may have been adapted upon lead garden statuary by John Cheere representing *Minerva*."[1] (For further information on Cheere, see cat. 86.) It is interesting that both of Derby's figures of Britannia and Minerva (cat. 81) were taken from the same model, though eventually they were modified with symbolic attributes to differentiate their identities. The model continued to be made throughout the eighteenth century, with the shape of the base also being adapted to suit the changing tastes of the period.

1. Bradshaw 1990, p. 328, citing Jewitt 1878, vol. 2, pp. 68–69; and Clifford 1969, p. 113, who suggests the adaptation from garden statuary.

81

Derby Mythological Figure of Minerva with Her Attributes of Wisdom, 1765–1770

Model number 298, 1st of three sizes (a larger version of the earlier model issued as number 121), adapted probably from a lead statue by John Cheere (1709–1787)
HEIGHT: 15½ in. (39.3 cm)
MARKS: Three faint patch marks, otherwise unmarked
PROVENANCE: Collection of Mrs. Henry D. Burnham, Boston, Massachusetts, sold at Parke-Bernet Galleries, Inc., New York City, March 15, 1946, lot 321
EXHIBITED: Dixon Gallery and Gardens, 1989
ACCESSION NUMBER: 2008.DA.2.81

See cat. 80 for a discussion of the model of Minerva.

82

Derby 'Birds in Branches' Candlestick Group, ca. 1765

HEIGHT: 8¹⁵⁄₁₆ in. (22.7 cm)
MARKS: Three patch marks, otherwise unmarked
PROVENANCE: Marshall Field & Company, Chicago, Illinois, 1946
ACCESSION NUMBER: 2008.DA.2.82

The coloring of the two birds in this bocage candlestick makes their ornithological identification difficult and suggests that the painter used some artistic license. Although the birds often are referred to as buntings, the model actually is included as "Redstart candlesticks" in "A List of Moulds and Models Which Belonged to the Estate of the Late Mr. [William] Duesbury in 1795, as Estimated by Messrs. Soar, Longdon, Farnsworth & Hardenberg."[1]

1. See Twitchett 2002, pp. 267 and 269.

83

Derby Arbor Figure of a Seated Musician Playing a Bagpipe, ca. 1770

Model number 301 (a reissue of model number 280); originally a candelabrum with flanking branches supporting pierced candle nozzles
HEIGHT: 14½ in. (36.8 cm)
MARK: None
PROVENANCE: The Cuthbertson Collection, sold at Parke-Bernet Galleries, Inc., New York City, May 26, 1949, lot 29
ACCESSION NUMBER: 2008.DA.2.77

84

Pair of Derby Arbor Figures of Seated Musicians Playing a Lute or a Bagpipe, ca. 1770

Model number 301 (a reissue of model number 280); originally a pair of candelabra with flanking branches supporting pierced candle nozzles
HEIGHT: 12⅜ and 11¼ in. (31.5 and 28.6 cm)
MARKS: Each with four patch marks, otherwise unmarked
PROVENANCE: The Cuthbertson Collection, sold at Parke-Bernet Galleries, Inc., New York City, May 26, 1949, lot 29
ACCESSION NUMBER: 2008.DA.2.83.1 (man) and .2 (lady)

ENGLISH PORCELAIN: DERBY

The Stag Looking into the Water, from Robert Sayer, *The Ladies Amusement*, 1762, pl. 116.

159, 160

159

Worcester 'Wet Blue'–Ground 'Fable' Plate, ca. 1770

Painted probably by Jefferyes Hamett O'Neale (ca. 1734–1801) with 'The Stag Looking into the Water,' after the engraving for Fable CVI in Francis Barlow's *Æsop's Fables* (1687), p. 213; and for Fable VIII in the Reverend Samuel Croxall's *Fables of Æsop and Others* (1722)

DIAMETER: 7⅝ in. (19.4 cm)
MARK: Pseudo-Chinese seal mark in underglaze blue
PROVENANCE: Collection of Reginald Bastard, D.S.O., and John Rodney Bastard, Kitley House, Yealmpton, Devon, England, sold at Christie's, London, April 21, 1953, lot 85 (a pair, with cat. 160); Winifred Williams Antiques, Eastbourne, Sussex, England, 1953
EXHIBITED: Dixon Gallery and Gardens, 1989
LITERATURE: Marshall 1954, p. 52, pl. 13, no. 15, illustrated, and pp. 54–55; C.M. Scott and G.R. Scott 1961, p. 198 and pl. 159, no. 550
ACCESSION NUMBER: 2008.DA.169

Little is known about the life and work of Jefferyes Hamett O'Neale, but the most thorough biographical account is given by Stephen Hanscombe.[1] O'Neale was a painter of Irish descent specializing in miniatures, which he exhibited at the Society for the Encouragement of the Arts in London from 1762 to 1768. In London he also worked, though perhaps not exclusively, for the Chelsea factory from about 1750/52 to 1758, painting monochrome landscapes and polychrome fable scenes, with which he is now most closely identified, although many have been reattributed to other unknown artists (see cat. 36 for O'Neale's painting on Chelsea porcelain). By April 1768 O'Neale had moved to Worcester, where he distinguished himself by his fable decoration, largely on blue-ground wares, which he occasionally signed, enabling a more positive identification of his skilled and imaginative hand in this genre—although fable subjects were painted by other factory artists as well. After "returning to London in March 1770, O'Neale subsequently did some work for William Duesbury and Josiah Wedgwood,"[2] but his work as an illustrator seems to have been his primary, if meager, source of income. He died unmarried and impoverished "in November 1801, and was buried at St. Pancras Old Church"[3] in the London borough of Camden.

Further information on this fable and its sources is supplied by Hanscombe, who illustrates the subject from Robert Sayer, and supplies the text from Mrs. Aphra Behn's synopses of Francis Barlow's *Æsop's Fables* (1687):

CVI The Stag looking in the Water
The Stag admires the beauty of his Horns,
But the ill graces of his Legs he scorns;
The Dogs approacht, and with those Legs he'd fled,
Had he not been entangled by his Head.
Morall: That which we value most may help us Least,
And often we despise what serves us best.[4]

Although a 1722 first edition of Samuel Croxall's *Æsop's Fables* was not accessible for current research, many revised editions were subsequently published. The fourteenth edition of 1789, "carefully Revised and Improved" (according to its title page), includes "The Stag looking into the Water" as Fable VIII, but illustrates the stag with a print showing the image in reverse and with variations. So while the subject was an illustrative source for O'Neale, the print in Croxall's *Æsop's Fables* clearly was not the direct source for the decoration on this Worcester plate.[5]

1. Hanscombe 2010, pp. 5–13.
2. J. Sandon 1993, p. 251.
3. Hanscombe 2010, p. 13.
4. Ibid., pp. 116–117, no. 107; and p. 170, illustrating the subject from Sayer 1762, pl. 116 (fig. 15).
5. Croxall 1789, pp. 13–15, illustrated on p. 13.

160

Worcester 'Wet Blue'–Ground 'Fable' Plate, ca. 1770

Painted probably by Jefferyes Hamett O'Neale (ca. 1734–1801) with an unidentified fable subject depicting three geese hissing at a fox hanging from a gibbet

DIAMETER: 7⅝ in. (19.4 cm)
MARK: Pseudo-Chinese seal mark in underglaze blue
PROVENANCE: Collection of Reginald Bastard, D.S.O., and John Rodney Bastard, Kitley House, Yealmpton, Devon, England, sold at Christie's, London, April 21, 1953, lot 85 (a pair, with cat. 159); Winifred Williams Antiques, Eastbourne, Sussex, England, 1953
EXHIBITED: Dixon Gallery and Gardens, 1989
LITERATURE: Marshall 1954, p. 52, pl. 13, no. 18, illustrated, and p. 55; C.M. Scott and G.R. Scott 1961, p. 198 and pl. 159, no. 551
ACCESSION NUMBER: 2008.DA.2.170

The collector Henry Rissik Marshall, whose collection is at the Ashmolean Museum, Oxford, commented that, in an attempt to identify the graphic sources of the fables represented on the series of Worcester plates to which cats. 159 and 160 belong,

> a large number of books dating prior to 1770, which is approximately the date on which this china was painted, [were] consulted, [but] four have yielded more results than the others, namely, *Æsop's Fables*, by Francis Barlow, 1687; *Æsop's Fables* by S. Croxall, 1722; *Fables Choisies par J de la Fontaine*, illustrated by J.B. Oudry, in four volumes, 1755–9; and *Æsop's Fables* by Dodsley, 1765.[1]

Some sources, however, could not be identified, which led "the author to believe there must be, or have been, some fable books or books of design intermediate between Barlow and O'Neale which he has not yet been lucky enough to find."[2] Subsequent searches still have not discovered the fable associated with the present plate.

1. Marshall 1954, p. 45.
2. Ibid.

ENGLISH PORCELAIN: WORCESTER

161

Worcester Plate Painted with Exotic Birds, 1765–1770
  Painted in the London atelier of James Giles (1718–1780)
  DIAMETER: 7½ in. (19.1 cm)
  MARK: None
  PROVENANCE: William H. Lautz, New York City, 1948
  ACCESSION NUMBER: 2008.DA.2.178

James Giles is the "China Painter" most familiarly associated with Worcester porcelain decorated outside of the factory. Giles is thought to have completed his apprenticeship in London in 1740, a year before the death of his father, who also was a "China Painter," and only three years before he opened his own decorating studio in Soho, which by 1747 had developed into a retail business as well. His early enameling work may have been primarily on Chinese export porcelain, but he also painted glass and English porcelain, eventually concentrating on undecorated or even partially decorated Worcester porcelain, which he obtained in great quantities from the factory, and which he advertised he could paint in any pattern his clients might choose. He also acquired finished pieces from various factories to enhance his retail business. "Giles's last purchase from Worcester was in December 1774,"[1] although by then his business had been in decline, as evidenced by the five-day sale at Christie's in March 1774, the 450 lots of which were composed entirely of "the STOCK in TRADE of Mr. *JAMES GILES*, CHINAMAN and ENAMELLER, Quitting that Business, brought from his shop in *Cockspur Street* opposite *Spring Gardens*."[2] In spite of the large sale, Giles continued in the retail business well into 1777 in the Cockspur Street shop that he had opened in 1767. While his subsequent activities have not been identified, it is possible that he lived his final three years in well-earned retirement.

1. Hanscombe 2005, p. 13.
2. Ibid.

162

Worcester Coffee Cup and Saucer, 1770–1772
  Painted in the London atelier of James Giles (1718–1780) with flower sprays and foliate vines
  Cup: H. 3 in. (7.7 cm); Saucer: DIAM. 5⅛ in. (13 cm)
  MARKS: Pseudo-Meissen crossed swords mark and numeral 9. in underglaze blue on each piece
  PROVENANCE: Collection of Frederick Walter Carter, Edinburgh, Scotland (Marshall Field catalogue number 48b); Marshall Field & Company, Chicago, Illinois, 1946
  ACCESSION NUMBER: 2008.DA.2.171a, b

163

Worcester Pink-Scale-Bordered Kidney-Shaped Dessert Dish, ca. 1770
  Painted in the London atelier of James Giles (1718–1780) after a Meissen porcelain original
  LENGTH: 11¼ in. (28.6 cm)
  MARK: None
  PROVENANCE: Albert Amor, Ltd., London, 1955
  ACCESSION NUMBER: 2008.DA.2.172

164

Worcester Pink-Scale-Bordered Waste Bowl, the porcelain ca. 1770
  Painted later in the style of James Giles (1718–1780) with a rural family scene in the manner of David Teniers the Younger (1610–1690)
  DIAMETER: 6 in. (15.3 cm)
  MARK: None
  PROVENANCE: Stoner & Evans, London, who sold the piece erroneously as having come from the Lady Ludlow Collection,

165

166

167

Luton Hoo, Bedfordshire, England; Collection of Marcel H. Stieglitz, New York City, sold at Parke-Bernet Galleries, Inc., New York City, January 23, 1954, lot 256
EXHIBITED: Chicago, Illinois, The Art Institute of Chicago, *The Stieglitz Collection of Dr. Wall Worcester Porcelain*, May 7–November 3, 1947, no. 134, catalogue pl. XXVI; Providence, Rhode Island, Rhode Island School of Design Museum, *Worcester Porcelain of the Dr. Wall Period Collected and Catalogued by Marcel H. Stieglitz*, July 1–October 15, 1949, no. 134; Dixon Gallery and Gardens, 1989
LITERATURE: McNair 2007, p. 293
ACCESSION NUMBER: 2008.DA.2.173

The waste bowl that Stoner & Evans assumed they were selling to WSS, because it so closely resembles the present example, is still in the Lady Ludlow Collection (now at the Bowes Museum, Barnard Castle, Co. Durham) as a component of what was originally a seventeen-piece tea and coffee service (now eleven pieces). It has been described by Arthur Hayden and illustrated and discussed by Anne McNair, who notes that this service, formerly fully attributed to Worcester with decoration by James Giles, actually is composed of pieces assembled from various factories, including Caughley (the waste bowl), Neale, and others.[1] Given the potential range of dates of the component pieces made after 1776 when Giles sold his workshop, the attribution for the decoration clearly had to be reassessed. As a result, it is currently thought that very little of the decoration on Worcester pink-scale pieces is actually of the period, although cat. 163 is a felicitous exception to this reassessment.

1. Hayden 1932, no. 71; McNair 2007, pp. 291–293, no. 9.

165
Worcester Faceted Teabowl and Saucer,
the porcelain ca. 1770
Painted at a later date with flowers and claret-ground panels
DIAMETERS: 3⅜ and 5⁷⁄₁₆ in. (8.6 and 13.8 cm)
MARK: Pseudo-Chinese seal mark in underglaze blue on each piece
PROVENANCE: Purportedly from the Rous Lench Collection of Thomas Burn, Rous Lench Court, Worcestershire, England; William H. Lautz, New York City, 1953
ACCESSION NUMBER: 2008.DA.2.174a, b

166
Worcester Coffee Cup and Saucer, the porcelain ca. 1770
Painted in the nineteenth century with bowknotted floral garlands and a chain border
Cup: H. 2½ in. (6.4 cm); Saucer: DIAM. 4⅞ in. (12.4 cm)
MARK: None
PROVENANCE: Collection of Frederick Walter Carter, Edinburgh, Scotland (Marshall Field catalogue number 23: a twenty-three-piece tea and coffee service); Marshall Field & Company, Chicago, Illinois, 1950
ACCESSION NUMBER: 2008.DA.2.177a, b

167
Worcester Plate Painted with the 'Marchioness of Huntly' Pattern, ca. 1770
DIAMETER: 8⅞ in. (22.5 cm)
MARK: None
PROVENANCE: Wilson Galleries, Chicago, Illinois, 1948
ACCESSION NUMBER: 2008.DA.2.175

ENGLISH PORCELAIN: WORCESTER   75

168

169

170

171

168

Worcester Quatrefoil Chestnut Basket, Pierced Cover, and a Pierced Stand, 1770–1772

The stand contemporary with, but not original to, the covered basket
LENGTHS: 7⅝ and 10⅜ in. (19.4 and 26.4 cm)
MARK: None
PROVENANCE: Stoner & Evans, London; Wilson Galleries, Chicago, Illinois, 1948
ACCESSION NUMBER: 2008.DA.2.176a–c

169

Worcester Square Dessert Dish Painted with the 'Earl Manvers' Pattern of Hops, Swags, and S-Scrolls, 1775–1778

WIDTH: 8½ in. (21.6 cm)
MARK: None
PROVENANCE: Collection of Frederick Walter Carter, Edinburgh, Scotland (Marshall Field catalogue number 20c: a pair); Marshall Field & Company, Chicago, Illinois, 1946; Mrs. Lilian B. Little, Oak Park, Illinois, 1947
ACCESSION NUMBER: 2008.DA.2.179

170

Worcester Scalloped Circular Dish Painted with a 'Hop Trellis' Pattern, 1780–1785

DIAMETER: 9⅝ in. (24.5 cm)
MARK: Open crescent mark in underglaze blue
PROVENANCE: Collection of Sir Oliver Welby, Bart., Denton Manor, Grantham, England, sold at Sotheby's, London, February 24, 1956, lot 4 (a forty-two-piece "tea and coffee equipage"); Winifred Williams Antiques, Eastbourne, Sussex, England, 1956
ACCESSION NUMBER: 2008.DA.2.181

171

Worcester Fluted Teacup and Saucer Painted with Floral Garlands above a Green Shagreen Border, 1780–1785

DIAMETERS: 3¹/₁₆ and 5⁹/₁₆ in. (7.8 and 14.2 cm)
MARK: The cup with a script *W* mark in underglaze blue; the saucer unmarked
PROVENANCE: Winifred Williams Antiques, Eastbourne, Sussex, England, 1956
ACCESSION NUMBER: 2008.DA.2.180a, b

172

Worcester 'Gros Bleu'–Bordered Dodecagonal Oval Dessert Dish, ca. 1780

LENGTH: 11⁷/₁₆ in. (29.1 cm)
MARKS: Script *W* mark and a small painter's mark in underglaze blue
PROVENANCE: Collection of Alfred Trapnell, Great Chalfield, Bournemouth, England; Albert Amor, Ltd., London (unconfirmed); Collection of Frederick Walter Carter, Edinburgh, Scotland (Marshall Field catalogue number 170); Marshall Field & Company, Chicago, Illinois, 1946
ACCESSION NUMBER: 2008.DA.2.185

172

173

174 175 176

173

Worcester Lozenge-Shaped Dessert Dish Painted with a 'Lord Henry Thynne Service'–Type Pattern, 1780–1785

Painted in the manner of Jefferyes Hamett O'Neale (ca. 1734–1801) with three leopards attacking a stag
LENGTH: 11¹⁵⁄₁₆ in. (30.3 cm)
MARK: Open crescent mark in underglaze blue
PROVENANCE: Collection of Marcel H. Stieglitz, New York City, sold at Parke-Bernet Galleries, Inc., New York City, January 23, 1954, lot 264 (a pair; the other dish bought by Bertram Cohn, Memphis, Tennessee)
EXHIBITED: Chicago, Illinois, The Art Institute of Chicago, *The Stieglitz Collection of Dr. Wall Worcester Porcelain*, May 7–November 3, 1947, no. 138, catalogue pl. XXVIII (bottom), the painting attributed to Jefferyes Hamett O'Neale; Providence, Rhode Island, Rhode Island School of Design Museum, *Worcester Porcelain of the Dr. Wall Period Collected and Catalogued by Marcel H. Stieglitz*, July 1–October 15, 1949, no. 138; Dixon Gallery and Gardens, 1989
ACCESSION NUMBER: 2008.DA.2.183

This dessert service certainly would have been a special commission. The border pattern is well known, but the unusually graphic central subject is uncharacteristic of the Worcester production; while it may represent an early fable, such as Aesop's fable of "The Deer and the Lion,"[1] neither the precise literary reference nor the pictorial source has been discovered.

1. "The Deer and the Lion" is Fable CXCI (191) in Croxall 1789, pp. 320–321.

174

Worcester Fluted Saucer Dish Painted with an 'Earl Dalhousie Service'–Type Pattern, 1780–1785

DIAMETER: 8⅜ in. (21.3 cm)
MARK: Open crescent mark in underglaze blue
PROVENANCE: Purportedly from the collection of F. Severne Mackenna, The Hollies, Droitwich, Worcestershire, England; T. Leonard Crow, Tewkesbury, Gloucestershire, England, 1950
LITERATURE: Mackenna 1950, pl. 37, fig. 76
ACCESSION NUMBER: 2008.DA.2.184

175

Worcester Plate Painted with the 'Lord Rodney Service' Pattern of 'Fancy Birds,' ca. 1785

DIAMETER: 8⅜ in. (21.3 cm)
MARK: Open crescent mark in underglaze blue
PROVENANCE: William H. Lautz, New York City, 1952
ACCESSION NUMBER: 2008.DA.2.182

176

Worcester 'Clobbered' Cup and Saucer Painted in Underglaze Blue with the 'Chantilly Sprig' Pattern, 1775–1780

Enhanced probably slightly later in iron-red
Cup: H. 2⅝ in. (6.7 cm); Saucer: DIAM. 4⁹⁄₁₆ in. (11.6 cm)
MARK: Pseudo-Chantilly hunting horn mark in underglaze blue on each piece
PROVENANCE: Stoner & Evans, London; Collection of Mr. [Herbert M. ?] Hughes, London and Leicestershire, England; Mrs. Lilian B. Little, Oak Park, Illinois, 1947
ACCESSION NUMBER: 2008.DA.2.186a, b

ENGLISH PORCELAIN: WORCESTER   77

177

Worcester Plate Painted in Underglaze Blue with the 'Royal Lily' Pattern, 1785–1790

Flight Period
DIAMETER: 6⅞ in. (17.5 cm)
MARK: Open crescent mark in underglaze blue
PROVENANCE: Marshall Field & Company, Chicago, Illinois, 1946
ACCESSION NUMBER: 2008.DA.2.187

178

Worcester Plate with a Crest and Monogram GEM, ca. 1790

Flight Period
DIAMETER: 8¾ in. (22.2 cm)
MARK: Open crescent mark in underglaze blue
PROVENANCE: The Georgian Experience, Memphis, Tennessee, at the Houston Museum Antique Show, Chattanooga, Tennessee, 1987
ACCESSION NUMBER: 2008.DA.2.356

179

Worcester Armorial Plate from the Duke of Clarence Service, ca. 1789

Flight Period
DIAMETER: 9¾ in. (24.7 cm)
MARKS: Crowned *Flight* and open crescent mark in underglaze blue
PROVENANCE: H.R.H. Prince William Henry (1765–1837), who became Duke of Clarence and St. Andrew in 1789, and King William IV in 1830; to his son, George Augustus Frederick FitzClarence, Earl of Munster (1799–1854) [the illegitimate son of the Duke of Clarence and Dorothy George]; to his sister, Elizabeth FitzClarence Hay, Countess of Erroll (1801–1856) [the illegitimate daughter of the Duke of Clarence and Mrs. Jordan], the wife of William George Hay, 18th Earl of Erroll (1801–1846); to her grandson, Charles Gore Hay (1852–1927), who succeeded his father in 1891 as 20th Earl of Erroll; to his widow, Mary Caroline L'Estrange Hay, Dowager Countess of Erroll (d. 1934), who sold ten plates at Messrs. Puttick & Simpson, London, October 14, 1927 (£171 3s), but whether this plate was among them is unconfirmable; Stoner & Evans, London; Collection of Frederick Walter Carter, Edinburgh, Scotland (Marshall Field catalogue number 1a); Marshall Field & Company, Chicago, Illinois, 1946
EXHIBITED: Atlanta, Georgia, High Museum of Art, *Fit for a King: Porcelains of Royalty and Nobility*, February 11, 1995–April 1, 1996; Dixon Gallery and Gardens, 1989
ACCESSION NUMBER: 2008.DA.2.188

This plate is from a service for dessert ordered in 1789 by H.R.H. Prince William Henry "to commemorate his elevation to Duke of Clarence and St. Andrew, and his investiture with the Order of the Thistle."[1] The duke's central coat of arms is encircled by the blue and gold Garter and motto HONI SOIT QUI MAL Y PENSE entwined with the green ribbon of the Thistle suspending the badge of the Thistle against flanking branches of oak ("a personal emblem of the Duke")[2] and olive leaves, and surmounted by the royal ducal coronet, all surrounded on the rim with a border formed by the husk-patterned entwined blue and green ribbons of the Orders of the Garter and the Thistle decorated in gold with motifs from the collars of the two orders and painted in the interstices at the top with The George, at the bottom with the badge of the Thistle, at the sides with the jewels of the Garter and Thistle, and in the eight remaining spaces with the pink rose and thistle flowers of the two orders.

1. Oakey 2012, p. 199.
2. Ibid.

180

Worcester Sauce Tureen, Cover, and Stand from the Duke of Clarence's 'Hope Service,' 1790–1792

Flight Period
Painted *en grisaille* by John Pennington (1765–1842) with allegorical scenes of 'Hope'
LENGTHS: 8⅝ and 9⅝ in. (21.9 and 24.5 cm)
MARKS: Crowned *Flight* and open crescent mark in underglaze blue on the tureen and stand
PROVENANCE: H.R.H. Prince William Henry (1765–1837), who became Duke of Clarence and St. Andrew in 1789, and King William IV in 1830; to his son, George Augustus Frederick FitzClarence, Earl of Munster (1799–1854) [the illegitimate son of the Duke of Clarence and Dorothy George]; to his sister, Elizabeth FitzClarence Hay, Countess of Erroll (1801–1856) [the illegitimate daughter of the Duke of Clarence and Mrs. Jordan], the wife of William George Hay, 18th Earl of Erroll (1801–1846); to her grandson, Charles Gore Hay (1852–1927), who succeeded his father in 1891 as 20th Earl of Erroll, and who sold 260 pieces of the service at Christie, Manson & Woods, London, May 11, 1893, lots 104–165, of which the eight pairs of sauce tureens were lots 106–112A; Marshall Field & Company, Chicago, Illinois, 1947
EXHIBITED: Dixon Gallery and Gardens, 1989
ACCESSION NUMBER: 2008.DA.2.189a–c

Little is known of John Pennington, but it is assumed that he was the son of James Pennington (1728–1804), who made porcelain at Brownlow Hill (ca. 1763–1767) and Park Lane (ca. 1767–1773) in Liverpool, and then at the short-lived Wirksworth China Factory (1772–1777) in Derbyshire (see cat. 271) before returning to

ENGLISH PORCELAIN: WORCESTER

180

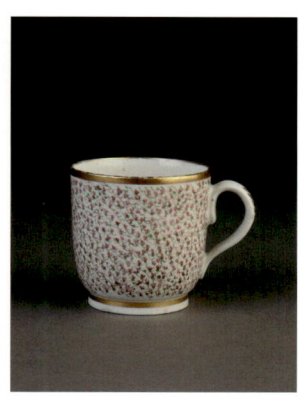

181

Liverpool. Born in Liverpool, John Pennington and his slightly older brother Robert were indentured in 1784 as apprentices to Josiah Wedgwood (1730–1795) to paint creamware in Wedgwood's London decorating shop. Within several years the brothers had joined the Flights' factory in Worcester, and John, having been hired in 1789, was set to work painting the important 'Hope Service' for the Duke of Clarence. John Pennington continued to work for the Worcester factory into and possibly through the Flight, Barr and Barr period (1813–1840) as a master of monochrome painting, but, because he never signed his work, much of what is less characteristic probably has remained unrecognized.[1]

The 'Hope Service,' the second of the two Worcester services ordered by H.R.H. Prince William Henry in 1789, the year in which he was created Duke of Clarence and St. Andrew, reflects his retirement and honorary elevation later that year to the rank of rear admiral of the British Navy, in which he had been enrolled at the age of thirteen by his father (King George III), and in which he had served admirably. As a sizable dinner service, the royal order seems to have been met with great celebration at John and Joseph Flight's factory, which up until that time had been struggling with technical difficulties.

According to Henry Sandon, John Flight's diary

> records the large order . . . for a service costing £700, the work to be completed in a year [though in fact it took three years to complete]. Two quality painters were enlisted [one of them the clever John Pennington, recruited] . . . from under the nose of Chamberlain; . . . and [the gilding was done by or under the supervision of Mrs. Charlotte Hampton, an expert gilder, who began working for the Flights in 1789]. John Flight makes the most interesting note that three specimen patterns were provided from which the Duke was to choose, on the themes of 'Arabesque,' 'Hope and Patience' and 'Peace and Abundance.' The Duke chose 'Hope and Patience' ['Hope's' symbol being an anchor,] and the local announcement of the order, coinciding with the "Grand Illuminations" in the city of Worcester to celebrate the Queen's Birthday [Queen Charlotte was born on May 19, 1744], brought prestige and publicity to the factory.[2]

The service remained in the family for a century until the majority of the surviving pieces were sold by the 20th Earl of Erroll at Christie, Manson & Woods in London, where the sale catalogue described it as:

THE CELEBRATED DINNER SERVICE OF OLD WORCESTER PORCELAIN (CONSISTING OF UPWARDS OF 260 PIECES), PRESENTED BY THE BRITISH NATION TO LORD NELSON "THE HERO OF THE NILE," by whom it was bequeathed to King William IV., and presented by him to Lord Frederick Fitzclarence, and now the property of the Earl of Erroll. Each piece is painted with a portrait of Lady Hamilton as Hope in varied attitudes on the seashore, a ship in the distance, the borders dark-blue, with rich decoration in gold, and is marked "Flight," with a crown above and crescent below in blue.[3]

This is an interesting example of family legend unnecessarily "enhancing" the true history and provenance of a possession—in this instance a service, which, with its legitimate royal provenance, needed no apocryphal and romanticized Nelsonian glorification. The service, listed in Christie's catalogue as lots 104 through 165, included 2 pairs of large oval tureens, covers, and stands; 8 pairs of oval sauce tureens, covers, and stands (among them the present tureen, cover, and stand); a large circular fluted bowl; another smaller; 50 oval platters in sizes from 11 to 20½ inches (27.9 to 52 cm); 144 plates (including "four broken"); and 46 soup plates. Unfortunately, inasmuch as the service was not illustrated in the catalogue, and it included eight pairs of sauce tureens (lots 106–112A, which sold for between £14 3s. 6d. and £15 4s. 6d. per pair), it is not possible to know which of the eight different purchasers bought the Stout and Hooker Collection example, or how often it changed hands during the ensuing half century until it was acquired by Marshall Field & Company and sold to WSS. Complicating without clarifying the provenance, on February 16, 1900, Christie, Manson & Woods in London offered as lots 228–246 fifty-four pieces of the 'Hope Service' previously sold from the 20th Earl of Erroll's collection in 1893, and representing the lots that were purchased by a buyer named Restell. Lot 230 was a pair of sauce tureens, covers, and stands that sold for £56 14s. to A. B. Daniell. Perhaps one of this pair is the present example.[4]

1. See Hillis 2011, p. 87; and J. Sandon 1993, pp. 163 and 258.
2. H. Sandon 1978a, pp. 27, 28, 230, and 231.
3. Christie, Manson & Woods, London, sale catalogue, May 11, 1893.
4. Christie, Manson & Woods, London, sale catalogue, February 16, 1900. Copies of the appropriate pages from these two catalogues, annotated with the prices and buyers, were kindly supplied by Lynda McLeod and Harriet Reed of Christie's Archives in London, whose assistance is acknowledged with thanks.

181

Flight and Barr Worcester Coffee Cup, ca. 1800
HEIGHT: 2⅝ in. (6.7 cm)
MARK: Crowned script *Flight & Barr* mark in blue enamel
PROVENANCE: Marshall Field & Company, Chicago, Illinois, 1946; Mrs. Lilian B. Little, Oak Park, Illinois, 1947 (sold with its saucer, now missing)
ACCESSION NUMBER: 2008.DA.2.190

182

*Flight, Barr and Barr Worcester 'Oeil-de-Perdrix'-
Ground Saucer and Teacup Foot*, ca. 1813

Saucer: DIAM. 5⅞ in. (14.9 cm)
MARKS: The cup with impressed crowned FBB, and the saucer with impressed crowned BFB
PROVENANCE: Taskey's Antiques, Chicago, Illinois, 1948 (who sold WSS an intact cup and saucer; the cup was broken during its ownership by CSH)
ACCESSION NUMBER: 2008.DA.2.191a, b

183

Flight, Barr and Barr Worcester Crested Plate, 1815–1820

DIAMETER: 9½ in. (24.2 cm)
MARKS: Prince of Wales feathers crest within the 'FLIGHT BARR & BARR Proprietors of the Royal Porcelain Works WORCESTER Established 1751, London Warehouse No 1 Coventry Street' mark printed in brown, and impressed crowned FBB mark
PROVENANCE: The Georgian Experience, Memphis, Tennessee, at the Houston Museum Antique Show, Chattanooga, Tennessee, 1986
EXHIBITED: Dixon Gallery and Gardens, 1989
ACCESSION NUMBER: 2008.DA.2.358

184

*Flight, Barr and Barr Worcester Crested
Oval Platter*, 1815–1820

With the motto DEUS ADJUVAT NOS [God assists us] of the Booth family of Essex, Baronets
LENGTH: 12⅛ in. (30.8 cm)
MARK: Impressed crowned FBB mark
PROVENANCE: Marshall Field & Company, Chicago, Illinois, 1948
EXHIBITED: Dixon Gallery and Gardens, 1989
ACCESSION NUMBER: 2008.DA.2.192

185

*Flight, Barr and Barr Worcester
Imari-Style Plate*, 1815–1820

DIAMETER: 9⅝ in. (24.4 cm)
MARK: Impressed crowned FBB mark
PROVENANCE: Atlanta Antiques Exchange, Atlanta, Georgia, 1982
ACCESSION NUMBER: 2008.DA.2.357

186

*Flight, Barr and Barr Worcester Teacup and Saucer
with Gilt 'Seaweed' Decoration*, ca. 1820

Cup: H. 2½ in. (6.3 cm); Saucer: DIAM. 5¹⁵⁄₁₆ in. (15.1 cm)
MARK: Impressed crowned FBB mark on each piece
PROVENANCE: Antiques on the Corner, Inc., Lookout Mountain, Tennessee, 1989
ACCESSION NUMBER: 2008.DA.2.359a, b

187

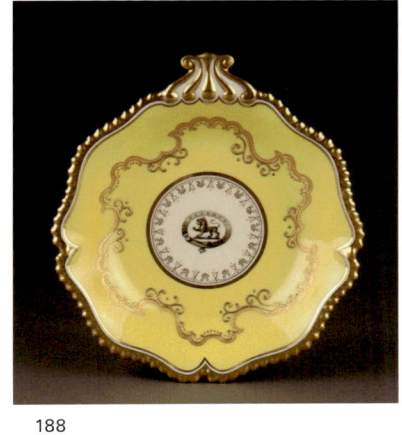

188

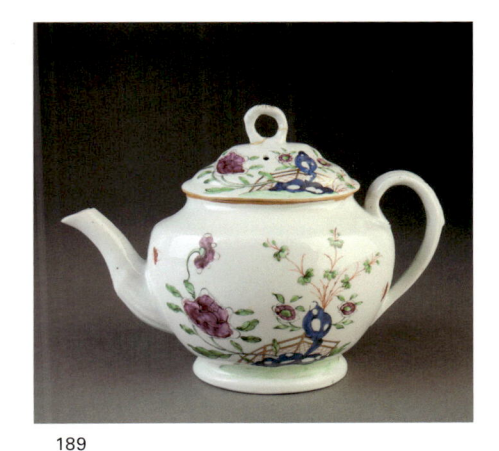

189

190

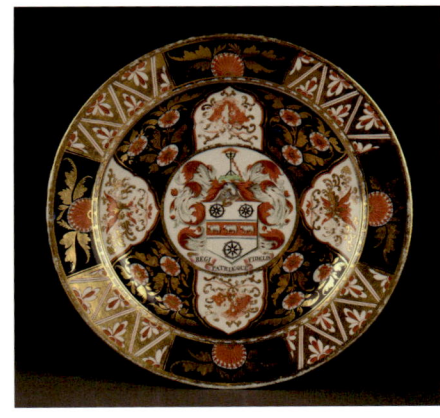

191

187
Flight, Barr and Barr Worcester Tripod Vase and Cover with Floral Decoration and Gilt Winged Mermen Supports, 1820–1825
- HEIGHT: 9⅝ in. (24.5 cm)
- MARKS: 'Flight Barr & Barr Royal Porcelain Works Worcester / London House 1 Coventry Street /' in brown script, and impressed crowned FBB mark
- PROVENANCE: B. Manheim, New Orleans, Louisiana, 1945
- ACCESSION NUMBER: 2008.DA.2.193 a, b

188
Flight, Barr and Barr Worcester Yellow-Ground Crested Dessert Dish, 1825–1830
- With the motto VICIMUS [We won]
- LENGTH: 8½ in. (21.6 cm)
- MARK: Indistinct impressed mark (presumably FBB)
- PROVENANCE: Mrs. Lilian B. Little, Oak Park, Illinois, 1947
- EXHIBITED: Dixon Gallery and Gardens, 1989
- ACCESSION NUMBER: 2008.DA.2.194

189
Chamberlain's Worcester Oval Teapot and Cover Painted with the 'Tasker's Chinese Bridge' Pattern, 1796–1798
- HEIGHT: 6⁵⁄₁₆ in. (16 cm)
- MARK: None
- PROVENANCE: M. Ford Creech Antiques, Memphis, Tennessee, 2000 (sold as "Factory X")
- ACCESSION NUMBER: 2008.DA.2.378a, b

190
Chamberlain's Worcester Quatrefoil Sauce Tureen, Cover, and Stand Painted with the 'Peacock' Pattern, 1805–1810
- LENGTHS: 7⁷⁄₁₆ and 8½ in. (18.9 and 21.6 cm)
- MARK: *Chamberlains Worcester* mark in brown script inside the cover; the tureen and stand unmarked
- PROVENANCE: Antiques on the Corner, Inc., Lookout Mountain, Tennessee, 1984
- ACCESSION NUMBER: 2008.DA.2.362a–c

191
Chamberlain's Worcester Imari-Style Armorial Plate, 1802–1805
- Painted with the arms and crest of Scott of Great Barr, Staffordshire, for Joseph Scott, M.P., before he was created 1st Baronet, above the motto REGI PATRIAEQUE FIDELIS [Faithful to king and country]
- DIAMETER: 9½ in. (24.1 cm)
- MARK: *Chamberlains Worcester* mark in iron-red script
- PROVENANCE: The Georgian Experience, Memphis, Tennessee, at the Houston Museum Antique Show, Chattanooga, Tennessee, 1986
- EXHIBITED: Dixon Gallery and Gardens, 1989
- ACCESSION NUMBER: 2008.DA.2.360

Sir Joseph Scott (1752–1828) was the High Sheriff of Staffordshire in 1779, and member of Parliament for Worcester from 1802 to 1806. In 1777 he married his cousin Margaret (d. 1822), the daughter and heiress of Edward Whitby, of Shut End, Staffordshire; and on April 30, 1806, he was created 1st Baronet of the Baronetage Scott of Great Barr[1] (Great Barr Hall, then in Staffordshire, being the name of his ancestral home, which he demolished and replaced with

192

193

194

195

196

a new structure around 1777). The coat of arms on this plate from a dessert service indicates that the service was ordered prior to Scott's elevation to the peerage, and probably soon after he became M.P. for Worcester.

1. Burke's 1970, p. 389.

192
Chamberlain's Worcester 'Dejeune' Shape Teacup Painted with a 'Japan' Pattern, 1805–1810
HEIGHT: 2⅜ in. (6 cm)
MARK: None
PROVENANCE: Antiques on the Corner, Inc., Lookout Mountain, Tennessee, 1987
ACCESSION NUMBER: 2008.DA.2.363

193
Chamberlain's Worcester Teacup and Saucer Painted with the 'Dragon in Compartments' Pattern, 1810–1815
Cup: H. 2⁵⁄₁₆ in. (5.9 cm); Saucer: DIAM. 5⅜ in. (13.6 cm)
MARK: Pattern number 75 in iron-red
PROVENANCE: Antiques on the Corner, Inc., Lookout Mountain, Tennessee, 1987
EXHIBITED: Dixon Gallery and Gardens, 1989
ACCESSION NUMBER: 2008.DA.2.361a, b

194
Chamberlain's Worcester 'Famille-Rose' Cabinet Cup Stand, ca. 1820
DIAMETER: 5⅛ in. (13 cm)
MARK: 'Chamberlains, WORCESTER. & 155, New Bond Street, LONDON. Royal Porcelain Manufacturers.' within crowned bound-reeds mark printed in brown
PROVENANCE: Antiques on the Corner, Inc., Lookout Mountain, Tennessee, 1985
ACCESSION NUMBER: 2008.DA.2.364

195
Chamberlain's Worcester Crested Lobed-Oval Dessert Dish Relief-Molded with the 'Union' Design, 1816–1820
LENGTH: 9¹¹⁄₁₆ in. (24.6 cm)
MARK: Crowned Chamberlains Regent China Worcester & 155 New Bond Street London mark printed in russet
PROVENANCE: Marshall Field & Company, Chicago, Illinois, 1948
EXHIBITED: Dixon Gallery and Gardens, 1989
ACCESSION NUMBER: 2008.DA.2.196

196
Pair of Chamberlain's Worcester Gilt Cailloute-Patterned Apricot-Ground Plates, 1820–1830
DIAMETERS: 8⁹⁄₁₆ and 8⅝ in. (21.7 and 22 cm)
MARK: '*Chamberlains*, WORCESTER, & 155, *New Bond Street*, London, .*Royal.Porcelain.Manufacturers*.' within crowned bound-reeds mark printed in gray
PROVENANCE: Mottahedeh & Company, New York City, 1945
ACCESSION NUMBER: 2008.DA.2.197.1 and .2

197

Cover of *The Bavarian Girl's Song: Buy a Broom!*, 1830. Baylor University, Crouch Fine Arts Library, Spencer Sheet Music Collection, E842_119.

W. Gunton, "The Broom Girl." Pencil and watercolor drawing that accompanied the purchase of cat. 198.

198

197
Chamberlain's Worcester Sèvres-Style Plate Painted with 'French Blue' Floral Garlands, ca. 1830

Made as a replacement for a Sèvres hard-paste porcelain original
DIAMETER: 9⅜ in. (23.8 cm)
MARKS: *Chamberlains Worcester* in iron-red script below a pseudo-Sèvres crowned interlaced Ls mark, date letters II for 1786, painter's mark FB for François-Marie Barrat, *oncle*, and gilder's mark BD for François Baudouin, *père*, all in blue enamel
PROVENANCE: Martin Pulver, London, England, 1993
ACCESSION NUMBER: 2008.DA.2.365

198
Chamberlain's Worcester Theatrical Figure of 'The Broom-Girl,' 1827–1835

Modeled as the actress and opera singer Madame Vestris (1797–1856)
HEIGHT: 5¼ in. (13.3 cm)
MARK: *Chamberlains Worcester* mark in iron-red script
PROVENANCE: Sotheby's, London, February 26, 1996, lot 569, with a framed nineteenth-century pencil and watercolor drawing of "The Broom Girl" by W. Gunton, signed lower left (image: 6 × 4⅞ in. [15.2 × 12.4 cm]; 2008.DA.2.367)
ACCESSION NUMBER: 2008.DA.2.366

"Madame Vestris" was the well-known stage name of Lucia Elizabeth Bartolozzi, the granddaughter of the equally renowned artist Francesco Bartolozzi (1727–1815), a founding member of the Royal Academy of Arts in 1768 who was also appointed Engraver to the King. Born Elizabetta Lucia in London in 1797, in 1813, at the age of sixteen, she married Auguste Armand Vestris and in 1815 she took the London stage by storm in the title role of Peter Winter's *Il Ratto di Proserpina* (*The Rape of Proserpina*) at the King's Theatre. Her attractive mien, skilled theatricality, and contralto voice gained her much acclaim in London and Paris. Although her husband deserted her in 1817, she continued to perform as "Madame Vestris" even after she remarried in 1835. With her second husband, Charles James Matthews, Madame Vestris, a canny businesswoman, undertook several successful ventures, including the management of both the Lyceum and Covent Garden Theaters, while continuing to perform until 1854, two years before her death.

This figure of Madame Vestris was a popular subject in English ceramics, inspired by her rendition of the song "Buy a Broom," which she sang on the London stage, costumed as a Bavarian broom-seller. Most of the models appear to have been based on the lithograph of "Madame Vestris as a Broom Girl" by Richard James Lane (1800–1872), published in 1826, and printed by C. Hullmandel, and the W. Gunton watercolor certainly is based on that print. The Chamberlain's figure, however, may have been taken more directly from the Derby porcelain model of 1826–1830, attributed to Samuel Keys Junior,[1] or even the Rockingham porcelain model.[2] The brooms for the Chamberlain's figures were not porcelain, and could be replaced at a cost of 6d each.[3]

1. See Bradshaw 1990, p. 419, pls. 341 and 342, no. G9.
2. See Rice 1971, pl. 152.
3. Godden 1982, pp. 242 and 243, pl. 291.

199

English 'Bute' Shape Teacup and Saucer, 1807–1810
  Attributed to Grainger, Wood & Co. Worcester
  Cup: H. 2⅜ in. (6 cm); Saucer: DIAM. 5⅜ in. (13.6 cm)
  MARK: None
  PROVENANCE: Antiques on the Corner, Inc., Lookout Mountain, Tennessee, 1990
  ACCESSION NUMBER: 2008.DA.2.368a, b

CSH recorded in her notebook that during a visit made by Henry Sandon in 1990, he attributed this cup and saucer to Grainger, Lee & Co. However, according to the 1989 book by Mr. Sandon and his knowledgeable son John, "the firm traded as 'Thomas Grainger & Co.' or 'Grainger & Co.' between March 1811 and October 1814 [when it] officially became Grainger Lee & Co.," a partnership that lasted until 1837 during a period that would be slightly too late stylistically for this cup and saucer.[1] In fact, it is more likely that these pieces were made during the early years of the Grainger factory, when Thomas Grainger was working in partnership with John Wood, who, like Grainger himself, had been "a leading early painter at the Chamberlain factory."[2]

1. H. Sandon and J. Sandon 1989, p. 17.
2. Godden 1988, p. 383.

200

Grainger, Lee & Co. Worcester Dessert Plate Printed in Underglaze Blue and Painted with the 'Old India' Pattern, 1815–1820
  DIAMETER: 7¹³⁄₁₆ in. (19.9 cm)
  MARK: *Grainger, Lee & Co. Worcester* script mark printed in underglaze blue
  PROVENANCE: Antiques on the Corner, Inc., Lookout Mountain, Tennessee, 1983
  ACCESSION NUMBER: 2008.DA.2.369

201

Grainger, Lee & Co. Worcester Gadroon-Edged Plate Printed in Underglaze Blue and Painted with the 'Old India' Pattern, ca. 1818
  DIAMETER: 8½ in. (21.6 cm)
  MARK: Pattern number 1276 in gold
  PROVENANCE: Antiques on the Corner, Inc., Lookout Mountain, Tennessee, 1983
  ACCESSION NUMBER: 2008.DA.370

202

Grainger, Lee & Co. Worcester Blue-Ground Shell-Shaped Dessert Dish, 1820–1830
  LENGTH: 8³⁄₁₆ in. (20.8 cm)
  MARK: *Grainger, Lee & Co. Worcester* mark in iron-red script
  PROVENANCE: Collection of Mrs. Carrington Jones, Memphis, Tennessee, a gift to CSH in 1965
  ACCESSION NUMBER: 2008.DA.2.371

203

204

205

206

203
Grainger, Lee & Co. Worcester Topographical Royal-Blue-Ground Oblong Dessert Dish, ca. 1825
  Inscribed in iron-red script on the base with the view identification: '*Kedleston house, Derbyshire, the seat of Lord Scarsdale*'
  LENGTH: 11⅞ in. (30.2 cm)
  MARK: None
  PROVENANCE: "Property of a Gentleman," sold at Sotheby's, New York, April 14, 2000, lot 171 (six pieces, including cats. 241, 268, and 321)
  ACCESSION NUMBER: 2008.DA.2.372

204
George Grainger & Co. Worcester Topographical Sky-Blue-Ground Shaped Oval Basket, 1840–1845
  Inscribed in black script on the base with the view identification: '*Worcester Bridge*'; the overhead handle missing
  LENGTH: 11½ in. (29.2 cm)
  MARK: Crowned G. GRAINGER. ROYAL PORCELAIN WORKS WORCESTER. mark printed in puce
  PROVENANCE: Collection of Mrs. Elizabeth H. Baldwin, Parkersburg, Virginia, sold at Parke-Bernet Galleries, Inc., New York City, October 10, 1947, lot 542
  EXHIBITED: Dixon Gallery and Gardens, 1989
  ACCESSION NUMBER: 2008.DA.2.198

205
George Grainger & Co. Worcester Low Circular Comport from a Turquoise-Bordered Dessert Service, ca. 1860
  Painted in the manner of John Stinton, Sr. (b. 1829, fl. ca. 1846–1895), with a castle on a hilltop
  DIAMETER: 9 5/16 in. (23.7 cm)
  MARK: 'CHEMICAL PORCELAIN GRAINGER & Co. Manufacturers, WORCESTER' mark printed in black, and pattern number 1498 painted in iron-red
  PROVENANCE: Sue Robinette Antiques, Monticello, Kentucky, 1991
  ACCESSION NUMBER: 2008.DA.2.373

206
George Grainger & Co. Worcester Coffee Cup and Saucer Printed in Iron-Red with the 'Bamboo' Pattern, ca. 1875
  Cup: H. 2 5/16 in. (5.9 cm); Saucer: DIAM. 5 in. (12.7 cm)
  MARKS: G & Co W. in a shield printed in iron-red, and pattern number 2/1959 painted in iron-red on each piece
  PROVENANCE: Unrecorded
  ACCESSION NUMBER: 2008.DA.2.374a, b

ENGLISH PORCELAIN: GRAINGER'S WORCESTER 85

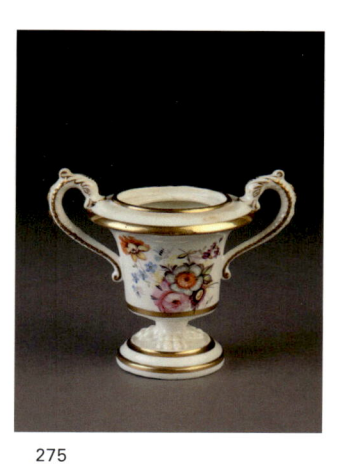

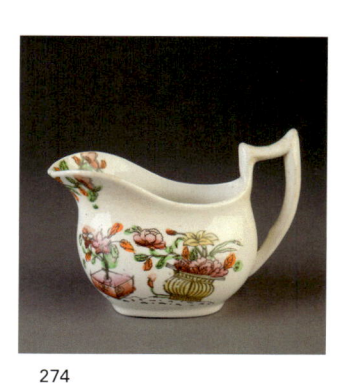

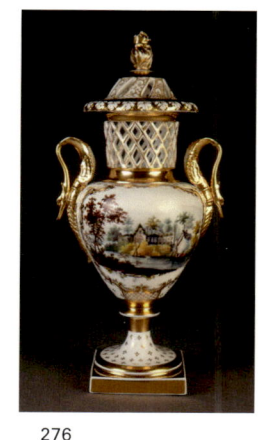

Francis Jukes, "View of Tintern Abbey on the River Wye," 1799. Engraving after a painting by Edward Dayes.

274
Staffordshire 'London' Shape Milk Jug Printed in Black and Painted with Chinese Vessels of Flowers, 1815–1825

A variation of the New Hall pattern number 2172
LENGTH: 5½ in. (14 cm)
MARK: Painter's X mark in iron-red
PROVENANCE: M. Ford Creech Antiques, Memphis, Tennessee, 2000 (sold as Hilditch)
ACCESSION NUMBER: 2008.DA.2.379

275
Staffordshire Potpourri Vase with Floral Decoration and Serpent Handles, 1820–1825

Taken from an original Swansea porcelain model
HEIGHT: 4⅛ in. (10.4 cm)
MARK: Pseudo-Swansea trident mark in red
PROVENANCE: Marshall Field & Company, Chicago, Illinois, 1950
ACCESSION NUMBER: 2008.DA.2.209

This vase was based on an original Swansea model of 1815–1820, a more finely molded example of which, with its pierced cover surmounted by a gilt seated squirrel-form knop, is illustrated by W.D. John and by A.E. Jones and Sir Leslie Joseph.[1] Although it is dangerous to attribute floral decoration to the known artists working in Swansea on both Swansea and Staffordshire porcelain blanks, it has been suggested that the painting on this vase might have been the work of Henry Morris (1799–1880). "Although Morris's flower painting was not outstanding, he painted garden flowers in the [William] Billingsley style and his painting was also influenced by the work of David Evans,"[2] another of Billingsley's protégés. For further discussions of William Billingsley and David Evans, see cats. 67 and 276, respectively; and for a further discussion of Henry Morris, see cat. 286.

1. John 1958, ill. 55B; Jones and Joseph 1988, p. 132, no. 2, and p. 227, no. 3.
2. Jones and Joseph 1988, p. 37.

276
English Potpourri Vase and Pierced Cover with Gilt Swan Handles, 1820–1830

Possibly decorated at the New China Works, Worcester
Painted on the front possibly by David Evans (ca. 1795–1881) with a flower spray, and on the reverse with a view of Tintern Abbey
HEIGHT: 12½ in. (31.8 cm)
MARK: None
PROVENANCE: D.M. & P. Manheim, New York City, 1954 (sold as Swansea with the floral painting attributed to William Billingsley [1758–1828], but the shape is not recorded in the Swansea literature)
ACCESSION NUMBER: 2008.DA.2.199a, b

No factory attribution has been discovered for this unusual potpourri vase; however, the decoration has been ascribed potentially to the New China Works, Worcester, about which little documentation has come to light. Some marked vases and 'London' shape tea wares are known, but they are thought to be of Staffordshire, rather than Worcester, porcelain, and it is now believed that the New China Works, Worcester was a decorating establishment in the 1820–1830 period, rather than an actual manufactory.[1] If this potpourri vase was decorated at the New China Works, Worcester, the attribution of the flower painting to David Evans must still be considered very tentative, as few details of Evans's life and work are known. "A superb painter of wild flowers, he worked at the Swansea porcelain works from 1815"[2] until possibly "1824, and seems to have been at Worcester by about 1825 or 1826,"[3] where he was employed at "the Grainger's factory. [Evans may have worked at Coalport, but] subsequently moved to Staffordshire, where he seems to have worked for several manufacturers, [possibly including Minton, Copeland & Garrett, and] Samuel Alcock & Co. some time around 1840."[4] It is possible that, while working in Worcester for Grainger Lee & Co., Evans took on extra assignments for the New China Works, but this is entirely speculative; it is equally possible that this piece was painted elsewhere by another talented, if unrecognized artist, whose technique resembled that of Evans. Comparing Evans to his supervisor at Swansea, William Billingsley (see cat. 67), who left the factory for Nantgarw at the end of 1816, E. Morton Nance comments,

> Evans' style, although mannered and no doubt considerably influenced by Billingsley's, is tighter, less tentative and more precise: the separate flowers are more sharply defined, there is a greater contrast between them both in colour and form; and the small delicately painted sprays, which Billingsley so frequently used to link up one flower with another, appear less often.... One of Evans' most striking peculiarities was his preference for a dense background of leaves for light-coloured flowers such as wild roses and bindweed and in his open wreath patterns for the use of loosely strung groups made up of more compact elements as a rule than Billingsley's, often joined by irregularly crossed stems upon which a certain emphasis is laid, especially on their protruding ends. In fact, clarity of outline and sharp contrast seems to have been his aim.... All this, however would hardly serve to distinguish his work from that of [William] Pollard [1803–1854] or [Henry] Morris [1799–1880] or any other imitator of Billingsley [at Swansea], although the mere fact of his predilection for wild flowers is sufficient to mark him off from all the other decorators except Pollard.[5]

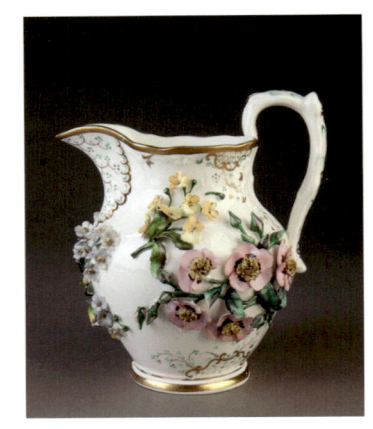

277　　　　　　　　　　　　278　　　　　　　　　　　　279

The suggestion that the view on this vase represents Tintern Abbey in Monmouthshire was made by Millie Manheim, who had attributed the vase to Swansea and the floral painting to William Billingsley. Miss Manheim, who as a young woman in Bristol, England, yearned to be a stage actress, was diverted by her brothers David and Peter into their antiques business in London, D.M. & P. Manheim (named for the three siblings), and eventually she was dispatched to New York City to open a branch on East 57th Street. Millie, however, made the best of her circumstances. Always generous with her time, knowledge, sense of humor, and delicious teas, she practiced her thespian talents on her customers, treating each to a convincing "performance," sometimes quite imaginative, but with an English accent that lent a certain credibility.

With respect to this vase, Millie's ideas seemed particularly creative, as many prints and most photographic views of the Gothic ruin bear little resemblance to what remained by the eighteenth century (and less today) of the Abbey of the Blessed Virgin Mary at Tintern, other than its location on the Welsh side of the navigable River Wye, from which it was best approached. Founded in 1131, the original Romanesque Norman structure was rebuilt as a Gothic abbey in 1256, but in 1536, when the Crown expelled the monks, the abbey began its inevitable structural disintegration. Paintings of the late eighteenth and early nineteenth centuries, however, do depict the picturesque ruin draped in ivy vines, which visitors found so romantic (but which were removed during Tintern's partial restoration in the early twentieth century), and reveal why it had become such an attraction for artists, literati, and tourists, some perhaps inspired by the 1798 poem by William Wordsworth (1770–1850) or the contemporary views by Joseph Mallord William Turner (1775–1851). One watercolor in particular, *Tintern Abbey from across the Wye*, painted in 1794 by Edward Dayes (1763–1804),[6] shows the abbey in the same state as it appears on this vase; Dayes then incorporated that view into a series of sixteen aquatints for his *Views on the River Wye*, engraved by Francis Jukes (1745–1812).[7] It is most likely that the Dayes print served as the source for the scene on this vase, and while because of its shape the artist was required to take slight license in his depiction of Tintern, he nevertheless validated Millie Manheim's initially questionable identification.

1. See Godden 1988, p. 560; J. Sandon 1993, pp. 246–247; and Hosking 1997.
2. H. Sandon and J. Sandon 1989, p. 34.
3. Renton 2005, p. 213.
4. Ibid.
5. Nance 1942, p. 294.
6. In the collection of the Whitworth Art Gallery, Manchester, England.
7. The print mentioned, titled "View of Tintern Abbey on the River Wye," and dedicated "To John Meyrick, Esqr. of Peterborough House Fulham," is the eighth of the sixteen aquatints of watercolor paintings by Edward Dayes for a series of *Views on the River Wye*, engraved by Francis Jukes and published by Jukes in London, 1799.

277
Staffordshire Comport with Sèvres-Style Floral Decoration, 1830–1840

DIAMETER: 9 7/16 in. (24 cm)
MARK: None
PROVENANCE: Antiques on the Corner, Inc., Lookout Mountain, Tennessee, 1989 (sold as Madeley)
EXHIBITED: Dixon Gallery and Gardens, 1989
ACCESSION NUMBER: 2008.DA.2.328

Attributions to the Madeley porcelain works in Shropshire (ca. 1825–1840) are almost entirely speculative because, according to Geoffrey Godden, Thomas Martin Randall (1786–1859), who "established this small works [ca. 1825] in an endeavour to reproduce the fine white translucent porcelains [of the recently closed Swansea and Nantgarw factories in Wales,] . . . did not use any Madeley factory-mark."[1] Randall was chiefly "a talented ceramic decorator who perhaps learnt ceramic painting at the Coalport factory prior to practicing his art or craft [at the Derby factory before moving in 1813 to London to work as an independent decorator in partnership with Richard Robins (see cat. 288), and then] to Madeley in the mid-1820s."[2] It is not known how much porcelain Randall produced at his Madeley factory, or whether it was predominantly "a decorating establishment, decorating imported French (or other) blanks"[3] largely in the style of Sèvres porcelain, which was in the height of fashion at the time, but by the late 1830s the taste had lost its edge, reducing Randall's business considerably. The Madeley "works were closed in 1840 and Mr. Randall moved to Shelton (Hanley) in North Staffordshire, taking his stock with him, [which he later offered] in the white to Mr. John Randall [1810–1910], his nephew, . . . who had worked with his uncle at Madeley."[4]

1. Godden 1988, p. 502.
2. Ibid.
3. Ibid.
4. Ibid., p. 503.

278
English Jug Applied with Floral Sprays, 1830–1840

HEIGHT: 7 1/2 in. (19.1 cm)
MARK: Pattern number 4180 in iron-red
PROVENANCE: The Robinson Collection, sold at Parke-Bernet Galleries, Inc., New York City, May 27, 1948, lot 459 (as "Rockingham, circa 1830")
ACCESSION NUMBER: 2008.DA.2.382

In 1948, when this jug was sold at Parke-Bernet Galleries, "Rockingham" and "Coalbrookdale" were the popular attributions for any unmarked English porcelain applied with flowers. Subsequently, the literature on English ceramics has expanded exponentially and has shown that ornamental pieces of this type, which enjoyed

280

281

282

a particular vogue between about 1825 and 1845, were made in a variety of shapes at a number of British factories, though they were a specialty of Minton and Coalport (Coalbrookdale). This jug is of a shape made at Minton by 1830, but it cannot be attributed to Minton with any certainty for several reasons cited by Geoffrey Godden: "pattern numbers occur only on repetitive, normally useful, wares [for example, dinner or tea and coffee services]—they are not to be found on figures, vases or other purely ornamental articles of the 1824–48 period unless these are of a stock pattern."[1] The pattern number 4180 on this jug would date from the late 1830s, which is stylistically appropriate, but the model does not appear in the Minton *Ornamental Design Books*, transcribed and annotated by Godden,[2] where, under "Jugs," he comments, "N.B. Most Minton jugs were produced in coloured earthenware or stoneware bodies . . . and it must be presumed that separate pattern books [were] used at the earthenware works, rather than at the porcelain factory."[3] With respect to Rockingham, the original attribution, the factory did make jugs of this general shape in porcelain and earthenware in the 1826–1842 period, but the contours and extremities were more exaggerated, and, according to Alwyn and Angela Cox, "pattern numbers *do not* occur on Rockingham ornamental porcelain, nor on the factory's earthenwares."[4] Most pattern numbers found on Rockingham porcelain tea, dinner, and dessert wares are in the three-digit range, and four-digit pattern numbers are rare and anomalous.

1. Godden 1978, p. 24.
2. Ibid., pp. 50–81.
3. Ibid., p. 53. See ibid., pls. 51 and 54 for a stoneware and earthenware version of this basic shape.
4. Cox and Cox 2001, p. 391.

279
English Plate Transfer-Printed and Painted with Oriental-Type Floral Decoration and Rocaillerie, ca. 1850
DIAMETER: 7^{15}⁄$_{16}$ in. (20.2 cm)
MARK: Pseudo-Meissen crossed swords mark in underglaze blue
PROVENANCE: Marshall Field & Company, Chicago, Illinois, 1948
ACCESSION NUMBER: 2008.DA.2.384

280
English Inkstand and Cover Formed as a Lotus Blossom and Leaves on a Gilt Seaweed-Patterned Dish, 1860–1880
The cover probably of different origin
WIDTH: 6⅝ in. (16.8 cm)
MARK: Spurious Chelsea red anchor mark
PROVENANCE: Unrecorded
ACCESSION NUMBER: 2008.DA.2.381a, b

Neither WSS's nor CSH's notebook records the purchase date, place, or price of this inkwell, but it is likely an early purchase by WSS, who probably was lured by its (spurious) red anchor mark into believing it was Chelsea porcelain. She eventually commented in her notebook, "I say this is a doubtful piece—the foot rim is smoked not usually found on Chelsea. While it is marked with the 'red anchor' the porcelain appears to be too hard for Chelsea. Until I find some one who knows more about this than I do I will continue to put it in the doubtful class." Later she elaborated, and CSH inscribed her mother's thoughts in her own notebook:

> It is not Chelsea but a faked mark. It is HARD PASTE & to be Chelsea it would be very soft. The Red Anchor & AR marks are the most faked of ALL marks. If genuine they were the most valuable. The world is full of faked gold anchor marks. I never did decide just what this is & often thought it English Bristol because of the smoking on the underside, but I never like to make attribution [*sic*] unless I KNOW more about it—so I always left it unrecorded. If Bristol I felt the factory would not resort to a faked mark for they were good enough in their own right that they would not care to try to pass off their work as something else.

The piece is, in fact, soft-paste porcelain, but its maker has not been identified.

281
Staffordshire Vase Modeled as a Squirrel Holding a Nut and Seated among Three Tree-Stumps, 1875–1885
HEIGHT: 6¾ in. (17.2 cm)
MARK: Number 355 in maroon enamel
PROVENANCE: Martin Pulver, London, England, 1994 (sold as John Bevington & Co.)
ACCESSION NUMBER: 2008.DA.2.302

282
English Teacup and Saucer Painted with Swansea-Type Roses, late nineteenth or early twentieth century
DIAMETERS: 3^{11}⁄$_{16}$ and 5⅝ in. (9.3 and 14.3 cm)
MARK: The cup unmarked; the saucer with a spurious sans-serif SWANSEA mark in puce
PROVENANCE: I. Freeman & Son, Inc., New York City, 1949
ACCESSION NUMBER: 2008.DA.2.385a, b

283

284

WELSH PORCELAIN

Swansea ❦ *Swansea, South Wales, 1814–1822*

283
Swansea Crested Oval Small Platter with a C-Scroll-Molded Rim, 1814–1817

The crest possibly added later
LENGTH: 10 11/16 in. (27.2 cm)
MARK: SWANSEA mark printed in red
PROVENANCE: Malcolm Franklin, Inc., Chicago, Illinois, 1948
ACCESSION NUMBER: 2008.DA.2.206

The history of the two Welsh porcelain factories, Swansea and Nantgarw, is complicated, but most succinctly described by Oliver Fairclough:

> The Welsh porcelain factories were the result of William Billingsley's [1758–1828] last and most ambitious attempt to manufacture porcelain. He came to Nantgarw late in 1813, moved to Swansea a year later, and returned to Nantgarw in 1817. The two factories are linked, and short-lived. Porcelain was made at Swansea between the late autumn of 1814 and the autumn of 1817 with a few subsequent firings up to 1822, and at Nantgarw for six months in 1814, and then between summer 1817 and spring 1820. Although the periods of manufacture were brief, the decoration of the stock of white wares continued at Nantgarw until 1822 and at Swansea until 1826, [the last year of the firm under the management of Timothy and his son John Bevington, but much of the blank porcelain was sold to outside decorators, particularly in London.] . . . Both Swansea and Nantgarw sought to produce high quality porcelains for a socially select market, [their] shapes often copied from French prototypes, but neither had a London showroom. They therefore sold their products through a network of London retailers, [the most important of which was John Mortlock's of Oxford Street; see cat. 288]. A wide range of porcelain decoration was undertaken in Swansea in 1815–26, [but] little decoration was undertaken at Nantgarw during the main production period of 1818 to 1820. . . . Any discussion of porcelain decoration at Swansea and Nantgarw, therefore, seeks to differentiate between factory and outside work.[1]

Attributions, even to known artists working primarily in London, can be highly speculative, not only because many were trained under William Billingsley and share his style, particularly in the painting of flowers, for which he is best known, but also because the decorators rarely marked their work.

With respect to the crest on this platter, it is difficult, if not impossible, to identify the occasionally imprecise rendering of heraldic devices on porcelain without a clear understanding of the significance of their distinct charges and tinctures (symbols and colors). No identical crest of a dove or even crow-type bird perched on a sprouting tree stump is illustrated by James Fairbairn. However, of the seventeen families associated with the two similar crests depicting either a hawk, a falcon, or a parrot perched on a sprouting tree stump,[2] the most likely family for the present crest is that of Welcome of Market Stanton, Lincolnshire, whose crest is described by Fairbairn as "on the stump of a tree ppr., sprouting branches vert, a bird close arg., beaked or" (on a properly colored tree stump sprouting green branches, a silver bird with its wings close to its body and a gold beak).[3] Alternatively, it is possible that the crest is apocryphal and was added at the request of the original (or a subsequent) owner to suggest a certain social achievement.

1. Fairclough 2000, p. 27.
2. Fairbairn 1905, illustrated in vol. 2, pl. 86, no. 11, and pl. 101, no. 9.
3. Ibid., vol. 1, p. 583.

284
Swansea 'London' Shape Teacup, Coffee Cup, and Saucer Painted with Stylized Floral Decoration on a Buff Ground, the porcelain 1814–1817

Pattern number 257; decorated on the factory site or elsewhere at Swansea, under Timothy and John Bevington, 1821–1826
Cups: H. 2 5/8 and 2 3/4 in. (6.7 and 7 cm); Saucer: DIAM. 5 7/8 in. (15 cm)
MARK: SWANSEA mark printed in red on each piece
PROVENANCE: The collection of M. Venis, Brighton, England, January 1953; Winifred Williams Antiques, Eastbourne, Sussex, England, 1953
ACCESSION NUMBER: 2008.DA.2.208.1a, b (teacup and saucer) and .2 (coffee cup)

See the first paragraph of cat. 283 for a brief history of the Swansea and Nantgarw factories.

Most of the information about the dating and decoration of the Welsh porcelain in this collection was kindly supplied by Jonathan Gray in consultation with Fergus Gambon, to whom I am most grateful for their intimate knowledge of Welsh ceramics, which they imparted so generously. We are all indebted, however, to the pioneering work of E. Morton Nance, who in this instance comments that "although collectors have as a rule given much more attention

285

286

287

to identifying and considering the work of individual free-hand painters [on Swansea and Nantgarw porcelain] than to the usually anonymous conventional patterns, there is no question that naturalistic flower-, landscape- or figure-painting is theoretically less appropriate to the material than the more traditional stylized designs, many of which . . . are of great interest and charm."[1] At Swansea some of these so-called set patterns have numbers, and "while their use was not consistent, it is quite evident that there must have been a 'pattern book,' or something equivalent to a book, perhaps merely a set of loose sheets, for designs which tend to approximate one another in colour or form are found to bear closely related series numbers."[2] Four tea wares in pattern number 257, including a teacup identical to the present example, are illustrated by Nance, which he describes as a "French tulip design."[3]

1. Nance 1942, p. 336.
2. Ibid.
3. Ibid., pl. CL A–C.

285
British 'London' Shape Teacup and Saucer with Floral Borders, ca. 1815
Possibly Swansea
DIAMETERS: 3⅝ and 5 9/16 in. (9.2 and 14.2 cm)
MARK: None
PROVENANCE: Taskey's Antiques, Chicago, Illinois, 1948 (sold as Swansea)
ACCESSION NUMBER: 2008.DA.2.205a, b

286
Swansea Plate Painted with Floral Sprays and Sprigs, the porcelain ca. 1820
Painted in the manner of Henry Morris (1799–1880) on the factory site or elsewhere at Swansea under Timothy and John Bevington until 1826
DIAMETER: 8⅞ in. (22.5 cm)
MARK: None
PROVENANCE: Winifred Williams Antiques, Eastbourne, Sussex, England, 1953 (with the painting attributed to David Evans)
ACCESSION NUMBER: 2008.DA.2.207

For a brief history of the Swansea and Nantgarw factories, see the first paragraph of cat. 283; for information on dating and attributions, see cat. 284; and for a comment on the painting style of Henry Morris, see cat. 275. Morris was one of the most enduring of the Swansea factory's painters, having apprenticed in 1813 under Lewis Weston Dillwyn (1778–1855), the factory's initial proprietor, and remaining through its sale by the Bevingtons in 1826. According to E. Morton Nance, the 1826 sale

> included in addition to Swansea china all that was left of the Nantgarw made by [William] Billingsley when he first came to Swansea [1814 through 1816]. Morris, who was never at Nantgarw, must have decorated on his own account pieces of Nantgarw which had been passed on with the lease of the China Works to the Bevingtons by Dillwyn [in 1817], and had evidently been left undecorated by them. Some time after this (the date is not known, but it could not have been long before the end of 1827 . . .), Morris went to London and is said to have been subsequently employed at Burslem and other Staffordshire potteries, ultimately returning to Swansea, probably about 1841, where he built a muffle [kiln] behind his house. "He imported a large quantity of Copeland's china in the white, painted and fired it for sale" (Turner 1897, p. 194). This may have continued perhaps merely as a side-line until he became blind as the result of a serious fall, in 1875, but no signed or dated work done during the last thirty or more years of his life appears to be known.[1]

1. Nance 1942, pp. 299–300.

Nantgarw China Works
Mid-Glamorgan, South Wales, ca. 1813 and ca. 1817–1820

287
Nantgarw Plate Painted with Flowers and Fruit, ca. 1820
Painted possibly in Swansea, 1821–1823, by William Pollard (1803–1854) or David Evans (ca. 1795–1881)
DIAMETER: 8½ in. (21.6 cm)
MARKS: Impressed NANT GARW and CW marks
PROVENANCE: The collection of Ivor Vachell, Park House, Cardiff; The Steele-Garnett Collection, property of Marcel Steele, Esq.; Guitel Montague, New York City, 1949
ACCESSION NUMBER: 2008.DA.2.201

For a brief history of the Swansea and Nantgarw factories, see the first paragraph of cat. 283; and for information on dating and attributions, see cat. 284. Although there is always a slight danger in attributing unsigned works to a particular porcelain painter, it has been suggested by Jonathan Gray and Fergus Gambon that this plate probably was a Nantgarw blank bought by the Bevingtons at one of the white ware disposal sales (possibly in 1821–1823), and decorated in Swansea by either William Pollard or David Evans. A plate from this service is illustrated by W. D. John with the comment that "it

288

289

290

appears to be decorated by a Swansea artist (William Pollard) indicating that it was probably purchased in the white glazed state at the final advertised sale at Nantgarw in 1822 for decoration in the muffle furnace at his own home."[1] Pollard was born near Swansea and is said to have been employed at a young age "in a solicitor's office, but such was his precocious propensity for drawing, that he covered even the parchments with sketches."[2] He may then have been apprenticed to the Swansea China Works, where he would "have received lessons in painting on porcelain from David Evans, who after [the factory's most skilled and experienced painter William] Billingsley's departure for Nantgarw in December 1816, was probably the chief decorator employed at the works."[3]

E. Morton Nance illustrates two further plates from this Nantgarw service and attributes them to "David Evans or perhaps London-painted."[4] Evans, of whom little is known (but see cat. 276), was, according to contemporary Swansea workers, "rather famous locally as a flower painter, and also as a fruit painter."[5] As Evans was the mentor of Pollard, their work and their choice of floral subjects—often wild flowers, which were Evans's particular specialty—is very similar, but slight differences have been detected. "Evans' style, although mannered . . . is tighter, . . . more precise, [and he had a] preference for a dense background of leaves for light-colored flowers, [whereas Pollard's flowers tend to have more] soft, rounded, less mannered petals and delicately drawn, slightly curved, and therefore less widely separated stamens," among other characteristics.[6]

1. John 1975, ill. 73.
2. Nance 1942, p. 317.
3. Ibid.
4. Ibid., pl. CXII B, C.
5. Ibid., p. 293.
6. See ibid., pp. 296–297.

288

Nantgarw Plate Painted in London with Sèvres-Style Flower Sprays and Gilt-Hatched Blue Lines, ca. 1820
DIAMETER: 9 13/16 in. (25 cm)
MARKS: Impressed NANT GARW and CW marks, and gilt script retailer's mark for John Mortlock
PROVENANCE: The Antique Dome, Inc., Miami Beach, Florida, 1952
ACCESSION NUMBER: 2008.DA.2.203

The firm of Mortlock on Oxford Street in London, established by John Mortlock in 1746, became "the leading retailer of china, earthenware and glass from about 1800 onwards."[1] By acting as the agent for the products of significant manufactories, Mortlock enhanced not only its own reputation but also the reputations of the factories whose wares it promoted and sold. Among them were Coalport, as well as Swansea and Nantgarw, which did not have their own showrooms in London, but whose porcelain was of particularly fine quality. In addition to fully decorated pieces, Mortlock bought English and French white wares, which the firm had painted to order in London by a group of talented artists—including Moses Webster ([1792–1870], formerly a Derby porcelain painter who later painted at Worcester and by 1820 had returned to Derby) and Thomas Martin Randall (1786–1859)—and then had the wares "fired at the enamel kiln of Messrs. Robins and Randall, in Spa Fields," Islington.[2] Randall also painted at Derby, but left for London in 1813 to join with Richard Robins from Pinxton to establish a decorating business in London, a partnership that Randall dissolved in 1825 to move on to Madeley in Shropshire, where he continued to decorate (and possibly produce) porcelain (see cat. 277). Mortlock rose to greatest prominence in the 1810–1830 period, largely through its association with Nantgarw, but continued as a retailer until 1932, and increasingly throughout the nineteenth century the pieces decorated for or sold by the firm bear various painted or printed marks.[3]

1. Godden 1988, p. 549.
2. Jewitt 1878, p. 220.
3. For a Mortlock chronology, see Hildyard 2004, pp. 484–485.

289

Nantgarw Plate Painted in London with Birds and Flowers, 1818–1820
Painted probably in the workshop of John Sims
DIAMETER: 9¾ in. (24.8 cm)
MARKS: Impressed NANT GARW and CW marks
PROVENANCE: T. Leonard Crow, Tewkesbury, Gloucestershire, England, 1949 (who attributed the painting to Thomas Pardoe [1770–1823])
ACCESSION NUMBER: 2008.DA.2.202

For a brief history of the Swansea and Nantgarw factories, see the first paragraph of cat. 283. John Sims (dates unrecorded) may be the least known of the outside decorators of Welsh porcelain. John Twitchett notes that Sims was "a painter who worked at [Derby's] Nottingham Road [factory], but left in the late 18th century to start his own decorating studio in Pimlico, London. Zachariah Boreman [1738–1810] worked for him,"[1] and Richard Askew (ca. 1730–1798) may have as well (see the last two paragraphs of cat. 59). John Haslem recounts a story revealing the measure of the man:

> The late Alderman Peat, of Derby, knew Sims before he went to London, and remembered a man once being put in the pillory for speaking disrespectfully of a fast-day which had been appointed on some occasion. Sims, the china painter, having engaged the only hackney coach which the town then possessed to take the man home after his release from the pillory, was afterwards so

291   292   293

teased for his humane act by the townspeople, that he left and went to London. It was at his establishment that much of the Nantgarw china, which was finished in London, was decorated.[2]

Sims's work was particularly fine, and he not only worked independently, but also completed orders for Mortlock (see cat. 288).

1. Twitchett 2002, p. 103.
2. Haslem 1876, p. 67.

290
Nantgarw Plate Painted in London with Fruit and Flowers on a Ledge, 1818–1820
   Painted possibly by John Sims for Mortlock or by Thomas Martin Randall for Robins and Randall
   DIAMETER: 8⅝ in. (21.9 cm)
   MARKS: Impressed I, NANT GARW and CW marks
   PROVENANCE: D.M. & P. Manheim, New York City, 1953
   ACCESSION NUMBER: 2008.DA.2.204

For a brief history of the Swansea and Nantgarw factories, see the first paragraph of cat. 283. For further remarks about John Sims, see cat. 289; about Mortlock, see cat. 288; and about Thomas Randall and Robins and Randall, see cats. 277 and 288.

SCOTTISH PORCELAIN

Note: For pieces made at the West Pans factory of William Littler, near Musselburgh, Midlothian, Scotland, ca. 1764–1777, see cats. 101–103.

John & Matthew Perston Bell & Co.
Glasgow, ca. 1841–1923

291
J. & M.P. Bell & Co. Turquoise-Ground Cabinet Cup, ca. 1865
   HEIGHT: 4 in. (10.2 cm)
   MARK: None
   PROVENANCE: M. Ford Creech Antiques, Memphis, Tennessee, 2000
   ACCESSION NUMBER: 2008.DA.2.386

ENGLISH POTTERY

Tin-Glazed Earthenware (Delftware)

292
London Delft Blue and White Plate with a Chinese River View, 1765–1775
   Abigail Griffith, Lambeth High Street
   DIAMETER: 9 1/16 in. (23 cm)
   MARK: None
   PROVENANCE: Collection of John Kenneth Byard, Silvermine, Norwalk, Connecticut, sold at Parke-Bernet Galleries, Inc., New York City, March 3, 1960, lot 16 (three plates, including cats. 293 and 294); Collection of "A Man Full of Trouble Tavern," Philadelphia, Pennsylvania, sold at Sotheby's, New York City, October 11, 1995, lot 27 (three plates, including cats. 293 and 294)
   ACCESSION NUMBER: 2008.DA.2.258

293
English Delft Manganese and Blue Plate with a European River View, 1770–1780
   Probably George Drinkwater's Factory, Duke Street, Liverpool
   DIAMETER: 8⅞ in. (22.6 cm)
   MARK: None
   PROVENANCE: Collection of John Kenneth Byard, Silvermine, Norwalk, Connecticut, sold at Parke-Bernet Galleries, Inc., New York City, March 3, 1960, lot 16 (three plates, including cats. 292 and 294); Collection of "A Man Full of Trouble Tavern," Philadelphia, Pennsylvania, sold at Sotheby's, New York City, October 11, 1995, lot 27 (three plates, including cats. 292 and 294)
   ACCESSION NUMBER: 2008.DA.2.259

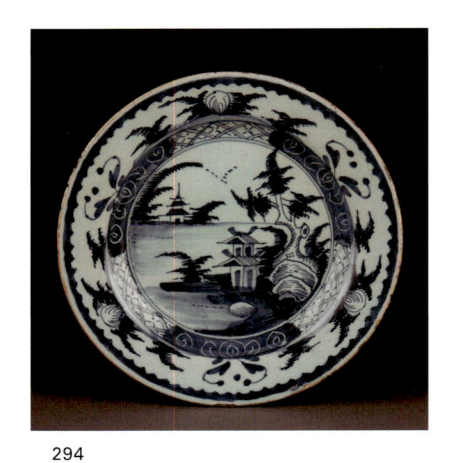

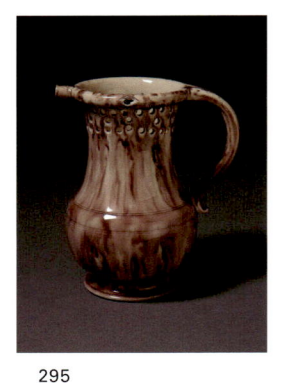

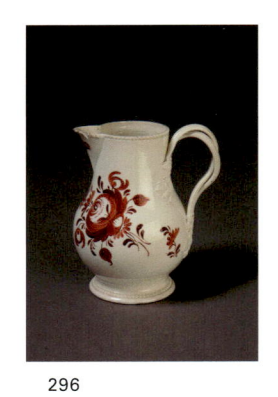

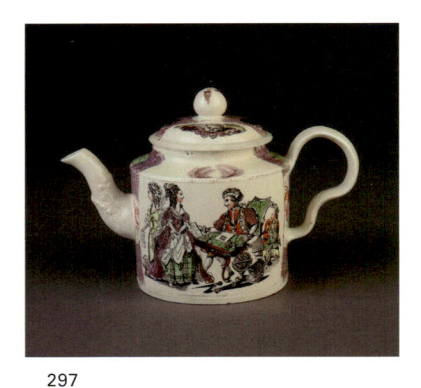

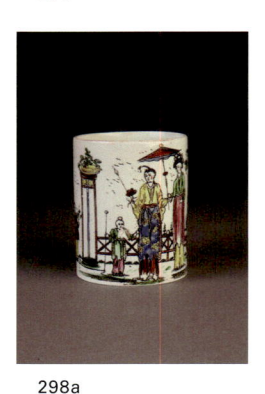

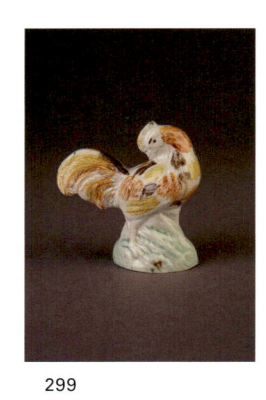

294

295

296

297

298a

298b

299

300

294
*London Delft Blue and White Plate
with a Chinese River View*, ca. 1780
>Thomas Morgan and Abigail Griffith, Lambeth High Street
>DIAMETER: 9 3/16 in. (23.3 cm)
>MARK: None
>PROVENANCE: Collection of John Kenneth Byard, Silvermine, Norwalk, Connecticut, sold at Parke-Bernet Galleries, Inc., New York City, March 3, 1960, lot 16 (three plates, including cats. 292 and 293); Collection of "A Man Full of Trouble Tavern," Philadelphia, Pennsylvania, sold at Sotheby's, New York City, October 11, 1995, lot 27 (three plates, including cats. 292 and 293)
>ACCESSION NUMBER: 2008.DA.2.260

Various Earthenwares

295
*Staffordshire Cream-Colored Earthenware Puzzle Jug
with Manganese Underglaze Oxide Decoration*, 1770–1775
>HEIGHT: 6 3/8 in. (16.2 cm)
>MARK: None
>PROVENANCE: "Property of an Eastern Educational Institution," sold at Parke-Bernet Galleries, Inc., New York City, September 21, 1946, lot 734 ("Three Staffordshire and Whieldon Puzzle Jugs [including cat. 301] and a Brown-Glazed Pottery Coffee Pot")
>ACCESSION NUMBER: 2008.DA.2.262

296
*English Creamware Milk Jug Enameled
with Iron-Red Flowers*, 1775–1780
>Probably Leeds
>HEIGHT: 4 5/8 in. (11.7 cm)
>MARK: None
>PROVENANCE: Marshall Field & Company, Chicago, Illinois, 1946
>ACCESSION NUMBER: 2008.DA.2.264

297
*Staffordshire Creamware Transfer-Printed and Enameled
Documentary Cylindrical Teapot and Cover*, 1778–1782
>William Greatbatch, Fenton
>One side with 'The Astrologer,' the other with 'The XII Houses of Heaven' inscribed beneath *"Published as the Act Directs Jany. 4 1778 by W. Greatbatch Lane Delf Stafford"*
>HEIGHT: 5 in. (12.7 cm)
>MARK: None
>PROVENANCE: Undesignated property, sold at Bonhams, London, June 8, 2005, lot 47
>ACCESSION NUMBER: 2008.DA.2.265a, b

298
*English Pearlware Cylindrical Mug Transfer-Printed
and Enameled with Chinoiserie Decoration*, 1780–1790
>HEIGHT: 3 11/16 in. (9.4 cm)
>MARK: None
>PROVENANCE: Taskey's Antiques, Chicago, Illinois, 1948
>ACCESSION NUMBER: 2008.DA.2.268

301

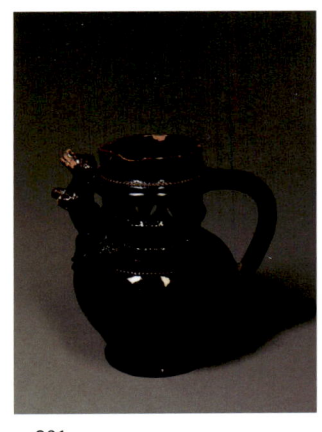

302

303

304

299
Staffordshire Pearlware Figure of a Preening Rooster Decorated in an Underglaze Pratt-Type Palette, ca. 1790

HEIGHT: 3¼ in. (8.2 cm)
MARK: None
PROVENANCE: Peter Williams, Tallarn Green, near Malpas, Cheshire, England, 1992
ACCESSION NUMBER: 2008.DA.2.266

300
Two Staffordshire Pearlware Allegorical Figures of 'Summer' and 'Winter,' 1790–1800

Possibly based on the Neale & Wilson (Hanley, Staffordshire [ca. 1784–1795]) models for a set of 'The Four Seasons,' 1785–1790
HEIGHTS: 4¹³⁄₁₆ and 5 in. (12.2 and 12.7 cm)
MARK: None
PROVENANCE: Undesignated property, sold at Parke-Bernet Galleries, Inc., New York City, 1947 (specific sale date and lot number unknown)
ACCESSION NUMBER: 2008.DA.2.267.1 ('Summer') and .2 ('Winter')

WSS commented in her notebook, "I have NO interest in Staffordshire of any sort much less their grotesque figure[s]. I purchased these just as an example of how poor they can be, as compared with those made of porcelain. I am not interested." Nevertheless, she did some research and decided that they were made by "Neale & Co. before 1788." Diana Edwards discusses and illustrates a marked NEALE & Co. set "of 'The Four Seasons' of which Neale apparently produced two versions."[1] This would not have been unusual for Neale, for "no other manufacturer, including the Leeds Pottery [in Yorkshire] and the Wood family [of Burslem, Staffordshire, who actually supplied some of the molds to Neale] could rival the variety of forms and composition in which they were produced."[2]

1. Edwards 1987, pp. 170 and 176–177, pl. 154.
2. Ibid., p. 170.

301
English 'Rockingham-Glazed' Red Earthenware Puzzle Jug with a Begging Dog Spout, early nineteenth century

HEIGHT: 6³⁄₁₆ in. (15.7 cm)
MARK: None
PROVENANCE: "Property of an Eastern Educational Institution," sold at Parke-Bernet Galleries, Inc., New York City, September 21, 1946, lot 734 ("Three Staffordshire and Whieldon Puzzle Jugs [including cat. 295] and a Brown-Glazed Pottery Coffee Pot")
ACCESSION NUMBER: 2008.DA.2.273

302
English Silver Resist Lustre Jug Reserved with Birds and Flowers, 1815–1820

Probably Leeds Pottery, Yorkshire
HEIGHT: 4⅞ in. (12.4 cm)
MARK: None
PROVENANCE: Collection of Dr. Maurice Harper, London, England; Casey & Casey, Inc., New Orleans, Louisiana, 1945
ACCESSION NUMBER: 2008.DA.2.279

303
Staffordshire Copper Lustre-Ground Transfer-Printed and Enameled Pearlware Chinoiserie Jug, dated 1825

Reserved below the spout with a panel inscribed *Richard & Mary Brammer 1825*
HEIGHT: 5⁵⁄₁₆ in. (13.5 cm)
MARK: None
PROVENANCE: Collection of Ralph H. Wark, Hendersonville, North Carolina (date of acquisition unrecorded)
ACCESSION NUMBER: 2008.DA.2.281

304
Staffordshire Copper and Pink Lustre Jug Reserved with Relief-Molded Classical Scenes, ca. 1820

Shorthose & Co. or Enoch Wood
HEIGHT: 3½ in. (8.9 cm)
MARKS: Lustrer's / mark in pink lustre, and impressed |||
PROVENANCE: Louis Gautier, London, England; Casey & Casey, Inc., New Orleans, Louisiana, 1945
ACCESSION NUMBER: 2008.DA.2.282

ENGLISH POTTERY: VARIOUS EARTHENWARES

305

British Pink Lustre Milk Jug Molded and Enameled with a Floral Border, 1830–1840

HEIGHT: 4⅞ in. (12.4 cm)
MARK: None
PROVENANCE: Louis Gautier, London, England; Casey & Casey, Inc., New Orleans, Louisiana, 1945
ACCESSION NUMBER: 2008.DA.2.280

306

Five British Pearlware Tea Wares Printed in Red and Enameled with the Chinoiserie 'Lady with Bird in Hand' Pattern within Pink Lustre Edges, 1830–1845

Probably Staffordshire
Dessert Plate: DIAM. 8 5/16 in. (21.1 cm); Bread-and-Butter Plate: DIAM. 6⅛ in. (15.6 cm); Octagonal Plate: W. 6¾ in. (17.2 cm); Toy Teacup and Saucer: DIAMS. 3 and 4¼ in. (7.7 and 10.8 cm)
MARK: None
PROVENANCE: Collection of Sir Leslie Joseph, Coedargraig, Mid Glamorgan, Wales, nos. P.12, P.18, P.22, P.410, and P.426, sold by Sotheby's at The Orangery, Margam Park, Port Talbot, Wales, May 15, 1992, lot 818 (thirteen tea wares, catalogued as "Glamorgan Pottery [Swansea], ca. 1813–1858")
ACCESSION NUMBER: 2008.DA.2.294.1, .2, .3, and .4 a, b

Wares of this type were produced inexpensively for popular consumption over a period of several decades. Noël Riley notes that "very few pieces are marked, and the same border patterns and engraved designs appear on plates made as far apart as Sunderland [in the Northeast] and Swansea [in South Wales] or Burslem [in Staffordshire] and Bovey Tracey [in Devon]. Buying, borrowing and even stealing of designs is evident, while copying went on indiscriminately."[1] As clear proof of this, Riley illustrates children's plates with Davenport factory marks dating from the mid-1840s and 1850s, and with the same blossom-molded rim pattern as the unmarked octagonal plate in this lot, but there is no evidence that Davenport ever used this chinoiserie print.[2] This pottery plagiarism has caused misattributions over the years, among them a 'toy cup and saucer' identical to the present example, illustrated by E. Morton Nance with the comment, "although unmarked save for splashes of green enamel on the base of both, [they] must also, I think, on account of the body, the enamels, and the style of the decoration, be assigned to the Glamorgan pottery. The main transfer basis is a peculiar red, to which are applied by hand green, blue and yellow, and there is a rim of pink lustre."[3] It probably was on the strength of this reasoning and without knowledge of the extent of the plagiarism throughout the British potteries that Sir Leslie Joseph, from whose collection these pieces were acquired, based his own attribution of these pieces to Glamorgan.

1. Riley 1991, p. 9.
2. For examples, see ibid., p. 191, nos. 720 and 722.
3. Nance 1942, pl. XCIII (between C and D), with the comment on p. 219.

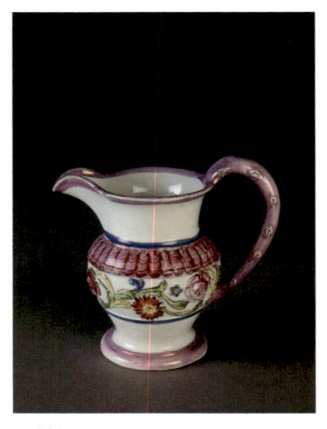

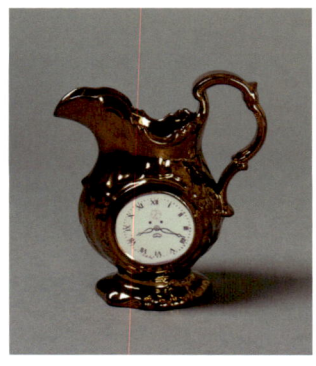

307

Staffordshire Copper Lustre Jug Reserved with a Clock Face and a Roundel of a Chinese Figure in a Garden, 1850–1860

HEIGHT: 5⅝ in. (14.3 cm)
MARK: None
PROVENANCE: Collection of Sir Leslie Joseph, Coedargraig, Mid Glamorgan, Wales, no. P.35, sold by Sotheby's at The Orangery, Margam Park, Port Talbot, Wales, May 15, 1992, lot 816 (with the jug [cat. 332], and catalogued as "Llanelli, ca. 1850")
ACCESSION NUMBER: 2008.DA.2.299

308

Wedgwood White Ware 'Leafage' Dessert Plate, ca. 1820
Etruria, Staffordshire
DIAMETER: 8 in. (20.3 cm)
MARKS: Impressed WEDGWOOD and letter O marks
PROVENANCE: Mottahedeh & Company, New York City, 1945
ACCESSION NUMBER: 2008.DA.2.289

309

Davenport Pearl-Glazed Earthenware Plate Transfer-Printed and Enameled in Chinese Export Porcelain Style with 'Pattern No. 6,' 1815–1820
Longport, Staffordshire
DIAMETER: 9 in. (22.8 cm)
MARKS: DAVENPORT mark printed in underglaze blue and impressed DAVENPORT between numeral 8 and an anchor, numeral 60 painted in black, and letter Y. in underglaze blue
PROVENANCE: Antiques on the Corner, Inc., Lookout Mountain, Tennessee, 1989
ACCESSION NUMBER: 2008.DA.2.271

In discussing Davenport's pattern 'No. 6,' Terence Lockett and Geoffrey Godden note that "this popular pattern with birds and branches is well known in Mason's ware, but also is common on pieces from Hicks and Meigh and several other potters."[1] It was, however, not only C.J. Mason's rival 'Patent Ironstone' but also the company's "methods of trading current at the period, especially their habit of selling at auction [that] greatly upset the established china wholesale and retailers,"[2] as revealed in a letter of January 12, 1818, from Child & Co., china dealers in Edinburgh, to John Davenport (1765–1848), the factory's proprietor, quoted here in part:

> At last the Masons have open'd out their *Forty Hhds. [hogsheads]* Stoneware and China here, and are selling by Auction, which circumstance of course for ever closes our Account with them. We fear it will, in some degree, injure our demand, but we must do the best we can, relying upon your support, for our mutual interest. We succeeded in competing for the Sale of two Dinner Services by the superior appearance of your No. 6, which we hope will not be allowed to fall off in whiteness, which is a great object.
> We are of the opinion that it would be a politic measure to Change the name of it to 'Metallic Porcelain' as we must now Cry down the Ironstone, at least the patent and it will warrant any one to do so as in fact it is now *bad earthenware*.
> Can you get us anything in ware for Masons to match up. To avoid suspicion they might be sent to Liverpool, for thence by sea to Glasgow and readdressed.
> We fear it is Masons intention to have a permanent Connection here with an auctioneer. If so we must devise some plan for opposing them. Say what you think of changing the name of the Stone ware and inform us the price of Breakfast and Tea ware No. 6 and the Broseley Pattern.
> We shall reply to your letter in a few posts. In the meantime,
> We are Dear Sirs,
> Yours truly, Child & Co.[3]

"Davenport did not change the name of the product; it remained as stone china,"[4] and "there is some evidence that stone china wares, particularly in the very popular pattern 142 [the 'Broseley' pattern; see cat. 267, a Rathbone porcelain plate] were being made certainly into the 1870s. A somewhat down-market version was also on offer called 'Opaque China,' ... [although] some very good pieces were made in the 'Opaque China' body, ... [and] white stoneware continued to be manufactured apparently until the closure of the factory" in March 1887.[5]

1. Lockett and Godden 1989, pp. 117–118 and pl. 91.
2. Ibid., p. 114.
3. Ibid.
4. Ibid., p. 115.
5. Ibid., pp. 188–189.

310

John Rogers & Son Pearl-Glazed Earthenware Plate Transfer-Printed in Underglaze Blue with the 'Camel' Pattern, ca. 1820
Longport, Staffordshire
Depicting the "Gate Leading to a Musjed, at Chunar Ghur" ["A Gate Leading to a Mosque, Chunargarh, Uttar Pradesh"] after Thomas and William Daniell in *Oriental Scenery*, 1795–1808
DIAMETER: 8 9/16 in. (21.7 cm)
MARKS: Impressed ROGERS and a potter's crescent mark
PROVENANCE: Martin Pulver, London, England, 1994
ACCESSION NUMBER: 2008.DA.2.272

An identical plate and the source views for the scene—two aquatints from Thomas and William Daniell's *Oriental Scenery*, published between 1795 and 1808—are illustrated by Michael Sack.[1] The database on the website of the Transferware Collectors Club also illustrates the source print for the building, "A Gate Leading to a Mosque, Chunargarh, Uttar Pradesh"; the source print for the camel (reversed on the Rogers plate), "The Western Entrance of Shere Shah's Fort, Delhi"; and the source print for the water buffaloes in the river, "North East View of the Cotsea Bhaug, on the River Jumna."[2] In her discussion of the historical climate in which such prints were popularized, Francesca Vanke notes that the depiction of the Orient "on mainstream British pottery dates from the beginning of the nineteenth century and stemmed from a growing enthusiasm among British architects for Islamic buildings, principally in India."[3]

1. Sack 2009, pp. 40 (right) and 41 (top and right).
2. See www.transcollectorsclub.org.
3. Vanke 2007, especially p. 545, pl. 12.

ENGLISH POTTERY: VARIOUS EARTHENWARES

311

312

313

314

315

311
J.D. Baxter [John Denton Bagster] Earthenware Square Dish Painted with Floral Clusters, 1823–1827

Hanley, Staffordshire
WIDTH: 8¾ in. (22.2 cm)
MARKS: Prince of Wales feathers mark within a coronet, JDB and Celtic China printed in red, pattern number 289 in black enamel, and impressed knot mark
PROVENANCE: Geoffrey Godden, Godden of Worthing Ltd., Worthing, Sussex, England, 1989; Antiques on the Corner, Inc., Lookout Mountain, Tennessee, 1989
EXHIBITED: Dixon Gallery and Gardens, 1989
ACCESSION NUMBER: 2008.DA.2.284

312
Don Pottery Green-Glazed Earthenware 'Thistle Pattern' Plate Molded with Roses, Thistles, and Shamrocks, ca. 1830

Swinton, Yorkshire
DIAMETER: 7¼ in. (18.4 cm)
MARK: None
PROVENANCE: Antiques on the Corner, Inc., Lookout Mountain, Tennessee, 1982
ACCESSION NUMBER: 2008.DA.2.286

313
Staffordshire Pearl-Glazed Earthenware Hexagonal Jug Sprigged in Blue Relief with Flowers, 1830–1850

HEIGHT: 9 in. (22.8 cm)
MARK: Impressed CAMBRIAN CHINA mark
PROVENANCE: Collection of Sir Leslie Joseph, Coedargraig, Mid Glamorgan, Wales, no. MP5, sold by Sotheby's at The Orangery, Margam Park, Port Talbot, Wales, May 15, 1992, lot 858 (with the teapot [cat. 331], and catalogued as "Cambrian Pottery, Swansea, ca. 1850")
ACCESSION NUMBER: 2008.DA.2.298

The 'Cambrian China' mark on this jug, while not intended to deceive, clearly misled the knowledgeable collector of Welsh ceramics, Sir Leslie Joseph, into assuming it was a product of the Cambrian Pottery in Swansea, and therefore an appropriate addition to his collection. Encouraged by a number of similarly misled collectors, Jonathan Gray, a Welsh pottery scholar, investigated the confusion and explained that "whilst the script mark 'CAMBRIAN' (or 'Cambrian') relates to wares made for the Cambrian Pottery's London Warehouse (1806–1808), the printed or impressed Cambria mark indicates the use of Welsh clay by a wide range of manufacturers, mainly in Staffordshire about 1818."[1] In this instance and so many others, the mark denotes Welsh clay but not Welsh manufacture.

1. Gray 2007, p. 559.

314
William Adams & Sons Pearl-Glazed Earthenware Teabowl and Saucer Printed in Crimson with the 'Cyrene' Pattern, 1855–1860

Stoke-on-Trent, Staffordshire
DIAMETERS: 4 1/16 and 6 3/16 in. (10.3 and 15.7 cm)
MARKS: The teabowl with numeral 20; and the saucer with a lion, boat, and Britannia mark inscribed on an oval shield: STONE CHINA CYRENE, and on a banderole below: W. ADAMS & SONS, all printed in crimson
PROVENANCE: The Galleries at Southside (Gallery 8), Chattanooga, Tennessee, 1997
ACCESSION NUMBER: 2008.DA.2.285 a, b

316

317

318

315
English Earthenware Wedgwood/Whieldon-Style Cauliflower-Molded Teapot and Cover, ca. 1875
HEIGHT: 4½ in. (11.4 cm)
MARK: None
PROVENANCE: WSS unrecorded source
ACCESSION NUMBER: 2008.DA.2.287a, b

Various Stonewares

316
Staffordshire White Salt-Glazed Stoneware Sauceboat Press-Molded in the 'Mosaic' or 'Basketwork' Pattern, ca. 1760
LENGTH: 5¹³⁄₁₆ in. (14.7 cm)
MARK: None
PROVENANCE: Marshall Field & Company, Chicago, Illinois, 1948
ACCESSION NUMBER: 2008.DA.2.261

Diana Edwards and Rodney Hampson illustrate a sauceboat of this model beside its master mold and comment that the model "was done by Aaron Wood, c. 1755–57."[1] Initially referred to as the 'Mosaic' pattern and "frequently mentioned as such in invoices and advertisements, by 1763 the description of the same still popular pattern was generally 'basketwork.'"[2]

1. Edwards and Hampson 2005, p. 87, fig. 75.
2. Ibid.

317
Staffordshire Black-Glazed Brown Stoneware Milk Jug with Three Paw Feet, ca. 1765
HEIGHT: 3¹¹⁄₁₆ in. (9.3 cm)
MARK: None
PROVENANCE: Martin Pulver, London, England, 1994
ACCESSION NUMBER: 2008.DA.2.263

318
Set of Ten Wedgwood and Bentley White Jasper Oval Medallions Relief-Molded with Figures of Apollo and the Nine Muses, 1775–1780
Etruria, Staffordshire
Modeled by John Flaxman (1755–1826), Wedgwood's master modeler from ca. 1775 until 1787, when he left England to travel to Rome
HEIGHT: 3¼ in. (8.3 cm)
MARKS: Impressed Wedgwood & Bentley marks and titles
PROVENANCE: Purportedly from the collection of Frederick A. Rhead, Staffordshire, England; Mrs. Lilian B. Little, Oak Park, Illinois, 1947 (who had purchased the medallions in London in 1947)
ACCESSION NUMBER: 2008.DA.2.288.1–.10, and .11 (the fitted case)

Frederick Alfred Rhead (1856–1933) was a ceramic designer and craftsman who worked for Wedgwood ca. 1877–1878, and in 1906 co-authored *Staffordshire Pots and Potters* with his brother, G. Woolliscroft Rhead. His more influential son, Frederick Hurten Rhead (1880–1942), became a major figure in the Arts and Crafts movement, but spent most of his potting career in the United States, where, among other achievements, he designed 'Fiesta Ware' for the Homer Laughlin China Company in Newell, West Virginia, where he worked as the art director from 1927 until his death.

October 20. Royal Copenhagen flower-painted plate, Margo, $12.50 [cat. 373; 2008.DA.2.248]
December 3. Caughley 'Dresden Flowers' pattern sugar bowl, Field, $25.00 [cat. 220; 2008.DA.2.33a, b]
December 5. 'Pair' of Bow figures: Ceres and Neptune, Parke-Bernet, $300.00 [cats. 25, 26; 2008.DA.2.26, .27]
December 5. Meissen group of three musicians, Parke-Bernet, $170.00 [cat. 357; 2008.DA.2.235]
December 6. Derby Group of Venus and Cupid, Parke-Bernet, $170.00 [cat. 76; 2008.DA.2.75]
December 12. Chinese export teabowl and saucer, Parke-Bernet, $18.00 [cat. 337; 2008.DA.2.212a, b]
December 12. Chinese export teabowl and saucer, Parke-Bernet, $15.00 [cat. 343; 2008.DA.2.218a, b]
December 30. New Hall flower-decorated plate, Field, $17.50 [cat. 226; 2008.DA.2.200]
No invoice. Chelsea 'Warren Hastings'–type plate, Waldhorn, $150.00 [cat. 37; 2008.DA.2.45]
No invoice. Derby plate painted with 'Chantilly sprigs,' B. Manheim, $25.00 [cat. 62; 2008.DA.2.68]
No invoice. Derby 'birds in branches' candlestick, Field, $325.00 [cat. 82; 2008.DA.2.82]
No invoice. Worcester coffee cup and saucer, Field, $45.00 [cat. 162; 2008.DA.2.171a, b]
No invoice. H. & R. Daniel breakfast cup and saucer, Field, $25.00 [cat. 255; 2008.DA.2.313a, b]
No invoice. Sampson Bridgwood & Son teacup, Field, $9.50 [cat. 261; 2008.DA.2.195]
No invoice. Chinese export floral-decorated plate, Charm, $6.00 [cat. 346; 2008.DA.2.220]
No invoice. Chinese export Near Eastern Market plate, Charm, $6.00 [cat. 347; 2008.DA.2.222]
No invoice. Wallendorf circular bowl and cover, Charm, $75.00 [cat. 359; 2008.DA.2.236a, b]
No invoice. Pair of Chinese export plates, Kessler, $35.00 [cat. 348; 2008.DA.2.223.1, .2]
No invoice. Meissen 'Onion' pattern cup and saucer, Field, price unrecorded [cat. 355; 2008.DA.2.234a, b]
No invoice. Bow 'Quail' pattern circular dish, Field, $85.00 [1985.DA.384]

1947

June 9. Worcester 'Hope' Service sauce tureen and stand, Field, $325.75 [cat. 180; 2008.DA.2.189a–c]
August 18. Lowestoft teabowl and saucer, Little, $60.00 [cat. 109; 2008.DA.2.109a, b]
August 18. Worcester transfer-printed mask jug, Little, $175.00 [cat. 124; 2008.DA.2.134]
August 18. Worcester 'Earl Manvers' pattern square dish, Little, $160.00 [cat. 169; 2008.DA.2.179]
August 18. Bristol teapot with neoclassical borders, Little, $85.00 [cat. 217; 2008.DA.2.31.1a, b]
August 18. Worcester 'clobbered' cup and saucer, Little, $50.00 [cat. 176; 2008.DA.2.186a, b]
September 5. Derby yellow-ground fluted plate, Little, $75.00 [cat. 67; 2008.DA.2.72]
September 5. Flight & Barr coffee cup, Little, $35.00 [cat. 181; 2008.DA.2.190]
September 5. Tournai dish decorated at The Hague, Little, $55.00 [cat. 367; 2008.DA.2.252]
September 13. Cozzi porcelain teabowl and saucer, Little, $45.00 [cat. 362; 2008.DA.2.238a, b]
September 13. Le Nove coffee can and saucer, Little, $50.00 [cat. 363; 2008.DA.2.241a, b]
September 13. Loosdrecht teabowl and saucer, Little, $50.00 [cat. 368; 2008.DA.2.250a, b]
September 13. Amstel yellow-ground topographical vase, Little, $80.00 [cat. 369; 2008.DA.2.251a, b]

September 24. Worcester breakfast teabowl and saucer, Little, $60.00 [cat. 120; 2008.DA.2.131a, b]
September 24. Worcester blue-scale plate, Little, $125.00 [cat. 158; 2008.DA.2.166]
September 24. Wedgwood teacup and saucer, Little, $37.50 [cat. 251; 2008.DA.2.115a, b]
October 10. Grainger's Worcester oval basket, Parke-Bernet, $45.00 [cat. 204; 2008.DA.2.198]
October 29. Derby 'Pastoral Group by a Fountain,' Parke-Bernet, $200.00 [cat. 85; 2008.DA.2.84]
October 29. Liverpool octagonal teacup and saucer, Parke-Bernet, $30.00 [cat. 105; 2008.DA.2.97a, b]
October 29. Worcester 'Walk in the Garden' pattern mug, Parke-Bernet, $35.00 [cat. 117; 2008.DA.2.126]
November 21. Meissen allegorical group of 'Victory,' Parke-Bernet, $120.00 [cat. 356; 2008.DA.2.232]
December 8. Two plaster slip molds and three casts, Little, $8.00 [cat. 328; 2008.DA.2.291.1–.5]
December 31. Ten Wedgwood & Bentley medallions in a case, Little, $500.00 [cat. 318; 2008.DA.2.288.1–.11]
No invoice. Bow '*famille-rose*' teabowl, Little, $120.00 [cat. 3; 2008.DA.2.5]
No invoice. Worcester chinoiserie sauceboat, Field, $125.00 [cat. 113; 2008.DA.2.122]
No invoice. Two flatware handles: Worcester and St.-Cloud, Little, $30.00 [cat. 118; 2008.DA.2.128, .129]
No invoice. Worcester 'Scarlet Japan' pattern teapot, Stern, $75.00 [cat. 145; 2008.DA.2.143a, b]
No invoice. Flight, Barr & Barr crested yellow dish, Little, $50.00 [cat. 188; 2008.DA.2.194]
No invoice. Caughley kidney-shaped dish, Field, $57.50 [cat. 221; 2008.DA.2.34]
No invoice. Two Staffordshire pearlware figures, Parke-Bernet, price unrecorded [cat. 300; 2008.DA.2.267.1, .2]
No invoice. Blanc-de-Chine libation cup, Little, $60.00 [cat. 336; 2008.DA.2.226]
No invoice. Meissen white sugar caster, Le Noble, $50.00 [cat. 354; 2008.DA.2.233]
No invoice. Samson 'Imari'-style ewer and basin, Le Noble, $200.00 [cat. 375; 2008.DA.2.227a, b]

1948

January 15. Bow prunus-molded '*famille-rose*' plate, Little, $125.00 [cat. 4; 2008.DA.2.2]
January 15. Chelsea plate painted with exotic birds, Little, $135.00 [cat. 44; 2008.DA.2.51]
January 15. Pair of Bow 'Quail' pattern handles, Little, $100.00 [1985.DA.385]
January 15. Staffordshire white salt-glazed stoneware sauceboat, Field, $85.00 [cat. 316; 2008.DA.2.261]
January 31. Chelsea 'Warren Hastings' pattern plate, Little, $150.00 [cat. 36; 2008.DA.2.44]
January 31. Pair of Derby groups of musicians, Parke-Bernet, $120.00 [cat. 77; 2008.DA.2.76.1, .2]
January 31. Pair of Derby 'Dresden Shepherds,' Parke-Bernet, $280.00 [cat. 87; 2008.DA.2.90.1, .2]
January 31. Longton Hall leaf-shaped dish, Little, $195.00 [cat. 100; 2008.DA.2.104]
January 31. Plymouth silver-shape sauceboat, Little, $135.00 [cat. 210; 2008.DA.2.113]
May 27. Derby group of 'Two Virgins Awaking Cupid,' Parke-Bernet, $180.00 [cat. 88; 2008.DA.2.85]
May 27. Derby figure of James Quin as 'Falstaff,' Parke-Bernet, $110.00 [cat. 92; 2008.DA.2.87]
May 27. English jug applied with floral sprays, Parke-Bernet, $50.00 [cat. 278; 2008.DA.2.382]
May 27. Volkstedt figure of Minerva, Parke-Bernet, $70.00 [cat. 358; 2008.DA.2.237]

June 9. Bow blue and white 'Image' pattern plate, Lautz, $90.00 [cat. 9; 2008.DA.2.11]

June 9. Bow powdered-blue octagonal small plate, Lautz, $35.00 [cat. 11; 2008.DA.2.13]

June 9. Chelsea scolopendrium beaker and saucer, Lautz, $125.00 [cat. 29; 2008.DA.2.37a, b]

June 9. Worcester decagonal coffee cup, Lautz, $27.50 [cat. 110; 2008.DA.2.120]

June 9. Worcester *famille-rose* coffee cup, Lautz, $22.50 [cat. 111; 2008.DA.2.121]

June 9. Bristol cylindrical small mug, Lautz, $50.00 [cat. 216; 2008.DA.2.28]

July 7. Worcester 'Red Bull' pattern teabowl and saucer, Lautz, $60.00 [cat. 128; 2008.DA.2.138a, b]

July 30. Lowestoft teabowl and saucer, Field, $30.00 [cat. 108; 2008.DA.2.108a, b]

July 30. Chamberlain's Worcester crested oval dish, Field, $50.00 [cat. 195; 2008.DA.2.196]

August 2. Derby blue-ground rococo vase and cover, Field, $300.00 [cat. 58; 2008.DA.2.63a, b]

August 2. Derby rococo potpourri vase and cover, Field, $375.00 [cat. 59; 2008.DA.2.65a, b]

August 2. Staffordshire oriental-style plate, Field, $10.00 [cat. 279; 2008.DA.2.384]

August 3. Chelsea 'Brocade Imari' pattern plate, Wilson, $68.00 [cat. 35; 2008.DA.2.43]

August 3. Chelsea-Derby caudle cup, cover, and stand, Wilson, $38.00 [cat. 54; 2008.DA.2.61a–c]

August 3. Worcester 'Marchioness of Huntly' pattern plate, Wilson, $55.00 [cat. 167; 2008.DA.2.175]

August 3. Flight, Barr & Barr teacup and saucer, Taskey's, $17.50 [cat. 182; 2008.DA.2.191a, b]

August 3. New Hall teacup and saucer, Taskey's, $15.00 [cat. 225; 2008.DA.2.112a, b]

August 3. Coalport 'Church Gresley' pattern botanical plate, Taskey's, $43.50 [cat. 228; 2008.DA.2.93]

August 3. British (Swansea ?) teacup and saucer, Taskey's, $18.50 [cat. 285; 2008.DA.2.205a, b]

August 3. St. Petersburg Paul I Service soup plate, Taskey's, $22.00 [cat. 371; 2008.DA.2.246]

August 30. Bow blue and white vine-molded dish, John's, $35.00 [cat. 12; 2008.DA.2.14]

August 30. Worcester blue and white teapot, John's, $20.00 [cat. 122; 2008.DA.2.132a, b]

October 14. Derby biscuit group of 'Two Virgins Awaking Cupid,' Plummer, $175.00 [cat. 89; 2008.DA.2.86]

October or November. Chelsea 'Kakiemon' octagonal plate, Lautz, $100.00 [cat. 31; 2008.DA.2.39]

October or November. Chelsea plate painted with green birds, Lautz, $75.00 [cat. 46; 2008.DA.2.53]

October or November. Strasbourg plate painted with a costumed man, Lautz, $50.00 [cat. 366; 2008.DA.2.253]

November 1. Flight, Barr & Barr crested oval platter, Field, $45.00 [cat. 184; 2008.DA.2.192]

November 9. Worcester 'Sir Joshua Reynolds' pattern teacup and saucer, Taskey's, $42.50 [cat. 137; 2008.DA.2.151a, b]

November 9. Coalbrookdale turquoise flower vase, Field, $95.00 [cat. 237; 2008.DA.2.95]

November 9. English pearlware cylindrical mug, Taskey's, $20.00 [cat. 298; 2008.DA.2.268]

November 9. Worcester 'Quail' pattern coffee cup and saucer, Taskey's, $40.00 [1985.DA.386]

November 30. Bow blue and white lobed sauceboat, Taskey's, $20.00 [cat. 8; 2008.DA.2.10]

November 30. Chelsea rocaillerie-molded plate, Taskey's, $100.00 [cat. 45; 2008.DA.2.52]

November 30. Derby wall pocket, Taskey's, $125.00 [cat. 56; 2008.DA.2.66]

November 30. West Pans leaf-molded sauceboat, Taskey's, $100.00 [cat. 101; 2008.DA.2.105]

November 30. Worcester 'Milkmaids' pattern teabowl and saucer, Taskey's, $25.00 [cat. 125; 2008.DA.2.135a, b]

November 30. Wedgwood 'Chinese Tigers' pattern plate, Taskey's, $7.50 [cat. 252; 2008.DA.2.116]

November 30. Wedgwood coffee can and saucer, Taskey's, $7.50 [cat. 253; 2008.DA.2.117a, b]

November 30. Doccia initialed coffee can and saucer, Taskey's, $20.00 [cat. 361; 2008.DA.2.242a, b]

No invoice. Bow white prunus-molded teabowl, Franklin, $5.00 [cat. 2; 2008.DA.2.4]

No invoice. Bow blue and white cylindrical mug, Stern, $100.00 [cat. 10; 2008.DA.2.12]

No invoice. Chelsea 'Kakiemon' shaped oval platter, Wilson, $75.00 [cat. 34; 2008.DA.2.41]

No invoice. Chelsea silver-shape dish, Wilson, $55.00 [cat. 40; 2008.DA.2.47]

No invoice. Chelsea kidney-shaped dish, Wilson, $78.00 [cat. 43; 2008.DA.2.50]

No invoice. Derby floral teabowl and saucer, Little, $37.50 [cat. 60; 2008.DA.2.67a, b]

No invoice. Derby gilt-striped coffee cup and saucer, Field, $75.00 [cat. 61; 2008.DA.2.59a, b]

No invoice. Worcester blue and white sauceboat, Wilson, $18.00 [cat. 116; 2008.DA.2.125]

No invoice. Worcester 'Chinese Family' pattern teapot, Hale, $37.50 [cat. 129; 2008.DA.2.153a, b]; and milk jug, coffee cup, and saucer, *en suite*, Hale, $87.50 [cat. 129; 2008.DA.2.154, 155a, b]

No invoice. Worcester cos lettuce leaf sauceboat, Franklin, $45.00 [cat. 151; 2008.DA.2.157]

No invoice. Worcester plate painted with Giles-type birds, Lautz, $105.00 [cat. 161; 2008.DA.2.178]

No invoice. Worcester chestnut basket, cover, and stand, Wilson, $200.00 [cat. 168; 2008.DA.2.176a–c]

No invoice. Coalport trellis-molded dessert plate, Field, $10.00 [cat. 232; 2008.DA.2.94]

No invoice. Swansea crested oval small platter, Franklin, $55.00 [cat. 283; 2008.DA.2.206]

No invoice. Meissen leaf-molded ladle and Meissen cos lettuce leaf-molded sauceboat, Lautz, $120.00 [cats. 352 and 353; 2008.DA.2.230, .231]

No invoice. Vinovo custard cup and cover, Lautz, $35.00 [cat. 364; 2008.DA.2.243a, b]

1949

January 15. Nantgarw plate painted with flowers and fruit, Montague, $120.00 [cat. 287; 2008.DA.2.201]

April 30. Four New Hall chinoiserie tea wares, Field, $60.00 [cat. 223; 2008.DA.2.111.1–.3]

May 18. Chelsea 'Kakiemon' peach-shaped dish, Lautz, $125.00 [cat. 30; 2008.DA.2.38]

May 19. Worcester 'Blind Earl' pattern plate, Manheim, $145.00 [cat. 153; 2008.DA.2.159]

May 26. Pair of Derby 'Ranelagh Dancers,' Parke-Bernet, $250.00 [cat. 78; 2008.DA.2.78.1, .2]

May 26. Derby arbor figure of a musician, Parke-Bernet, $150.00 [cat. 83; 2008.DA.2.77]

May 26. Derby large figure of James Quin as 'Falstaff,' Parke-Bernet, $70.00 [cat. 93; 2008.DA.2.92]

May 26. Pair of Derby arbor figures of musicians, Parke-Bernet, $300.00 [cat. 84; 2008.DA.2.83.1, .2]

October 8. Chelsea pine cone–molded coffee cup and saucer, Crow, $84.00 [cat. 47; 2008.DA.2.54a, b]

October 8. Derby rococo vase, Crow, $76.00 [cat. 57; 2008.DA.2.64]

October 8. Nantgarw London-decorated plate, Crow, $154.00 [cat. 289; 2008.DA.2.202]

No invoice. Bow pine cone–molded teacup and saucer, Lautz, $50.00 [cat. 15; 2008.DA.2.17a, b]

No invoice. Chelsea botanical plate, Lautz, $65.00 [cat. 42; 2008.DA.2.49]

No invoice. Chelsea-Derby neoclassical plate, Lautz, $75.00 [cat. 52; 2008.DA.2.62]
No invoice. Worcester 'Chrysanthemum' pattern teapot, Field, $45.00 [cat. 119; 2008.DA.2.130a, b]
No invoice. Worcester faceted coffee cup and saucer, Lautz, $67.50 [cat. 148; 2008.DA.2.146a, b]
No invoice. Plymouth 'pleated' sauceboat, Field, $165.00 [cat. 212; 2008.DA.2.114]
No invoice. English Swansea-style teacup and saucer, Freeman, $60.00 [cat. 282; 2008.DA.2.385a, b]
No invoice. Chinese export rice bowl and cover, Freeman, $40.00 [cat. 340; 2008.DA.2.214a, b]
No invoice. Doccia relief-molded teacup and saucer, Lautz, price unrecorded [cat. 360; 2008.DA.2.239a, b]
No invoice. Meissen 'Quail' pattern cinquefoil dish, Lautz, $65.00 [1985.DA.379]

1950

January 26. Worcester 'Old Mosaick Japan' pattern plate, Blair's, $45.00 [cat. 142; 2008.DA.2.147]
January 26. Chinese export 'Quail' pattern plate, Blair's, $60.00 [1985.DA.380]
September 23. Worcester 'Sir Joshua Reynolds' pattern plate, Parke-Bernet, $86.70 [cat. 138; 2008.DA.2.150]
No invoice. Worcester 'famille-verte' sauceboat, Wilson, $75.00 [cat. 112; 2008.DA.2.123]
Invoice undated. Worcester teabowl coffee cup and saucer, Crow, $23.50 [cat. 132; 2008.DA.2.139a–c]
Invoice undated. Worcester 'Dalhousie'-type saucer dish, Crow, $133.00 [cat. 174; 2008.DA.2.184]
Invoice undated. Bristol octofoil plate with floral garlands, Crow, $76.00 [cat. 214; 2008.DA.2.29]
No invoice. Worcester coffee cup and saucer, Field, $30.00 [cat. 166; 2008.DA.2.177a, b]
No invoice. Staffordshire potpourri vase, Field, $45.00 [cat. 275; 2008.DA.2.209]

1951

June 16. Bristol figure of a girl with a puppy, Willson, $276.00 [cat. 213; 2008.DA.2.32]
July 16. Bow 'famille-rose' plate, Taskey's, $50.00 [cat. 6; 2008.DA.2.1]
July 16. Bristol ogee-shaped teacup and saucer, Taskey's, $37.50 [cat. 217; 2008.DA.2.31.2a, b]
July 26. Chelsea circular écuelle and cover, Wilson, $210.00 [cat. 39; 2008.DA.2.46a, b]
July 26. Derby figure of Harlequin, Field, $137.50 [cat. 79; 2008.DA.2.79]
July 26. Worcester blue-scale teacup and saucer, Field, $20.00 [cat. 139; 2008.DA.2.165a, b]
July 26. Worcester blue-scale teapot, Wilson, $60.00 [cat. 140; 2008.DA.2.164a, b]
July 26. Worcester blue-scale butter tub, cover, and stand, Wilson, $163.00 [cat. 157; 2008.DA.2.162a–c]
August 1. Chelsea 'Hans Sloane' botanical plate, Hale $150.00 [cat. 41; 2008.DA.2.48]
August 1. Derby figure of J.P. Kemble as 'Richard III,' Hale, $245.00 [cat. 91; 2008.DA.2.91]
August 1. Worcester powder-blue-ground coffee cup and saucer, Hale, $125.00 [cat. 154; 2008.DA.2.161a, b]
No invoice. Derby topographical coffee cup and saucer, Crow, $22.00 [cat. 66; 2008.DA.2.71a, b]
No invoice. Worcester Imari-style coffee cup, Wilson, $25.00 [cat. 133; 2008.DA.2.140]
No invoice. Meissen white coffee cup and saucer, Art Exchange, $56.00 [cat. 351; 2008.DA.2.229a, b]
No invoice. Royal Copenhagen figure of a woman, Treasure, $125.00 [cat. 374; 2008.DA.2.249]

1952

January 2. Worcester 'Tall Chelsea Ewer' milk jug, Lautz, $50.00 [cat. 130; 2008.DA.2.152]
January 28. Chelsea white 'Goat and Bee' jug, Lewis, $350.00 [cat. 28; 2008.DA.2.36]
May 23. Worcester 'Jabberwocky' pattern teabowl and saucer, Parke-Bernet, $100.00 [cat. 146; 2008.DA.2.148a, b]
May 23. Worcester 'Jabberwocky' pattern covered milk jug, Parke-Bernet, $110.00 [cat. 147; 2008.DA.2.149a, b]
September 4. Bow botanical 'Cotton Tree' dish, Lautz, $121.50 [cat. 13; 2008.DA.2.6]
September 4. Bow figure of a monk, Lautz, $247.50 [cat. 22; 2008.DA.2.23]
September 4. Worcester 'Lord Rodney' pattern plate, Lautz, $135.00 [cat. 175; 2008.DA.2.182]
September 4. West Pans 'Quail' pattern cup and saucer, Lautz, $85.00 [1985.DA.382]
October 22. Worcester kidney-shaped dish, Lautz, $137.50 [cat. 149; 2008.DA.2.145]
December 19. English armorial octagonal plate, Lautz, $85.00 [cat. 273; 2008.DA.2.8]
No invoice. Nantgarw London-decorated plate, Antique Dome, $100.00 [cat. 288; 2008.DA.2.203]
No invoice. Chantilly 'Quail' pattern beaker and saucer, Heuser, $145.00 [1985.DA.381]

1953

January 2. Worcester 'penciled' teabowl and saucer, Lewis, $75.00 [cat. 114; 2008.DA.2.124a, b]
January 2. Worcester chinoiserie teabowl and saucer, Lewis, $160.00 [cat. 127; 2008.DA.2.137a, b]
February 17. Derby six-shell sweetmeat or pickle stand, Manheim, $650.00 [cat. 55; 2008.DA.2.316]
February 17. Derby biscuit group of 'Two Bacchantes Adorning Pan,' Manheim, $360.00 [cat. 87; 2008.DA.2.89]
February 17. Nantgarw London-decorated plate, Manheim, $180.00 [cat. 290; 2008.DA.2.204]
June 29. Chelsea 'Kakiemon' octagonal soup plate, Williams, $109.20 [cat. 32; 2008.DA.2.40]
June 29. Longton Hall hollyhock leaf-molded dish, Williams, $246.00 [cat. 97; 2008.DA.2.101]
June 29. Pair of Worcester 'Fable' plates, Williams, $525.00 [cats. 159, 160; 2008.DA.2.169, .170]
July 20. Bow white bust of a Mongolian, Williams, $413.00 [cat. 16; 2008.DA.2.18]
July 20. Bow figure of a priest, Williams, $118.00 [cat. 23; 2008.DA.2.24]
September 7. Worcester yellow-ground sauceboat, Amor, $226.00 [cat. 131; 2008.DA.2.160]
October (no date). Worcester faceted teabowl and saucer, Lautz, $350.00 [cat. 165; 2008.DA.2.174a, b]
November 12. Swansea plate painted with floral sprays, Williams, $40.00 [cat. 286; 2008.DA.2.207]
November 26. Liverpool chinoiserie spherical teapot, Williams, $63.00 [cat. 104; 2008.DA.2.98a, b]
November 26. Swansea teacup, coffee cup, and saucer, Williams, $54.00 [cat. 284; 2008.DA.2.208.1a, b, .2]
No invoice. Chinese Qingbai lobed small dish, Wark, $37.50 [cat. 333; 2008.DA.2.225]

1954

January 23. Worcester pink-scale waste bowl, Parke-Bernet, $650.00 [cat. 164; 2008.DA.2.173]
January 23. Worcester 'Lord Henry Thynne Service'–type dish, Parke-Bernet, $350.00 [cat. 173; 2008.DA.2.183]
March 2. Bow chinoiserie octagonal plate, Williams, $90.00 [cat. 7; 2008.DA.2.16]
June 30. Worcester 'King of Prussia' mug, Taskey's, $85.00 [cat. 123; 2008.DA.2.133]

August 5. Bow 'Island House' pattern plate, Williams, $95.00 [cat. 5; 2008.DA.2.7]
August 5. Worcester cabbage leaf–shaped dish, Williams, $170.00 [cat. 152; 2008.DA.2.158]
August 5. English (M. Mason ?) dodecagonal platter, Williams, $125.00 [cat. 264; 2008.DA.2.9]
August 20. Longton Hall strawberry-molded plate, Manheim, $380.00 [cat. 98; 2008.DA.2.102]
August 20. English potpourri vase and cover, Manheim, $330.00 [cat. 276; 2008.DA.2.199a, b]
October 7. Derby group of 'Isabella, Gallant and Jester,' Manheim, $880.00 [1985.DA.54]
October 27. Chelsea 'Quail' pattern small oval dish, Williams, $125.00 [1985.DA.383]
Invoice undated. Bow white figure of a nun, Amor, $154.00 [cat. 21; 2008.DA.2.25]
Invoice undated. Derby white figure of Kitty Clive, Amor, $700.00 [cat. 74; 2008.DA.2.73]

1955

August (no date). Two Longton Hall allegorical figures, Katz, $375.00 [cat. 95; 2008.DA.2.99.1, .2]
August 12. Worcester blue-scale 'cabbage leaf' jug, Amor, $225.00 [cat. 155; 2008.DA.2.167]
August 12. Worcester pink-scale kidney-shaped dish, Amor, $308.00 [cat. 163; 2008.DA.2.172]
August 12. Bristol coffee cup and saucer, Amor, $106.40 [cat. 215; 2008.DA.2.30a, b]
October 18. Charles Gouyn white figure of a bird, Amor, $672.00 [cat. 27; 2008.DA.2.35]
November 16. Worcester figure of a Turk, Tilley, $1,100.00 [cat. 150; 2008.DA.2.118]

1956

February 3. Chelsea *'famille-rose'* octagonal soup plate, Amor, $128.00 [cat. 33; 2008.DA.2.42]
February 27. Derby 'Smith's Blue'–bordered jug, Williams, $75.00 [cat. 64; 2008.DA.2.69]
March 10. Worcester 'Hop Trellis' pattern dish, Williams, $180.00 [cat. 170; 2008.DA.2.181]
May 6. Bow figure of a sailor: 'Tom Bowling,' Katz, $250.00 [cat. 18; 2008.DA.2.21]
May 6. Bow figure of a sailor's lass, Katz, $250.00 [cat. 19; 2008.DA.2.22]
May 6. Chelsea figure of a carpenter, Katz, $500.00 [cat. 48; 2008.DA.2.56]
May 6. Chelsea figure of 'Narcisin,' Katz, $500.00 [cat. 49; 2008.DA.2.55]
May or June. Worcester reeded coffee cup, Katz, date and price unrecorded [cat. 115; 2008.DA.2.119]
June 6. Bow allegorical group of 'Charity,' Katz, $650.00 [cat. 20; 2008.DA.2.19]
June 6. Chelsea group of a bagpiper and dog, Katz, $700.00 [cat. 50; 2008.DA.2.57]
July 20. Chelsea sweetmeat figure of a lady, Amor, $210.00 [cat. 51; 2008.DA.2.58]
July 20. Derby 'dry-edge' shepherd group, Amor, $266.00 [cat. 75; 2008.DA.2.74]
July 20. West Pans leaf-molded oval stand, Katz, $125.00 [cat. 102; 2008.DA.2.106]
August 4. Bow figure of an actor, probably David Garrick, Katz, $600.00 [cat. 17; 2008.DA.2.20]
September 3. Worcester fluted teacup and saucer, Williams, $56.00 [cat. 171; 2008.DA.2.180a, b]
No invoice. Longton Hall white group of a lady and dog, Stern, $180.00 [cat. 96; 2008.DA.2.100]
No invoice. Eight Minton cups and eight saucers, Manheim, price unrecorded [cat. 242; 2008.DA.2.335.1a, b–.8a, b]

1957

No invoice. Meissen Kakiemon-style small bowl, Langeloh, $125.00 [cat. 350; 2008.DA.2.228]

1958

No British acquisitions.

1959

No invoice. Worcester 'Bodenham Service' teabowl and saucer, Scott, $200.00 [cat. 141; 2008.DA.2.161a, b]

1960–1964

No British acquisitions.

1965

February 2. Longton Hall finger bowl and stand, Williams, $450.00 [cat. 99; 2008.DA.2.103a, b]
February 2. West Pans rococo vase and cover, Williams, $560.00 [cat. 103; 2008.DA.2.107a, b]
No invoice. Grainger's Worcester shell-shaped dish, Jones Gift [cat. 202; 2008.DA.2.371]

1966–1967

No British acquisitions.

1968

April 29. Chinese export 'Resurrection' plate, Art Exchange $600.00 [cat. 328; 2008.DA.2.213]
No invoice. Spode 'New Stone' hot water dish, Sisters, $55.00 [cat. 322; 2008.DA.2.274]

1969

No British or Continental acquisitions.

1970

April (no date). Continental (French ?) Chelsea-style plate, Schindler, $10.00 [cat. 379; 2008.DA.2.257]

1971

No British or Continental acquisitions.

1972

October 15. Chinese export ovoid tea canister, Sharpe, $265.00 [cat. 341; 2008.DA.2.216]
October 16. St. Petersburg 'Kremlin Service' plate, Bull & Bear, $325.00 [cat. 372; 2008.DA.2.247]

1973

No British or Continental acquisitions.

1974

March 12. Pair of Spode 'Chelsea figures,' Zell, $250.00 [cat. 250; 2008.DA.2.351.1, .2]
May 31. Chelsea spirally molded saucer, Williams, $180.00 [cat. 38; 2008.DA.2.306]
August (no date). Derby 'King's' pattern plate, Lookout, $65.00 [cat. 70; 2008.DA.2.321]
August (no date). Derby 'Brocade Imari' pattern plate, Lookout, $55.00 [cat. 71; 2008.DA.2.322]
November (no date). Davenport 'Imari' stone china soup plate, Lookout, $50.00 [cat. 324; 2008.DA.2.276]
No invoice. Royal Worcester dessert plate, Murfrees, $15.00 [cat. 209; 2008.DA.2.377]

1975
No British or Continental acquisitions.

1976
November 11. English (Alcock ?) three-vase garniture, Estate sale, $150.00 [cat. 259; 2008.DA.2.380.1–.3]
November 11. Chinese export armorial waste bowl, Estate sale, $35.00 [cat. 339; 2008.DA.2.215]

1977–1979
No British or Continental acquisitions.

1980
November 28. Spode tan-ground plate with sepia flowers, Corner, $45.00 [cat. 247; 2008.DA.2.348]
November 29. Coalport reticulated circular comport, Corner, $150.00 [cat. 236; 2008.DA.2.311]

1981
March 7. Mason's ironstone 'Imari' oval dish, Northgate, $186.00 [cat. 323; 2008.DA.2.277]
April 10. Plymouth leaf-shaped pickle dish, Sayman, $175.00 [cat. 211; 2008.DA.2.341]
November. Chinese export 'Mandarin palette' soup plate, Miller, $150.00 [cat. 342; 2008.DA.2.217]
December 10. Caughley 'Royal Lily' pattern saucer dish, Godden, $78.80 [cat. 219; 2008.DA.2.305]
December 10. Chinese export covered custard cup, Godden, $78.80 [cat. 345; 2008.DA.2.221a, b]

1982
March 18. Derby Kakiemon-style shell-shaped dish, Atlanta, $130.00 [cat. 69; 2008.DA.2.320]
March 18. Flight, Barr & Barr Imari-style plate, Atlanta, $35.00 [cat. 185; 2008.DA.2.357]
March 18. Coalport 'Finger and Thumb' pattern teacup, Atlanta, $14.00 [cat. 230; 2008.DA.2.308]
August 13. Don Pottery green-glazed earthenware plate, Corner, $65.00 [cat. 312; 2008.DA.2.286]

1983
February (no date). Grainger's Worcester 'Old India' pattern plate, Corner, $85.00 [cat. 200; 2008.DA.2.369]
August 18. Grainger's Worcester 'Old India' pattern plate, Corner, $65.00 [cat. 201; 2008.DA.2.370]
September 8. Ashworth & Bros. ironstone pudding plate, Corner, $128.00 [cat. 325; 2008.DA.2.278]
December 2. New Hall 'Red Ribbon' pattern saucer, Stockbridge, $33.00 [cat. 222; 2008.DA.2.337]

1984
July 19. Pair of (Samson ?) allegorical figures of 'Spring' and 'Summer,' Ida's, $160.00 [cat. 378; 2008.DA.2.256.1, .2]
August 10. Chamberlain's Worcester sauce tureen and stand, Corner, $185.00 [cat. 190; 2008.DA.2.362a–c]
August 10. Spode black-printed oval sugar bowl, Corner, $160.00 [cat. 246; 2008.DA.2.347a, b]
November 13. Royal Worcester pink 'Blind Earl' pattern plate, Corner, $45.00 [cat. 208; 2008.DA.2.376]

1985
November 13. H. & R. Daniel 'Mayflower Shape' plate, Corner, $150.00 [cat. 256; 2008.DA.2.314]
No invoice. Chamberlain's Worcester cup stand, Corner, $75.00 [cat. 194; 2008.DA.2.155]

1986
August (no date). Derby '*Angoulême* Sprig' pattern plate, Corner, $65.00 [cat. 63; 2008.DA.2.317]
October 2. Chamberlain's Worcester armorial plate, Georgian, $300.00 [cat. 191; 2008.DA.2.360]
October 3. Flight, Barr & Barr crested plate, Georgian, $270.00 [cat. 183; 2008.DA.2.358]
No invoice. Samson Worcester-style blue-scale plate, Corner, $130.00 [cat. 377; 2008.DA.2.255]

1987
October (no date). Worcester plate monogrammed *GEM*, Georgian, $536.00 [cat. 178; 2008.DA.2.356]
December 7. Chamberlain's Worcester teacup, Corner, $5.00 [cat. 192; 2008.DA.2.363]
December 7. Chamberlain's Worcester teacup and saucer, Corner, $110.00 [cat. 193; 2008.DA.2.361a, b]
December 7. New Hall 'Imari'-style oval milk jug, Corner, $120.00 [cat. 224; 2008.DA.2.338]
December 7. New Hall teacup, coffee cup, and saucer, Corner, $175.00 [cat. 227; 2008.DA.2.339.1a, b, .2]

1988
April 15. Derby 'Witches' pattern inkstand, Corner, $245.00 [cat. 72; 2008.DA.2.319]
No invoice. Derby saucer painted with a prunus tree, Corner, $60.00 [cat. 68; 2008.DA.2.318]

1989
April 17. Derby circular pastille burner, Corner, $225.00 [cat. 73; 2008.DA.2.323]
April 17. Staffordshire Sèvres-style comport, Corner, $190.00 [cat. 277; 2008.DA.2.328]
April 17. J. D. Baxter earthenware square dish, Corner, $100.00 [cat. 311; 2008.DA.2.284]
October 30. Flight, Barr & Barr teacup and saucer, Corner, $120.00 [cat. 186; 2008.DA.2.359a, b]
November 4. Coalport botanical dessert plate, Corner, $175.00 [cat. 234; 2008.DA.2.310]
November 4. Davenport pearlware Chinese-style plate, Corner, $40.00 [cat. 309; 2008.DA.2.271]

1990
May (no date). Grainger's Worcester cup and saucer, Corner, $100.00 [cat. 199; 2008.DA.2.368a, b]
May (no date). Bowers sugar bowl painted with flowers, Corner, $200.00 [cat. 260; 2008.DA.2.304a, b]
June 8. Pair of Minton white biscuit figures, Becker, $918.00 [cat. 244; 2008.DA.2.336.1, .2]
November (no date). Miles Mason 'Bute' shape teacup and saucer, Corner, $85.00 [cat. 265; 2008.DA.2.329a, b]
No invoice. Minton 'Bute' shape teacup and saucer, Corner, $150.00 [cat. 238; 2008.DA.2.331a, b]
No invoice. Minton plate printed and painted with oriental shrubbery, Corner, $100.00 [cat. 239; 2008.DA.2.332]

1991
February (no date). Bow allegorical figure of 'Asia,' Lundeen, $1,200.00 [cat. 24; 2008.DA.2.303]
September 6. Grainger's Worcester low comport, Robinette, $150.00 [cat. 205; 2008.DA.2.373]
October (no date). Alcock teacup, coffee cup, and saucer, Corner, $150.00 [cat. 258; 2008.DA.2.301.1a, b, .2]

1992
April 16. Pratt-type pearlware figure of a rooster, P. Williams, $977.00 [cat. 299; 2008.DA.2.266]

May 15. Five Staffordshire pearlware tea wares, Sotheby's, London, $325.00 [cat. 306; 2008.DA.2.294.1–4a, b]

May 15. Staffordshire copper lustre clock face jug, Sotheby's, London, $250.00 [cat. 307; 2008.DA.2.299]

May 15. Staffordshire pearlware hexagonal jug, Sotheby's, London, $184.00 [cat. 313; 2008.DA.2.298]

May 15. Glamorgan pearlware milk jug, Sotheby's, London, $152.00 [cat. 329; 2008.DA.2.296]

May 15. Two Glamorgan Pottery pearlware plates, Sotheby's, London, $341.00 [cat. 330; 2008.DA.2.295.1, .2]

May 15. Glamorgan Pottery pearlware teapot, Sotheby's, London, $150.00 [cat. 331; 2008.DA.2.297a, b]

May 15. Llanelli pearlware 'Nautillus' pattern jug, Sotheby's, London, $250.00 [cat. 332; 2008.DA.2.300]

September 22. Copeland & Garrett parian 'Vintage' jug, Gina, $306.00 [cat. 249; 2008.DA.2.350]

September 22. John Yates black basalt cylindrical teapot, Gina, $1,071.00 [cat. 320; 2008.DA.2.269a, b]

November 4. Kerr & Binns Worcester dish, Pulver, $573.75 [cat. 207; 2008.DA.2.375]

November 20. Coalport 'Japan' pattern teapot and stand, Walker and Hoover, $650.00 [cat. 231; 2008.DA.2.309a–c]

November 20. Turner feldspathic stoneware teapot, Walker and Hoover, $950.00 [cat. 319; 2008.DA.2.270a, b]

1993

June 3. Chamberlain's Worcester plate, Pulver, $618.70 [cat. 197; 2008.DA.2.365]

July 20. Charles Meigh drab stoneware teapot, Sotheby's, London, $198.37 [cat. 327; 2008.DA.2.293a, b]

October 21. Herculaneum 7-piece part tea service, Sotheby's, New York, $250.00 [cat. 107; 2008.DA.2.325.1–5a, b]

October 21. Minton saucer dish, Sotheby's, New York, $50.00 [cat. 240; 2008.DA.2.333]

1994

February 9. Rockingham spill vase, Pulver, $150.00 [cat. 270; 2008.DA.2.345]

February 9. J. Rogers & Son pearlware plate, Pulver, $45.00 [cat. 310; 2008.DA.2.272]

March 1. Vauxhall chamber candlestick, Sotheby's, London, $1,382.13 [cat. 94; 2008.DA.2.352]

March 24. Wedgwood teacup and saucer, Pulver, $95.00 [cat. 254; 2008.DA.2.353a, b]

March 24. Staffordshire black-glazed milk jug, Pulver, $350.00 [cat. 317; 2008.DA.2.263]

June 15. Coalport teacup, coffee cup, and saucer, Pulver, $264.00 [cat. 233; 2008.DA.2.312.1a, b, .2]

June 15. Copeland & Garrett toy teacup and saucer, Pulver, $179.00 [cat. 248; 2008.DA.2.349a, b]

June 15. Staffordshire squirrel-form vase, Pulver, $120.00 [cat. 281; 2008.DA.2.302]

Unrecorded. Worcester large teabowl and saucer, CC of A, Gift [cat. 144; 2008.DA.2.354a, b]

1995

October 11. Three English delft landscape plates, Sotheby's, New York, $517.00 [cats. 292–294; 2008.DA.2.258–260]

1996

February 26. Chamberlain's Worcester 'Broom Girl' figure and a watercolor drawing, Sotheby's, London, $736.00 [cat. 198; 2008.DA.2.366, .367]

February 27. French white allegorical group of 'Africa,' Sotheby's, London, $1,840.00 [cat. 365; 2008.DA.2.244]

1997

No invoice. W. Adams pearlware teabowl and saucer, Corner, $185.00 [cat. 314; 2008.DA.2.285a, b]

1998

No British or Continental acquisitions.

1999

October 3. Liverpool teabowl and saucer, Creech, $238.00 [cat. 106; 2008.DA.2.327a, b]

2000

April 14. Grainger's Worcester topographical dish, Sotheby's, New York, $1,200.00 [cat. 203; 2008.DA.2.372]

April 14. Minton 'Oxford Embossed' oval dish, Sotheby's, New York, $750.00 [cat. 241; 2008.DA.2.334]

April 14. Pair of John Ridgway dessert plates, Sotheby's, New York, $220.00 [cat. 268; 2008.DA.2.343.1, .2]

April 14. Pair of Hicks & Meigh stone china dishes, Sotheby's, New York, $230.00 [cat. 321; 2008.DA.2.275.1, .2]

May (no date). Staffordshire oval milk jug, Creech, $98.50 [cat. 274; 2008.DA.2.379]

June 22. S. & J. Rathbone 'Broseley' pattern dessert plate, Creech, $120.00 [cat. 267; 2008.DA.2.342]

August 3. Chamberlain's Worcester teapot, Creech, $295.00 [cat. 189; 2008.DA.2.378a, b]

August 3. Hilditch & Son chinoiserie cake dish, Creech, $98.00 [cat. 263; 2008.DA.2.326]

October 10. S. Alcock & Co. stoneware 'Gypsy Encampment' jug, Creech, $315.00 [cat. 326; 2008.DA.2.292]

2001

May 16. Caughley 'Mansfield' pattern teabowl, Creech, $115.00 [cat. 218; 2008.DA.2.355]

May 16. J. & M.P. Bell & Co. coffee cup, Creech, $76.50 [cat. 291; 2008.DA.2.386]

September 12. Derbyshire (Wirksworth ?) teapot, Phillips, $705.00 [cat. 271; 2008.DA.2.324a, b]

2002–2004

No British or Continental acquisitions.

2005

June 6. Greatbatch creamware documentary teapot, Bonhams, $1,839.00 [cat. 297; 2008.DA.2.265a, b]

Acquisition Date Unknown

Unrecorded. Bow child's toy teabowl, Katz, Gift [cat. 14; 2008.DA.2.15]

No invoice. Grainger's Worcester coffee cup and saucer, provenance and price unrecorded [cat. 206; 2008.DA.2.374a, b]

No invoice. H. & R. Daniel teacup, coffee cup, and saucer, Corner, price unrecorded [cat. 257; 2008.DA.2.315.1a, b, .2]

No invoice. Robinson & Leadbeater Shakespeare bust, provenance and price unrecorded [cat. 269; 2008.DA.2.344]

No invoice. Staffordshire lotus-form inkstand, provenance and price unrecorded [cat. 280; 2008.DA.2.381a, b]

Unrecorded. Staffordshire copper lustre jug dated 1825, Wark, price unrecorded, perhaps a gift [cat. 303; 2008.DA.2.281]

No invoice. English earthenware cauliflower teapot, provenance and price unrecorded [cat. 315; 2008.DA.2.287a, b]

No invoice. Chinese export rice bowl and cover, provenance unrecorded, $75.00 [cat. 349; 2008.DA.2.224a, b]

No invoice. Samson 'faïence' reticulated teapot, provenance and price unrecorded [cat. 376; 2008.DA.2.254a, b]

BIBLIOGRAPHY

Specific catalogues from Parke-Bernet Galleries in New York and Christie's and Sotheby's auctions in London and New York, dating back into the late nineteenth century and preserved in the Thomas J. Watson Library at the Metropolitan Museum of Art in New York, were so useful for investigating and confirming provenances, but these references are too numerous to list here, as are the most current Bonhams, London sale catalogues, in which the scholarship and expertise have been invaluable.

Abraham, Birte. *Commedia dell'Arte: The Patricia & Rodes Hart Collection of European Porcelain and Faience.* Amsterdam: Aronson Concepts, 2010.

Adams, Elizabeth. *Chelsea Porcelain.* London: Barrie & Jenkins, 1987.

———. *Chelsea Porcelain.* 2nd ed. London: The British Museum Press, 2001.

Adams, Elizabeth, and David Redstone. *Bow Porcelain.* Rev. ed. London: Faber and Faber, 1991.

Albert Amor Ltd. [Anne George and Anton Gabszewicz]. *An Exhibition of The Yarbrough Collection of Bow Porcelain, the London Theatre.* March 11–24, 1999. London: Albert Amor Ltd., 1999.

Archer, Michael. *Delftware: The Tin-Glazed Earthenware of the British Isles.* London: Victoria and Albert Museum, 1997.

———. *Delftware at the Fitzwilliam Museum.* London: Philip Wilson Publishers, and Cambridge: The Fitzwilliam Museum, 2013.

The Arts Council of Great Britain. *The Age of Neo-Classicism.* The Fourteenth Exhibition of the Council of Europe at the Royal Academy and the Victoria and Albert Museum, London, September 9–November 19, 1972. London: The Arts Council of Great Britain, 1972.

Ashton, Geoffrey, with Kalman A. Burnim and Andrew Wilton. *Pictures in the Garrick Club.* London: Garrick Club, 1997.

Aslin, Elizabeth, and Paul Atterbury. *Minton 1798–1910.* Catalogue of an exhibition at the Victoria and Albert Museum and Thomas Goode & Company Ltd., London, August–October 1976. London: Victoria and Albert Museum, 1976.

Atkins, Garry. *An Exhibition of English Pottery.* Catalogue of an exhibition and sale, March 9–20, 1999. London: Garry Atkins, 1999.

Atterbury, Paul, ed. *The Parian Phenomenon: A Survey of Victorian Parian Porcelain Statuary & Busts.* Shepton Beauchamp, Somerset, England: Richard Dennis, 1989.

Atterbury, Paul, and Maureen Batkin. *The Dictionary of Minton.* Woodbridge, Suffolk, England: Antique Collectors' Club, 1990.

Auchincloss, Louis. *J.P. Morgan: The Financier as Collector.* New York: Harry Abrams, 1990.

Austin, John C. *Chelsea Porcelain at Williamsburg.* Williamsburg, Virginia: The Colonial Williamsburg Foundation, 1977.

Ayres, John. *Blanc de Chine: Divine Images in Porcelain.* New York: China Institute, 2002.

Ayres, John, Oliver Impey, and J.V.G. Mallet. *Porcelain for Palaces: The Fashion for Japan in Europe, 1650–1750.* Catalogue of an exhibition organized jointly with the British Museum, July 6–November 4, 1990. London: Oriental Ceramic Society, 1990.

Barker, David. *William Greatbatch: A Staffordshire Potter.* London: Jonathan Horne Publications, 1990.

Barker, David, and Pat Halfpenny. *Unearthing Staffordshire.* Catalogue to accompany an exhibition at the International Ceramics Fair and Seminar, London, June 1990. Stoke-on-Trent, Staffordshire, England: City of Stoke-on-Trent Museum & Art Gallery, 1990.

Barkla, Robin, and Ross Barkla. "Andrew Planché—Life after Derby." *English Ceramic Circle Transactions* 15, no. 3 (1995): 367.

———. "Andrew Planché—Life after Derby." In A.P. Ledger, ed., *Derby Porcelain International Society Journal* 3 (1996): 26–43.

Barlow, Francis. *Aesop's Fables With his Life in English, French & Latin Newly Translated Illustrated with One hundred and twelve Sculptures.* London: H. Hills jun. for Francis Barlow, 1687.

Barrett, Franklin A. *Caughley and Coalport Porcelain.* Leigh-on-Sea, England: F. Lewis Publishers, 1951.

Barrett, Franklin A., and Arthur L. Thorpe. *Derby Porcelain, 1750–1848.* Cirencester, England: The Collectors' Book Club, 1973.

Beevers, David, ed. *Chinese Whispers: Chinoiserie in Britain, 1650–1930.* Brighton and Hove, England: The Royal Pavilion & Museums, 2008.

Begg, Patricia, and Barry Taylor. *A Treasury of Bow: A Survey of the Bow Factory from First Patent until Closure, 1744–1774.* Catalogue of an exhibition at The Gold Treasury, Melbourne, August 7–October 8, 2000; Ballarat Fine Art Gallery, Ballarat, November 24, 2000–January 8, 2001; and Hamilton Art Gallery, Hamilton, February 2–April 8, 2001. Hawksburn, Australia: The Ceramics and Glass Circle of Australia, 2000.

Berthoud, Michael. *H. & R. Daniel, 1822–1846.* Wingham, Kent, England: Micawber Publications, 1980.

———. *A Compendium of British Cups.* Bridgnorth, Shropshire, England: Micawber Publications, 1990.

———. *A Cabinet of British Creamers.* Bridgnorth, Shropshire, England: Micawber Publications, 1999.

Berthoud, Michael, and Lynne Price. *Daniel Patterns on Porcelain.* Bridgnorth, Shropshire, England: Micawber Publications, 1997.

Biancalana, Alessandro. *Porcellane e maioliche a Doccia: La fabbrica dei marchesi Ginori. I primi cento anni.* Florence: Edizioni Polistampa, 2009.

Bimson, Mavis. "The Missing Muse." *English Ceramic Circle Transactions* 19, no. 3 (2007): 569–572.

Binns, W. Moore. *The First Century of English Porcelain.* London: Hurst and Blackett, 1906.

Blake Roberts, Gaye. "Sources of Decoration on an Unrecorded Caughley Dessert Service." *English Ceramic Circle Transactions* 10, no. 1 (1976): 59–68.

———. "Wirksworth–The Elusive Manufactory." In "Recent Research on Ceramics of Derbyshire," edited by Gerald Daniel, *Derby Porcelain International Society Journal* 2 (1991): 64–72.

———. *Mason's: The First Two Hundred Years.* London: Merrell Holberton Publishers, 1996.

Blumenfield, Robert H. *Blanc de Chine: The Great Porcelain of Dehua.* Berkeley, California: Ten Speed Press, 2002.

Blunt, Reginald. *The Cheyne Book of Chelsea China and Pottery.* London: Geoffrey Bles, 1924.

Boicourt, Jane. "Oriental Designs in English Ceramics." *The Magazine Antiques* 58, no. 4 (October 1950): 278–280.

Bonehill, John, and Stephen Daniels, eds. *Paul Sandby: Picturing Britain.* Catalogue for *Paul Sandby (1731–1809): Picturing Britain, A Bicentenary Exhibition* at the Nottingham Museum and Art Gallery, July 25–October 18, 2009; the National Gallery of Scotland, Edinburgh, November 7, 2009–February 7, 2010; and the Royal Academy of Arts, London, March 13–June 13, 2010. London: Royal Academy of Arts, 2009.

Bonhams. *The Billie Pain Collection.* November 26, 2003. Sale no. 10559. London: Bonhams, 2003.

———. *The Zorensky Collection of Worcester Porcelain.* Part 1. March 16, 2004. Sale no. 10816. London: Bonhams, 2004.

———. *The Zorensky Collection of Worcester Porcelain.* Part 2. February 23, 2005. Sale no. 11900. London: Bonhams, 2005.

———. *The Zorensky Collection of Worcester Porcelain.* Part 3. February 22, 2006. Sale no. 14279. London: Bonhams, 2006.

———. *The Sir Jeremy Lever Collection [of Worcester Porcelain].* March 7, 2007. Sale no. 15267. London: Bonhams, 2007.

———. *The Frank Wheeldon Collection of English Porcelain.* January 23, 2008. Sale no. 15925. London: Bonhams, 2008.

Bradley, Gilbert, with Judith Anderson and Robin Barkla. *Derby Porcelain, 1750–1798.* London: Thomas Heneage, 1990.

Bradley, H. G[ilbert]. *Ceramics of Derbyshire, 1750–1975.* London: Gilbert Bradley, 1978.

Bradshaw, Peter. *18th Century English Porcelain Figures, 1745–1795.* Woodbridge, Suffolk, England: Antique Collectors' Club, 1981.

———. *Derby Porcelain Figures, 1750–1848.* London: Faber and Faber, 1990.

———. *Bow Porcelain Figures circa 1748–1774.* London: Barrie & Jenkins, 1992.

Brandimarte, Cynthia A. "Darling Dabblers: American China Painters and Their Work, 1870–1920." *The American Ceramic Circle Journal* (New York), 6 (1988): 6–27.

Branyan, Lawrence, Neal French, and John Sandon. *Worcester Blue and White Porcelain, 1751–1790: An Illustrated Encyclopaedia of the Patterns.* 2nd ed. London: Barrie & Jenkins, 1989.

[British Museum.] *Rare and Documentary 18th Century English Porcelain from The British Museum: The International Ceramics Fair and Seminar, London, June 1987.* Catalogue to accompany an exhibition at The International Ceramics Fair and Seminar, London, 1987. London: Christie's, 1987.

Brosio, Valentino. *Rossetti, Vische, Vinovo: Porcellane e maioliche torinesi del Settecento.* Milan: Görlich Editore, 1973.

Brown, E. Myra, and Terence A. Lockett. *Made in Liverpool: Liverpool Pottery & Porcelain, 1700–1850.* Catalogue of the Seventh Exhibition from the Northern Ceramic Society, Walker Art Gallery, Liverpool, June 27–September 19, 1993. Liverpool: Board of Trustees of the National Museums & Galleries on Merseyside and the Northern Ceramic Society, 1993.

Bruce-Mitford, R.L.S. *Bow Porcelain, 1744–1776.* Catalogue of a Special Exhibition of Documentary Material to commemorate the bicentenary of the retirement of Thomas Frye, manager of the factory and "inventor and first manufacturer of porcelain in England." The British Museum, London, October 1959–April 1960. London: The Trustees of the British Museum, 1959.

Burke's Genealogical and Heraldic History of the Peerage, Baronetage and Knightage. Edited by Peter Townend. 105th ed. London: Burke's Peerage, 1970.

Burnim, Kalman A., and Andrew Wilton. *The Richard Bebb Collection in the Garrick Club: A Catalogue of Figures, Sculpture and Paintings.* London: Garrick Club, 2001.

Burresi, Mariagiulia. *La manifattura Toscana dei Ginori Doccia 1737–1791.* Ospedaletto (Pisa), Italy: Pacini Editore, 1998.

Bushnell, Gordon. *The Illustrated Guide to 19th Century Coalport 'Coalbrookdale' Floral Encrusted Porcelain.* United Kingdom: Gordon Bushnell, 2006.

Calmann, Gerta. *Ehret: Flower Painter Extraordinaire.* Boston: Little Brown and Company for the New York Graphic Society, 1977.

Cassidy-Geiger, Maureen. *The Arnhold Collection of Meissen Porcelain, 1710–50.* New York: The Frick Collection and the Arnhold Foundation Inc. in association with D. Giles, London, 2008.

Caughley in Colour: Exhibition Catalogue 2005. Coalbrookdale, Telford, Shropshire, England: Ironbridge Gorge Museum Trust, 2005.

Caviró, Balbina Martínez. *Porcelana del Buen Retiro: Escultura.* Madrid: Instituto Diego Velázquez, 1973.

Chaffers, William. *Marks and Monograms on European and Oriental Pottery and Porcelain.* Edited by Geoffrey A. Godden, Frederick Litchfield, and R.L. Hobson. 2 vols. 15th rev. ed. London: William Reeves Bookseller, 1965.

Charleston, R.J., and Donald Towner. *English Ceramics, 1580–1830.* Commemorative catalogue to celebrate the 50th Anniversary of the English Ceramic Circle, 1927–1977. London: Sotheby Parke Bernet Publications, 1977.

Chilton, Meredith. *Harlequin Unmasked: The Commedia dell'Arte and Porcelain Sculpture.* Toronto: The George R. Gardiner Museum of Ceramic Art, 2001.

Clarke, T.H. "French Influences at Chelsea." *English Ceramic Circle Transactions* 4, no. 5 (1959): 45–57.

Clifford, Timothy. "Derby Biscuit." *English Ceramic Circle Transactions* 7, no. 2 (1969): 108–117.

———. "J.J. Spängler, a Virtuoso Swiss Modeler at Derby." *The Connoisseur* 198, no. 796 (June 1978): 146–155.

Coke, David, and Alan Borg. *Vauxhall Gardens: A History.* New Haven and London: The Paul Mellon Centre for Studies in British Art, 2011.

Coke, Gerald. *In Search of James Giles (1718–1780).* Wingham, Kent, England: Micawber Publications, 1983.

Cook, Cyril. *The Life and Work of Robert Hancock.* London: Chapman and Hall, 1948.

———. *Supplement to The Life and Work of Robert Hancock.* London: Published by the Author, 1955.

Copeland, Robert. *Spode & Copeland Marks and Other Relevant Intelligence.* 2nd ed. London: Studio Vista, 1997.

Cox, Alwyn, and Angela Cox. *Rockingham Pottery and Porcelain, 1745–1842.* London: Faber and Faber, 1983.

———. *Rockingham, 1745–1842.* Woodbridge, Suffolk, England: Antique Collectors' Club, 2001.

Coysh, A.W. *Blue and White Transfer Ware, 1780–1840.* Rutland, Vermont: Charles E. Tuttle Company, 1971.

Coysh, A.W., and R.K. Henrywood. *The Dictionary of Blue and White Printed Pottery, 1780–1880.* Woodbridge, Suffolk, England: Antique Collectors' Club, 1982.

———. *The Dictionary of Blue and White Printed Pottery, 1780–1880.* Vol. 2. Woodbridge, Suffolk, England: Antique Collectors' Club, 1989. Reprinted 1990.

Crane, Paul. "Zoomorphic, Phyllomorphic and Marine Forms." In *Scrolls of Fantasy: The Rococo and Ceramics in England, c 1735–c 1775,* edited by Charles Dawson, pp. 95–109. London: English Ceramic Circle, 2015a.

———. "Nature, Porcelain and the Age of the Enlightenment." In

Art Antiques London Handbook, pp. 92–102. London: Haughton International Fairs, 2015b.

Craven, Babette. "Derby Figures of Richard III." *English Ceramic Circle Transactions* 10, no. 2 (1977): 95–98.

Crossley, Robert. "Circulatory Systems of Puzzle Jugs." *English Ceramic Circle Transactions* 15, no. 1 (1993): 73–98 and plate V.

Croxall, Samuel. *Fables of Æsop and Others: Translated into English with Instructive Applications; And a Print before each Fable*. 14th rev. ed. London: Printed and sold by the booksellers in Town and Country, 1789. First published in 1722. British Library edition online.

Cumming, Robert, and Michael Berthoud. *Minton Patterns of the First Period*. Bridgnorth, Shropshire, England: Micawber Publications, 1997.

Dacier, Émile, and Albert Vuaflart. *Jean de Jullienne et les graveurs de Watteau au XVIIIe siècle*. 4 vols. Paris: Société pour l'étude de la gravure française, 1921.

Danckert, Ludwig. *Directory of European Porcelain*. Rev. ed. London: Robert Hale, 2004.

Davis, Howard. *Chinoiserie: Polychrome Decoration on Staffordshire Porcelain, 1790–1850*. London: Howard Davis, 1991.

Dawson, Aileen. *The Art of Worcester Porcelain, 1751–1788: Masterpieces from the British Museum Collection*. London: The British Museum Press, 2007.

De Castro, Nuno. *Chinese Porcelain and the Heraldry of the Empire*. London: Philip Wilson Publishers; Oporto, Portugal: Livraria Editora Civilização, 1988.

Den Blaauwen, Abraham L. *Het Meissen servies van Stadhouder Willem V* [The Meissen Service of Stadholder Willem V]. Catalogue of an exhibition at Paleis Het Loo, Apeldoorn, September 25, 1993–March 14, 1994. Apeldoorn, the Netherlands: Paleis Het Loo; Zwolle, the Netherlands: Waanders Uitgevers, 1993.

———. *Meissen Porcelain in the Rijksmuseum*. Amsterdam: Rijksmuseum and Waanders Publishers, 2000.

Deroubaix, Christiane. *Les porcelaines de Tournai du Musée de Mariemont*. Mariemont, Belgium: Ministère de l'instruction publique et le Patrimoine du domaine de Mariemont, 1958.

Díaz, Rocío. *Chinese Armorial Porcelain for Spain*. London: Jorge Welsh Books, 2010.

Dobler, Andreas, and Meinolf Siemer. *Das weisse Gold des Nordens: Kopenhagener Porzellan des 18. und 19. Jahrhunderts*. Catalogue of an exhibition at Hessische Hausstiftung Museum Schloss Fasanarie. Eichenzell near Fulda, Germany: Hessische Hausstiftung Museum Schloss Fasanarie, 1992.

Dragesco, Bernard. *English Ceramics in French Archives*. London: English Ceramic Circle, 1993.

Drakard, David. *Printed English Pottery: History and Humour in the Reign of George III, 1760–1820*. London: Jonathan Horne Publications, 1992.

Draper, J. *Jugs in Northampton Museum*. Northampton, England: Northampton Borough Council Leisure Activities Committee for Northampton Museums and Art Gallery, 1978.

Ducret, Siegfried. *Keramik und Graphik des 18. Jahrhunderts: Vorlagen für Maler und Modelleure*. Brunswick, Germany: Klinkhardt & Biermann, 1973.

Eberle, Martin. *Cris de Paris: Meissener Porzellanfiguren des 18. Jahrhunderts, Meissen Porcelain Figurines of the 18th Century*. Published for the exhibition *Sachsens Gold im Schlösschen*, at the Gohliser Schlösschen, Leipzig, April 29–June 10, 2001. Leipzig: Kulturamtes der Stadt Leipzig and Freundeskreis "Gohliser Schlösschen," 2001.

Eberlein, Harold Donaldson, and Roger Wearne Ramsdell. *The Practical Book of Chinaware*. New York: Halcyon House, 1925.

E.C.C. [English Ceramic Circle]. *English Ceramic Circle 1927–1948: English Pottery and Porcelain*. Commemorative catalogue of an exhibition held at the Victoria and Albert Museum, London, May 5–June 20, 1948. London: Routledge and Kegan Paul, 1948.

———. "Some Chelsea Advertisements." *English Ceramic Circle Transactions* 7, no. 3 (1970): 160–161b.

———. *Creamware and Pearlware Re-examined*. Edited by Tom Walford and Roger Massey. A collection of papers presented at a colloquium held by the English Ceramic Circle at the Victoria and Albert Museum on June 4th and 5th, 2005. London: English Ceramic Circle, 2005.

Edmundson, Roger S. "Billingsley and His China Artists, 1796–1808." In Gray 2005, pp. 151–169.

Edwards, Diana. *Neale Pottery and Porcelain: Its Predecessors and Successors, 1763–1820*. London: Barrie & Jenkins, 1987.

———. *Black Basalt: Wedgwood and Contemporary Manufacturers*. Woodbridge, Suffolk, England: Antique Collectors' Club, 1994.

Edwards, Diana, and Rodney Hampson. *White Salt-Glazed Stoneware of the British Isles*. Woodbridge, Suffolk, England: Antique Collectors' Club, 2005.

Emmerson, Robin. *British Teapots and Tea Drinking, 1700–1850*. London: HMSO, 1992.

Fairbairn, James. *Fairbairn's Book of Crests of the Families of Great Britain and Ireland*. 4th rev. ed. 2 vols. London and Edinburgh: T.C. & E.C. Jack, 1905.

Fairclough, Oliver. "The Decoration of Welsh Porcelain." *Derby Porcelain International Society Journal* 4 (2000): 27–37.

Ferguson, Patricia. "The Earls of Enniskillen at Florence Court, a 1754 Chelsea Auction in Dublin and the Irish Market, and the So-called 'Warren Hastings' Pattern." *English Ceramic Circle Transactions* 24 (2013): 1–30.

Fleming, J. Arnold. *Scottish Pottery*. Glasgow: MacLehose, Jackson & Co., 1923.

Friedman, Terry, and Timothy Clifford. *The Man at Hyde Park Corner: Sculpture by John Cheere, 1709–1787*. Catalogue of an exhibition at Temple Newsam, Leeds, May 15–June 15, 1974, and at Marble Hill House, Twickenham, July 19–September 8, 1974. Leeds, England: Leisure Services Committee and Leeds Art Galleries, 1974.

Fritzsche, Christoph. *Die Aelteste Volkstedter Porzellanmanufaktur: Ihre Geschichte von der Gründung bis heute*. Stuttgart, Germany: Arnoldsche Art Publishers and Christoph Fritzsche, 2013.

Gabszewicz, Anton. *Made at New Canton: Bow Porcelain from the Collection of the London Borough of Newham*. London: The English Ceramic Circle in association with the London Borough of Newham and the Newham Millennium Celebrations 2000 Committee, 2000.

Gabszewicz, Anton, and Geoffrey Freeman. *Bow Porcelain: The Collection Formed by Geoffrey Freeman*. London: Lund Humphreys, 1982.

Gabszewicz, Anton, and Roderick Jellicoe. *Isleworth Porcelain*. Catalogue of a 1998 exhibition (details unpublished). London: Roderick Jellicoe, 1998.

Gallagher, Brian D. *British Ceramics, 1675–1825: The Mint Museum*. Charlotte, North Carolina: The Mint Museum in association with D. Giles Ltd., London, 2015.

Gardner, Dr. H. Bellamy. "An Early Allusion to English Porcelain, Gouyn's Will, and Some Chelsea Models." *English Porcelain Circle Transactions*, no. 2 (1929): 23–27.

———. "Primitive Chelsea Porcelain." *The Connoisseur* 109 (January–June 1942): 35–39.

Gibbs-Smith, C.H. *The Great Exhibition of 1851*. 2nd ed. London: Victoria and Albert Museum, 1981. First published in 1951.

Gibson, Michael. *19th Century Lustreware*. Woodbridge, Suffolk, England: Antique Collectors' Club, 1999.

Gilhespy, F. Brayshaw. *Crown Derby Porcelain*. Leigh-on-Sea, England: F. Lewis Publishers, 1951.

Ginori Lisci, Leonardo. *La Porcellana di Doccia*. Milan: Electa Editrice, 1963.

Glendenning, Mr. O., and Mrs. Donald MacAlister. "Chelsea, The Triangle Period." *English Ceramic Circle Transactions* 1, no. 3 (1935): 20–36.

Godden, Geoffrey A. *Encyclopaedia of British Pottery and Porcelain Marks*. New York: Bonanza Books, 1964. Later revised editions have been published in the United Kingdom, e.g., Barrie & Jenkins, 1979; and Hutchinson, 1991.

———. *An Illustrated Encyclopedia of British Pottery and Porcelain*. New York: Bonanza Books, 1966.

———. *Caughley and Worcester Porcelains, 1775–1800*. New York: Frederick A. Praeger, 1969. Reprinted with an expanded introduction, Woodbridge, Suffolk, England: Antique Collectors' Club, 1981.

———. *Minton Pottery and Porcelain of the First Period, 1793–1850*. New York: Frederick A. Praeger, 1968. Reprinted, London: Barrie & Jenkins, 1978.

———. *Oriental Export Market Porcelain and Its Influence on European Wares*. London: Granada Publishing, 1979.

———. *Godden's Guide to Mason's China and the Ironstone Wares*. Woodbridge, Suffolk, England: Antique Collectors' Club. 1980.

———. *Coalport and Coalbrookdale Porcelains*. Woodbridge, Suffolk, England: Antique Collectors' Club, 1970. Reprinted with a new introduction, 1981.

———. *Chamberlain-Worcester Porcelain, 1788–1852*. London: Barrie & Jenkins, 1982. Reprinted in 1992.

———., ed. *Staffordshire Porcelain*. London: Granada Publishing, 1983.

———. *Eighteenth-Century English Porcelain: A Selection from the Godden Reference Collection*. London: Granada Publishing, 1985a.

———. *English China*. London: Barrie & Jenkins, 1985b.

———. *Lowestoft Porcelains*. Rev. ed. Woodbridge, Suffolk, England: Antique Collectors' Club, 1985c.

———. *Ridgway Porcelains*. 2nd ed. Woodbridge, Suffolk, England: Antique Collectors' Club, 1985d.

———. *Encyclopaedia of British Porcelain Manufacturers*. London: Barrie & Jenkins, 1988.

———. *Godden's Guide to Mason's China and the Ironstone Wares*. Revised and enlarged from the 1971 and 1980 editions. Woodbridge, Suffolk, England: Antique Collectors' Club, 1991.

———. *Godden's Guide to Ironstone, Stone and Granite Wares*. Woodbridge, Suffolk, England: Antique Collectors' Club, 1999.

———. *Godden's Guide to English Blue and White Porcelain*. Woodbridge, Suffolk, England: Antique Collectors' Club, 2004a.

———. *Godden's New Guide to English Porcelain*. London: Miller's; London: Octopus Publishing, 2004b.

———. *New Hall Porcelains*. Woodbridge, Suffolk, England: Antique Collectors' Club, 2004c.

Godden, Geoffrey A., and Michael Gibson. *Collecting Lustreware*. London: Barrie & Jenkins, 1991.

Graesse, Dr. J. G. Th., and E. Jaennicke. *Führer für sammler von Porzellan und Fayence, Steinzeug, Steingut usw*. 23rd ed. Brunswick, Germany: Klinkhardt & Biermann, 1974.

Grandjean, Bredo L. *Kongelig Dansk Porcelæn 1775–1884*. Copenhagen: Thaning & Appels Forlag, 1962.

———. *200 Years of Royal Copenhagen Porcelain*. The catalogue of a retrospective exhibition circulated by the Smithsonian Institution, 1974–1976. Washington, D.C.: The Smithsonian Institution, 1974.

Grandjean, Bredo L., Dyveke Helsted, and Merete Bodelsen. *The Royal Copenhagen Porcelain Manufactory, 1775–1975*. Copenhagen: The Royal Copenhagen Porcelain Manufactory, 1975.

Gray, Jonathan, ed. *Welsh Ceramics in Context*. Part 1. Swansea, Wales: Royal Institution of South Wales, 2003.

———, ed. *Welsh Ceramics in Context*. Part 2. Swansea, Wales: Royal Institution of South Wales, 2005.

———. "Cambria or Cambrian: Two Different Aspects of the Welsh Ceramic Industry." *English Ceramic Circle Transactions* 19, no. 3 (2007): 559–568.

———. *The Cambrian Company: Swansea Pottery in London, 1806–1808*. Great Britain: Jonathan Gray, 2012.

Griffin, John D. *A Celebration of Yorkshire Pots*. The Eighth Exhibition from the Northern Ceramic Society, June 29–September 21, 1997. Rotherham, England: Clifton Park Museum, 1997.

———. *The Don Pottery, 1801–1993*. Doncaster, England: Doncaster Museum Service, 2001.

———. *The Leeds Pottery, 1770–1881*. 2 vols. Leeds, England: The Leeds Art Collections Fund, 2005.

Grigsby, Leslie B. *English Pottery: Stoneware and Earthenware, 1650–1800, The Henry H. Weldon Collection*. London: Sotheby's Publications, 1990.

Grimwade, Arthur G. *London Goldsmiths, 1697–1837: Their Marks and Lives*. 3rd rev. ed. London: Faber and Faber, 1990.

Guest, Montague John, ed. *Lady Charlotte Schreiber's Journals*. 2 vols. London and New York: John Lane, 1911.

Gurnett, Robin. "Mr Tebo at Wedgwood's and an Alternative Occupation." *English Ceramic Circle Transactions* 19, no. 1 (2005): 73–78.

Guy-Jones, Gordon, and Sue Guy-Jones. *Bow Porcelain On-glaze Prints and Their Sources*. London: English Ceramic Circle, 2013.

Hackenbroch, Yvonne. *Chelsea and Other English Porcelain, Pottery, and Enamel in the Irwin Untermyer Collection*. Cambridge, Massachusetts: Harvard University Press for The Metropolitan Museum of Art, New York, 1957.

Haggar, Reginald, and Elizabeth Adams. *Mason Porcelain and Ironstone, 1796–1853: Miles Mason and the Mason Manufactories*. London: Faber and Faber, 1977.

Halfpenny, Pat. *English Earthenware Figures, 1740–1840*. Woodbridge, Suffolk, England: Antique Collectors' Club, 1991.

———, ed. *Penny Plain, Twopence Coloured: Transfer-Printing on English Ceramics, 1750–1850*. Stoke-on-Trent, Staffordshire, England: Stoke-on-Trent City Museum and Art Gallery, 1994.

Halfpenny, Pat, and Terry Lockett, eds. *Staffordshire Porcelain, 1740–1851*. Catalogue of The Third Exhibition of the Northern Ceramic Society, City Museum and Art Gallery, Hanley, Stoke-on-Trent, Staffordshire, October 20–December 29, 1979. Stafford, England: The Northern Ceramic Society, 1979.

Hallesy, Helen L. *The Glamorgan Pottery, Swansea, 1814–38*. Llandysul, Dwyfed, Wales: Gomer Press, 1995.

———. "The Glamorgan Pottery, Swansea and Some Comparisons with the Cambrian." In Gray 2003, pp. 99–119.

———. *Swansea Pottery Collectors' Exhibition 2006 / Arddangosfa Casglwyr Crochenwaith Abertawe 2006*. Swansea, Wales: Gomer Press, 2006.

Hammer Galleries. *Art Objects and Furnishings from the William Randolph Hearst Collection: Catalogue Raisonné*. Exhibited and sold at Gimbel Brothers, New York, in cooperation with Saks Fifth Avenue, 1941. New York: William Bradford Press, 1941.

Handley, Joseph. *18th Century English Transfer-Printed Porcelain and Enamels: The Joseph M. Handley Collection*. Carmel, California: Mulberry Press, 1991.

Hanscombe, Stephen. *James Giles: China and Glass Painter (1718–1780)*. Published in conjunction with a loan exhibition at Stockspring Antiques, London, June 9–21, 2005. London: Stockspring Antiques, 2005.

———. *The Early James Giles and His Contemporary London Decorators*. Published in conjunction with a loan exhibition at Stockspring Antiques, London, June 5–17, 2008. London: Stockspring Antiques, 2008.

———. *Jefferyes Hamett O'Neale: China Painter and Illustrator (d. 1801)*. Published in conjunction with a loan exhibition at Stockspring Antiques, London, June 3–15, 2010. London: Stockspring Antiques, 2010.

Haslem, John. *The Old Derby China Factory: The Workmen and Their Productions*. London: George Bell and Sons, 1876.

Haughton Gallery. *A Taste of Elegance: Dining in Eighteenth Century Europe*. Catalogue of an exhibition and sale. London: Brian Haughton Gallery, 2010.

———. *Nature, Porcelain and Enlightenment*. Catalogue of an exhibition and sale. London: Brian Haughton Gallery, 2014.

———. *A Private Collection: Chelsea and Other Early English Porcelain*. Catalogue of an exhibition and sale. London: Brian Haughton Gallery, 2015.

Hayden, Arthur. *Old English Porcelain: The Lady Ludlow Collection*. London: John Murray, 1932.

Helke, Gun-Dagmar. *Johann Esaias Nilson (1721–1788): Augsburger Miniaturmaler, Kupferstecher, Verleger und Kunstakademiedirek-*

tor. Beiträge zur Kunstwissenschaft 82. Munich: Scaneg Verlag, 2005.

Henderson, Arthur E. *Tintern Abbey: Then and Now*. London: Simkin Marshall, 1935.

Henrywood, R. K. *Relief-Moulded Jugs, 1820–1900*. Woodbridge, Suffolk, England: Antique Collectors' Club, 1984.

———. *An Illustrated Guide to British Jugs from Medieval Times to the Twentieth Century*. Shrewsbury, England: Swan Hill Press, an imprint of Airlife Publishing, 1997.

———. *Staffordshire Potters, 1781–1900*. Woodbridge, Suffolk, England: Antique Collectors' Club, 2002.

Hermann, Luke. *Paul and Thomas Sandby*. London: B. T. Batsford in association with the Victoria and Albert Museum, 1986.

Hildyard, Robin. "London Chinamen." *English Ceramic Circle Transactions* 18, no. 3 (2003): 447–524.

Hillis, Maurice. *Liverpool Porcelain, 1756–1804*. Great Britain: Maurice Hillis, 2011.

Hillis, Maurice, and Roderick Jellicoe. *The Liverpool Porcelain of William Reid*. A Catalogue of Porcelain and Excavated Shards, exhibited at Roderick Jellicoe, 3a Campden Street, London, March 15–April 1, 2000. London: Roderick Jellicoe, 2000.

Hodgson, Zorka. "Survey of the Sources of Inspiration for the Goat and Bee Jug and Some Other Noted Chelsea Creations." *English Ceramic Circle Transactions* 14, no. 1 (1990): 34–47.

Hofer, Philip. "Francis Barlow's Aesop." *Harvard Library Bulletin* 2, no. 3 (1948): 279–295.

Holgate, David. "Polychrome and Hard Paste Caughley Porcelain." *English Ceramic Circle Transactions* 7, no. 1 (1968): 39–45.

———. *New Hall*. London: Faber and Faber, 1987.

Holloway, Dr. Chris, and Felicity Marno. *Paul Sandby and Related Influences on Caughley Porcelain*. Monographs on Caughley Porcelain 2. Based on a loan exhibition at Stockspring Antiques, London, April 2003.

Honey, William B. *Old English Porcelain*. New York: Whittlesey House, McGraw-Hill Book Company, 1946.

———. *European Ceramic Art from the End of the Middle Ages to about 1815*. London: Faber and Faber, 1952.

Hosking, Mollie. "New China Works, Worcester." *Northern Ceramic Society Journal* (Stoke-on-Trent, England) 14 (1997): 131–142.

Howard, David Sanctuary. *Chinese Armorial Porcelain*. London: Faber and Faber, 1974.

———. *Chinese Armorial Porcelain*. Vol. 2. Chippenham, Wiltshire, England: Heirloom & Howard Limited, 2003.

Howard, David, and John Ayers. *China for the West: Chinese Porcelain & Other Decorative Arts for Export Illustrated from the Mottahedeh Collection*. 2 vols. London and New York: Sotheby Parke Bernet Publications, 1978.

Howell, John. "Transfer-printed Lowestoft Porcelain." *English Ceramic Circle Transactions* 7, no. 3 (1970): 210–219.

Hoyte, Anthony. *The Charles Norman Collection of 18th Century Derby Porcelain*. Abingdon, England: The Nuffield Press and the Proprietors of the Charles Norman Collection, 1996.

———. *The Charles Norman Collection of 18th Century Derby Porcelain. Supplementary Catalogue I*. Abingdon, England: The Nuffield Press and the Proprietors of the Charles Norman Collection, 1999.

———. *The Charles Norman Collection of 18th Century Derby Porcelain. Supplementary Catalogue II*. Abingdon, England: The Nuffield Press and the Proprietors of the Charles Norman Collection, 2000.

Hughes, Bernard, and Therle Hughes. *The Collector's Encyclopaedia of English Ceramics*. New York: The Macmillan Company, [1957].

Hurlbutt, Frank. *Bow Porcelain*. London: G. Bell and Sons, 1926.

———. *Bristol Porcelain*. London: Medici Society, 1928.

Hutton, A. de Saye. *A Guide to New Hall Porcelain Patterns*. London: Barrie & Jenkins, 1990.

Jacob-Hanson, Charlotte. "Maria Sibylla Merian: Artist-Naturalist." *The Magazine Antiques* 158, no. 2 (August 2000): 174–183.

———. "'Deux-viviers?' A Critical Re-appraisal of the Duvivier Family Tree." *English Ceramic Circle Transactions* 19, no. 3 (2007): 477–483.

Jansen, Reinhard, ed. *Commedia dell'arte, Fest der Komödianten*. 3 vols., including an English translation and print sources. Stuttgart: Arnoldsche Art Publishers with the Gesellschaft der Keramikfreunde, Düsseldorf, 2001.

Jean-Richard, Pierrette. *L'oeuvre gravé de François Boucher dans la Collection Edmond de Rothschild*. Musée du Louvre, Cabinet des Dessins, Collection Edmond de Rothschild. Paris: Éditions des Musées Nationaux, 1978.

Jedding, Hermann. *Europäisches Porzellan*. Vol. 1, *Von den Anfängen bis 1800*. Munich: Keysersche Verlagsbuchhandlung, 1974.

Jenkins, Dilys. *Llanelly Pottery*. Swansea, Wales: Deb Books, 1968.

Jewitt, Llewellynn. *The Ceramic Art of Great Britain: From Prehistoric Times Down to the Present Day*. 2 vols. London: Virtue and Co., 1878.

John, W. D. *Nantgarw Porcelain*. Newport, Monmouthshire, Wales: R. H. Johns, 1948.

———. *Swansea Porcelain*. Newport, Monmouthshire, Wales: Ceramic Book Company, 1958.

———. *William Billingsley (1758–1828): His Outstanding Achievements as an Artist and Porcelain Maker*. Newport, Monmouthshire, Wales: Ceramic Book Company, 1968.

John, W. D., and Warren Baker. *Old English Lustre Pottery*. Newport, Monmouthshire, Wales: R. H. Johns, 1951.

John, W. D., with G. J. Coombes and Katherine Coombes. *The Nantgarw Porcelain Album*. Newport, Gwent, Wales: Ceramic Book Company, 1975.

Jones, A. E. (Jimmy), and Sir Leslie Joseph. *Swansea Porcelain Shapes and Decoration*. Cowbridge, Wales: D. Brown and Sons, 1988.

Jones, Joan. *Minton: The First Two Hundred Years of Design and Production*. Shrewsbury, England: Swan Hill Press and Royal Doulton Limited, 1993.

Jörg, Christiaan J. A. "A Pattern of Exchange: Jan Luyken and *Chine de Commande* Porcelain." *Metropolitan Museum Journal* (New York) 37 (2002): 171–176.

Jörg, Christiaan J. A., with Jan van Campen. *Chinese Ceramics in the Collection of the Rijksmuseum, Amsterdam: The Ming and Qing Dynasties*. London: Philip Wilson in association with the Rijksmuseum, Amsterdam, 1997.

Kelly, Henry E. *Scottish Ceramics*. Atglen, Pennsylvania: Schiffer Publishing, 1999.

———. *The Glasgow Pottery of John and Matthew Perston Bell: China and Earthenware Manufacturers in Glasgow*. Photographs, layout, and computer work by Douglas A. Leishman. Online revised edition. Glasgow: Privately published, 2006.

Kevill-Davies, Sally. *Chelsea China from Private Collections*. Catalogue of an exhibition organized by The Chelsea Society in association with Sally Kevill-Davies at Chelsea Old Town Hall, London, June 20–26, 1999. London: Chelsea Society and S. Kevill-Davies, 1999.

Kevill-Davies, Sally, in association with Antonia Agnew and Felicity Marno. *Sir Hans Sloane's Plants on Chelsea Porcelain*. Published in conjunction with a loan exhibition at Stockspring Antiques, London, June 2–16, 2015. London: Elmhirst & Suttie, 2015.

King, W. A. H. "Early Chelsea Figures," and O. Glendenning, "Girl in a Swing Figures." *English Ceramic Circle Transactions* 2, no. 8 (1942): 153–154.

King, William. *Chelsea Porcelain*. London: Benn Brothers, 1922.

———. *English Porcelain Figures of the Eighteenth Century*. London and Boston: Medici Society, 1924.

Kleinman, Bella. "Mr. Tebo vs. John Toulouse." *English Ceramic Circle Transactions* 15, no. 2 (1994): 327–328.

Kroes, Dr. Jochem. *Chinese Armorial Porcelain for the Dutch Market: Chinese Porcelain with Coats of Arms of Dutch Families*. Zwolle: Waanders Publishers and The Hague: Centraal Bureau voor Genealogie, 2007.

Lane, Arthur. *Italian Porcelain*. London: Faber and Faber, 1954.

———. *English Porcelain Figures of the Eighteenth Century*. London: Faber and Faber, 1961a.

———. "William Littler of Longton Hall and West Pans, Scotland." *English Ceramic Circle Transactions* 5, no. 2 (1961b): 82–92b.

Laursen, Bodil Busk, and Steen Nottelmann, eds. *Royal Danish Porcelain, 1775–2000*. Copenhagen: Nyt Nordisk Forlag Arnold Busck and The Danish Museum of Decorative Art, 2000.

Lawrence, Heather. *Yorkshire Pots and Potteries*. Newton Abbot, Devon, England: David & Charles, 1974.

Lebel, Antoine. *Armoiries Françaises et Suisses sur la porcelaine de Chine au XVIIIe Siècle* [French and Swiss Armorials on Chinese Export Porcelain of the 18th Century]. Brussels: Antoine Lebel, 2009.

Le Corbeiller, Clare, et al. *The Jack and Belle Linsky Collection in the Metropolitan Museum of Art*. New York: The Metropolitan Museum of Art, 1984.

Ledger, Andrew P. *Derby Porcelain Archive Research*. Vol. 1, *European Competition, Trade and Influence, 1786–1796*. References from original documents. Derby, England: Derby Museum and Art Gallery, 1998.

———. "Richard Askew, Derby Painter: Unsafe Attributions." *English Ceramic Circle Transactions* 22 (2011): 39–47.

Lee, T. A. *Seekers of Truth: The Scottish Founders of Modern Public Accountancy*. Studies in the Development of Accounting Thought 9. Oxford, Amsterdam, and San Diego: Elsevier, 2006.

Legge, Margaret. *Flowers and Fables: A Survey of Chelsea Porcelain, 1745–69*. The catalogue of an exhibition at the National Gallery of Victoria, Victoria, Australia, November 1, 1984–February 10, 1985. Melbourne, Australia: National Gallery of Victoria, 1984.

Lewis, John, and Griselda Lewis. *Pratt Ware: English and Scottish Relief Decorated and Underglaze Coloured Earthenware, 1780–1840*. 2nd ed. Woodbridge, Suffolk, England: Antique Collectors' Club, 2006.

Lockett, T[erence] A. *Davenport Pottery and Porcelain, 1794–1887*. Rutland, Vermont: Charles E. Tuttle, 1972.

———. "Problems of Attribution." In Northern Ceramic Society 1986, pp. 52–58.

Lockett, Terence A., and Geoffrey A. Godden. *Davenport China, Earthenware & Glass, 1794–1887*. London: Barrie & Jenkins, 1989.

Lockett, T[erence] A., and P[atricia] A. Halfpenny, eds. *Creamware & Pearlware*. The Fifth Exhibition from the Northern Ceramic Society, May 18–September 7, 1986. Stoke-on-Trent, England: City Museum and Art Gallery, 1986.

MacAlister, Mrs. Donald A. "Longton Hall Porcelain: Some Uncommon Specimens." *Apollo* (London) 5, no. 25 (January 1927): 27–31.

———. "Longton Hall: The Domestic Wares of William Littler, Part II." *Apollo* (London) 10, no. 60 (December 1929): 338–342.

Mackenna, F. Severne. *Cookworthy's Plymouth and Bristol Porcelain*. Leigh-on-Sea, England: F. Lewis Publishers, 1946.

———. *Champion's Bristol Porcelain*. Leigh-on-Sea, England: F. Lewis Publishers, 1947.

———. *Chelsea Porcelain: The Triangle and Raised Anchor Wares*. Leigh-on-Sea, England: F. Lewis Publishers, 1948.

———. *Worcester Porcelain: The Wall Period and Its Antecedents*. Leigh-on-Sea, England: F. Lewis Publishers, 1950.

———. *Chelsea Porcelain: The Red Anchor Wares*. Leigh-on-Sea, England: F. Lewis Publishers, 1951.

———. *Chelsea Porcelain: The Gold Anchor Wares*. Leigh-on-Sea, England: F. Lewis Publishers, 1952.

———. "William Stephens, China Painter, I: An End to Speculation." *Apollo* (London) 57, no. 342 (August 1953a): 34–36.

———. "William Stephens, China Painter, II: Attribution Clarified." *Apollo* (London) 58, no. 343 (September 1953b): 69–72.

———. "William Stephens, China Painter: A Postscript." *Apollo* (London) 58, no. 344 (October 1953c): 95.

———. "William Stephens: Bristol China Painter." *English Ceramic Circle Transactions* 4, no. 1 (1957): 33–44.

———. *The F. S. Mackenna Collection of English Porcelain*. Part 3, *Plymouth and Bristol*. Leigh-on-Sea, England: F. Lewis Publishers, 1975.

Malenchini, Livia Frescobaldi, ed. *The Victoria and Albert Museum Collection*. Amici di Doccia, *Quaderni*, no. 7, 2013. Florence: Edizioni Polistampa, 2014.

Mallet, J.V.G. "Rococo in English Ceramics." In *Rococo Art and Design in Hogarth's England*, edited by Michael Snodin with Elspeth Moncrieff, pp. 235–263. The catalogue to accompany the exhibition, May 16–September 30, 1984. London: Victoria and Albert Museum in association with Trefoil Books, 1984.

———. "Agostino Carlini, Modeller of 'Dry-Edge' Derby Figures." In *British Ceramic Design, 1600–2002*, edited by Tom Walford and Hilary Young, pp. 42–57. London: English Ceramic Circle, 2003.

Malowney, Megan-Anne. "Defining Trembly Rose: Enamel Decoration at Longton Hall and West Pans." In "William Littler: An English Earth Potter, 1724–1784." *Proceedings of the Mint Museum of Art Ceramic Seminar, September 24–26, 1998*, edited by Margery Adams, pp. 29–35. Charlotte, North Carolina: Delhom Service League and Mint Museum of Art, 1999.

Manners, Errol. "A Documentary 'Girl-in-a-Swing' Seal and Other Considerations on the Porcelain of Charles Gouyn's Factory." *English Ceramic Circle Transactions* 18, no. 3 (2003): 398–407.

———. "Some Continental Influences on English Porcelain." *English Ceramic Circle Transactions* 19, no. 3 (2007): 429–470.

———. "Meissen and England: The Baroque Influence." In *Fire and Form: The Baroque and Its Influence on English Ceramics, c 1660–c 1770*, edited by Charles Dawson, pp. 27–41. London: English Ceramic Circle, 2013.

Marchant. *Blanc de Chine*. Catalogue of a selling exhibition, November 1–17, 2006. London: Marchant, 2006.

———. *Blanc de Chine*. Catalogue of a selling exhibition, October 30–November 21, 2014. London: Marchant, 2014.

Marno, Felicity. "The Shells of Bow and Derby." *English Ceramic Circle Transactions* 20, no. 2 (2008): 361–368.

———. "The Pleasure Gardens of London and Their Influence on Ceramics in England." In *Scrolls of Fantasy: The Rococo and Ceramics in England, c 1735–c 1775*, edited by Charles Dawson, pp. 123–144. London: English Ceramic Circle, 2015.

Marshall, Henry Rissik. *Coloured Worcester Porcelain of the First Period (1751–1783)*. Newport, Monmouthshire, Wales: Ceramic Book Company, 1954.

Massey, Roger. "Andrew Planché after Derby." *English Ceramic Circle Transactions* 19, no. 1 (2005a): 71–72.

———. "Independent China Painters in Eighteenth Century London." *English Ceramic Circle Transactions* 19, no. 1 (2005b): 153–189.

———. "Thomas Hughes Revisited." *English Ceramic Circle Transactions* 19, no. 1 (2005c): 190–192.

Massey, Roger, Felicity Marno, and Simon Spero. *Ceramics of Vauxhall: 18th Century Pottery and Porcelain*. Published to accompany the exhibition *Ceramics of Vauxhall*, held by the English Ceramic Circle at Stockspring Antiques, London, June 7–18, 2007. London: English Ceramic Circle, 2007.

Massey, Roger, Jacqueline Pearce, and Ray Howard. *Isleworth Pottery and Porcelain: Recent Discoveries*. Catalogue to accompany the eponymous exhibition held by the English Ceramic Circle and the Museum of London Specialist Services at Stockspring Antiques, London, June 5–13, 2003. London: English Ceramic Circle, 2003.

McNair, Anne, with Patricia Begg and Howard Coutts. *Catalogue of the Lady Ludlow Collection of English Porcelain at the Bowes Museum*. London: Bowes Museum [Barnard Castle, County Durham] and Unicorn Press, 2007.

Menzhausen, Ingelore. *In Porzellan verzaubert: Die Figuren Johann Joachim Kändlers in Meissen aus der Sammlung Pauls-Eisenbeiss Basel*. Basel: Wiese Verlag, 1993.

Merian, Maria Sibylla. *Metamorphosis insectorum Surinamensium*. Amsterdam: Gerardum Valk, 1705. Facsimile of the Latin edition with reproductions of the original watercolors on vellum in the collection of Her Majesty Queen Elizabeth II, in the Royal Library at Windsor Castle, a limited edition of 990. 2 vols. London: Pion, 1980.

———. *Dissertatio de Generatione et Metamorphosibus Insectorum Surinamensium*. Engravings by J. Mulder, P. Sluyter, and D. Stoopendaal. The Hague: Gosse, 1726.

Messenger, Michael. *Caughley Porcelains: A Bi-Centenary Exhibition*. Exhibition catalogue. Shrewsbury, England: Shrewsbury Art Gallery, 1972.

———. *Caughley and Coalport Porcelain in the Collection of Clive House, Shrewsbury*. London: Remploy, 1976.

———. *Coalport, 1795–1926*. Woodbridge, Suffolk, England: Antique Collectors' Club, 1995.

Miller, Philip, and Michael Berthoud. *An Anthology of British Teapots*. Brosely, Shropshire, England: Micawber Publications, 1985.

Molfino, Alessandra Mottola. *L'Arte della Porcellana in Italia*. 2 vols. Busto Arsizio, Italy: Bramante Editrice, 1976 and 1977.

Monti, Raffaele, ed. *La Manifattura Richard-Ginori di Doccia*. Milan: Arnoldo Mondadori Editore, and Rome: De Luca Editore, 1988.

Morrison, Alasdair. "Derby 1780–1786: The Useful Wares." In Brian George, ed., *Derby Porcelain International Society Journal* 5 (2004): 48–67.

Murdoch, John, and John Twitchett. *Painters and the Derby China Works*. Published on the occasion of the eponymous exhibition at the Victoria and Albert Museum, London, March–June 1987. London: Trefoil Publications, 1987.

Murdoch, Tessa, et al. *The Quiet Conquest: The Huguenots, 1685–1985*. The catalogue of an exhibition at the Museum of London. London: Board of Governors of the Museum of London, 1985.

Musée Cernuschi. *Pagodes et dragons: Exotisme et fantaisie dans l'Europe rococo, 1720–1770*. Catalogue of an exhibition at the Musée Cernuschi, Musée des arts de l'Asie de la Ville de Paris, February 24–June 17, 2007. Paris: Musée Cernuschi, 2007.

Nance, E. Morton. *The Pottery and Porcelain of Swansea and Nantgarw*. London: B.T. Batsford, 1942.

Nelson, Christina H., and Letitia Roberts. *A History of Eighteenth-Century German Porcelain: The Warda Stevens Stout Collection*. Memphis: The Dixon Gallery and Gardens, 2013.

Nightingale, J.E. *Contributions towards the History of Early English Porcelain from Contemporary Sources*. To which are added Reprints from Messrs. Christie's Sale Catalogues of the Chelsea, Derby, Worcester and Bristol Manufactories from 1769 to 1785. Salisbury, England: Bennett Brothers, Printers, Journal Office, 1881.

Noss, Aagot. *Statuane i Nordmandsdalen: Utgjeven I Samarbeid med Norsk Folkemuseum*. Oslo: Det Norske Samlaget, 1977.

Oakey, David. "Celebratory Ceramics: A Royal History." *English Ceramic Circle Transactions* 23, no. 1 (2012): 193–212.

Oppé, A.P. *The Drawings of Paul and Thomas Sandby in the Collection of His Majesty the King at Windsor Castle*. Oxford and London: Phaidon Press, 1947.

Oxford Dictionary of National Biography. Edited by H.C.G. Matthew and Brian Harrison. 60 vols. Oxford: Oxford University Press, 2004.

Pauls-Eisenbeiss, Erika. *German Porcelain of the 18th Century*. 2 vols. London: The Antique Porcelain Company, and New York: The Antique Company of New York, 1972.

Pedrocco, Filippo. *La Porcellana di Venezia nel '700: Vezzi, Hewelcke, Cozzi*. The catalogue of an exhibition at the Museum of the Eighteenth Century at Ca' Rezzonico, Venice, February 20–May 20, 1998. Venice: Marsilio Editori, 1997.

Pelichet, Edgar. *Merveilleuse Porcelaine de Nyon*. Paris: La Bibliothèque des Arts, 1973.

Pemberton, Rosemary. "Francis Thomas and the Sale of the Chelsea Manufactory." *English Ceramic Circle Transactions* 25 (2014): 23–44.

Pierson, Stacey. *Chinese Ceramics*. London: V&A Publishing, Victoria and Albert Museum, 2009.

Preller, Patricia. *A Partial Reconstruction of the New Hall Pattern Book*. Bude, Cornwall: Pat Preller, 2003.

Priore, Alicia M. "François Boucher's Designs for Vases and Mounts." *Studies in the Decorative Arts* (Bard Graduate Center for Studies in the Decorative Arts, New York) 3, no. 2 (Spring–Summer 1996): 2–51.

Rackham, Bernard. *Catalogue of the Herbert Allen Collection of English Porcelain*. London: Victoria and Albert Museum, 1917.

———. *Catalogue of English Porcelain Earthenware Enamels and Glass Collected by Charles Schreiber Esq. M.P. and the Lady Charlotte Elizabeth Schreiber and Presented to the Museum in 1884*. Vol. 1, *Porcelain*; vol. 2, *Earthenware*; vol. 3, *Enamels and Glass*. London: Board of Education, 1928, 1930, 1924, respectively.

Reilly, Robin. *Wedgwood*. 2 vols. London: Macmillan London, and New York: Stockton Press, 1989.

———. *Wedgwood: The New Illustrated Dictionary*. Woodbridge, Suffolk, England: Antique Collectors' Club, 1995.

Reilly, Robin, and George Savage. *The Dictionary of Wedgwood*. Woodbridge, Suffolk, England: Antique Collectors' Club, 1980.

Reinheckel, Günter. "Die erste Folge der Pariser Ausrufer in Meissner Porzellan" in: *Keramos* (Gesellschaft der Keramikfreunde, Düsseldorf) 50 (October 1970): 115–121.

Renton, Andrew. "The Swansea Diaspora: The Later Careers of David Evans, Henry Morris and William Pollard." In Gray 2005, pp. 209–234.

Riccoboni, Luigi. *Histoire du Théâtre Italien depuis la décadence de la Comédie Latine; avec un Catalogue des Tragédies et Comédies Italiennes imprimées depuis l'an 1500 jusqu'à l'an 1660. Et une Dissertation sur la Tragédie Moderne. Avec des figures qui représentent leurs differens habillemens. Par Loüis Riccoboni*. Paris: Pierre Delormel, 1728.

Rice, D.G. *Rockingham Ornamental Porcelain*. London: The Adam Publishing Company, 1965.

———. *Illustrated Guide to Rockingham Pottery and Porcelain*. New York: Praeger Publishers, 1971.

Riley, Noël. *Gifts for Good Children: The History of Children's China, Part 1, 1790–1890*. Ilminster, Somerset, England: Richard Dennis, 1991.

Rogers, J. Pope. *Notice of Henry Bone, R.A., and His Works, Together with Those of His Son, Henry Pierce Bone, and Other Members of the Family*. Truro, Cornwall, England: Lake & Lake, 1880.

Rondot, Bertrand, ed. *Discovering the Secrets of Soft-Paste Porcelain at the Saint-Cloud Manufactory, ca. 1690–1766*. In conjunction with the eponymous exhibition at The Bard Graduate Center for Studies in the Decorative Arts, New York, July 15–October 24, 1999. New Haven and London: Yale University Press for The Bard Graduate Center for Studies in the Decorative Arts, New York, 1999.

Röntgen, Robert E. *Marks on German, Bohemian and Austrian Porcelain: 1710 to the Present*. Revised and expanded 3rd ed. Atglen, Pennsylvania: Schiffer Publishing, 2007.

Roth, Linda H., and Clare Le Corbeiller. *French Eighteenth-Century Porcelain at the Wadsworth Atheneum: The J. Pierpont Morgan Collection*. Hartford, Connecticut: The Trustees of the Wadsworth Atheneum, 2000.

Rowan, Pamela. "Derby Models and Moulds." In "Recent Research on Ceramics of Derbyshire," edited by Gerald Daniel, *Derby Porcelain International Society Journal* 2 (1991): 28–34.

Rucellai, Oliva, ed. *Museo Richard Ginori della Manifattura di Doccia*. English translation by Elana Okun. Sesto Fiorentino, Italy: Museo Richard-Ginori della Manifattura di Doccia, 2003.

Rücker, Elisabeth, and William T. Stearn. Commentary to the Windsor Library facsimile edition of *Metamorphosis Insectorum Surinamensium*, Amsterdam, 1705. 2 vols. London: Pion, 1980–1982.

Rückert, Rainer. *Meissener Porzellan, 1710–1810*. Catalogue of an exhibition at the Bayerischen Nationalmuseum, Munich. Munich: Hirmer Verlag, 1966.

Rust, W. J. *Nederlands Porselein*. Schiedam, the Netherlands: Interbook International, 1978.

Sack, Michael. *India on Transferware: A Compendium of Indian Scenes on Transferware Together with Their Source Prints*. [No location]: Transferware Collectors Club, 2009.

Sandon, Henry. *Flight and Barr Worcester Porcelain, 1783–1840*. Woodbridge, Suffolk, England: Antique Collectors' Club, 1978a.

———. *Royal Worcester Porcelain from 1862 to the Present Day*. 3rd ed. London: Barrie & Jenkins, 1978b.

Sandon, Henry, and John Sandon. *Grainger's Worcester Porcelain*. London: Barrie & Jenkins, 1989.

Sandon, John. *The Phillips Guide to English Porcelain of the 18th and 19th Centuries*. London: Merehurst Press, 1989.

———. *The Dictionary of Worcester Porcelain*. Vol. 1, *1751–1851*. Woodbridge, Suffolk, England: Antique Collectors' Club, 1993.

———. *British Porcelain*. Oxford: Shire Publications, 2009.

Sargent, William R. *Treasures of Chinese Export Ceramics from the Peabody Essex Museum*. Salem, Massachusetts: Peabody Essex Museum, 2012.

Sassoon, Adrian. *Vincennes and Sèvres Porcelain: Catalogue of the Collections*. Malibu, California: J. Paul Getty Museum, 1991.

Sattler, Ralf-Jürgen. *Thüringer Porzellan des 18. und 19. Jahrhunderts: Sammlung Jan Ahlers*. Schlossmuseum Jever. Oldenburg, Germany: Isensee Verlag, 1993.

Savage, George. *18th-Century English Porcelain*. London: Rockliff Publishing, 1952.

———. "The Enigmatic Mr. Tebo." *Apollo* (London) 57, no. 341 (1953): 11–14.

Sayer, Robert. *The Ladies Amusement and Designer's Assistant; Being a Curious Collection of . . . Upwards of One Thousand Different Devices, Drawn by Pillement, O'Neale, and other Masters*. London: Robert Sayer, 1762.

———. *The Ladies Amusement, or Whole Art of Japanning Made Easy*. 2nd ed. London: Robert Sayer, 1762. Facsimile editions, Newport, England: Ceramic Book Company, 1959 and 1966.

———. *The Artist's Vade Mecum; Being the Whole Art of Drawing Taught in a New Work*. "Third Edition with considerable Additions." London: Printed and Published according to Act of Parliament: And Sold by R. Sayer, and J. Bennett, 1776.

Scherf, Helmut, and Jürgen Karpinski. *Thüringer Porzellan unter besonderer Berücksichtigung der Erzeugnisse des 18. und frühen 19. Jahrhunderts*. Leipzig: E. A. Seemann Verlag, 1985.

Scholten, Constance. "Inspiration or Imitation? Decorating Dutch Porcelain." In *Pretty Dutch: 18de-eeuws Hollands porselein, 18th Century Dutch Porcelain*, edited by Ank Trumpie, pp. 38–45. Rotterdam: Princessehof Leeuwarden, 2007.

Schroder, Timothy. "Rococo Silver." In *Scrolls of Fantasy: The Rococo and Ceramics in England, c 1735–c 1775*, edited by Charles Dawson, pp. 7–26. London: English Ceramic Circle, 2015.

Scott, Cleo M., and George Ryland Scott, Jr. *Antique Porcelain Digest*. Newport, Monmouthshire, Wales: Ceramic Book Company, 1961.

Sharp, Rosalie Wise. *Ceramics, Ethics and Scandal*. [Toronto, Canada]: RWD Books, 2002.

———. *China to Light Up a House*. Vol. 1, *Mainly Mid-Eighteenth Century English and French Porcelain from the Sharp Collection*. Vol. 2, *English Pottery and Later Porcelain from the Sharp Collection*. Toronto, Canada: ECW Press, 2015 and 2016.

Sheppard, C. Barry. *Pinxton Porcelain, 1795–1813, and the Porcelain of Mansfield and Brampton-in-Torksey*. Shirland, Alfreton, England: Published by the Author, 1996.

Shono, Masako. *Japanisches Aritaporzellan im sogenannten "Kakiemonstil" als Vorbild für die Meissener Porzellanmanufaktur*. Munich: Editions Schneider, 1973.

Skerry, Janine E., and Suzanne Findlen Hood. *Salt-Glazed Stoneware in Early America*. Williamsburg, Virginia: The Colonial Williamsburg Foundation in association with the University Press of New England, 2009.

Skinner, Deborah S., and Velma Young. *Miles Mason Porcelain: A Guide to Patterns and Shapes*. Stoke-on-Trent, England: City Museum and Art Gallery, 1992.

Slitine, Florence. *Samson génie de l'imitation*. Paris: Editions Charles Massin, 2002.

Smith, Alan. "The Herculaneum China and Earthenware Manufactory, Toxteth, Liverpool." *English Ceramic Circle Transactions* 7, no. 1 (1968): 16–38.

———. *The Illustrated Guide to Liverpool Herculaneum Pottery, 1796–1840*. London: Barrie & Jenkins, 1970.

Spero, Simon. *Worcester Porcelain: The Klepser Collection*. London: Lund Humphries Publishers and The Minneapolis Institute of Arts, 1984.

———. *The Bowles Collection of 18th-Century English and French Porcelain*. San Francisco: Fine Arts Museums of San Francisco, 1995.

———. *English Porcelain, 1745–1792*. Catalogue of an exhibition and sale, October 7–18, 2003. London: Simon Spero, 2003a.

———. "Vauxhall Porcelain: A Tentative Chronology." *English Ceramic Circle Transactions* 18, no. 2 (2003b): 349–372.

———, with a contribution by Richard Burt. *Lund's Bristol and Early Worcester Porcelain, 1750–58: The A. J. Smith Collection*. London: C. and J. Smith, 2005.

———. *Liverpool Porcelain, 1755–1799*. Catalogue of an exhibition and sale, March 14–25, 2006. London: Simon Spero, 2006a.

———. *English Porcelain, 1745–1785*. Catalogue of an exhibition and sale, October 10–21, 2006. London: Simon Spero, 2006b.

———. *English and French Porcelain, 1740–1775*. Catalogue of an exhibition and sale, October 6–15, 2011. London: Simon Spero, 2011.

———. "Fifteen Years among Furnaces": Bow Porcelain from a Private Collection. Catalogue of an exhibition and sale, April 19–28, 2012. London: Simon Spero, 2012a.

———. *English Porcelain and Enamels, 1745–1770*. Catalogue of an exhibition and sale, October 11–20, 2012. London. Simon Spero, 2012b.

———. *50th Anniversary Exhibition, 1964–2014: Early English Porcelain 1748–1783*. Catalogue of an exhibition and sale, April 24–May 3, 2014. London: Simon Spero, 2014.

Spero, Simon, and John Sandon. *Worcester Porcelain, 1751–1790: The Zorensky Collection*. Woodbridge, Suffolk, England: Antique Collectors' Club, 1996.

Stazzi, Francesco. *Italian Porcelain*. New York: G. P. Putnam's Sons, 1964.

Stieglitz, Marcel H. *The Stieglitz Collection of Dr. Wall: Worcester Porcelain*. Catalogue of an exhibition under the auspices of the Antiquarian Society at the Art Institute of Chicago, May 7–November 3, 1947. [Chicago]: Art Institute of Chicago, 1947.

Stockspring Antiques. *25th Anniversary Exhibition and Sale: Private Collections and Noteworthy Acquisitions*. November 12–19, 2012. London: Stockspring Antiques, 2012.

———. *The Stephen Hanscombe Porcelain Collection: James Giles and His Contemporary Decorators*. Catalogue of an exhibition and sale, June 10–21, 2014. London: Stockspring Antiques, 2014.

———. *Private Collections and Noteworthy Acquisitions*. Exhibition and sale, November 16–21, 2015. London: Stockspring Antiques, 2015.

Stoner, Frank. *Chelsea, Bow and Derby Porcelain Figures: Their Distinguishing Characteristics*. Newport, Monmouthshire, Wales: Ceramic Book Company, 1955.

Stout, Warda Stevens. "Mr. and Mrs. Warder W. Stevens" (1965), pp. 29–35; "Recollections of Mrs. Warda Stevens Stout" (1971), pp. 40–68; and "Early Traditions, Customs and Superstitions" (1968), pp. 69–80. In *Stevens Memorial Museum and the John Hay Center: An Historical Review*. Compiled by Alice Stout Edwards. Point Lookout, Missouri: S of O Press, The School of The Ozarks, 1975.

Synge-Hutchinson, Patrick. "Sir Hans Sloane's Plants and Other Botanical Subjects on Chelsea Porcelain." In *The Connoisseur Year Book, 1958*, pp. 18–25. London: The Connoisseur, 1958a.

———. "G. D. Ehret's Botanical Designs on Chelsea Porcelain." *The Connoisseur* 142, no. 572 (October 1958b): 88–94.

Tait, Hugh. "Some Consequences of the Bow Porcelain Special Exhibition. Part I: The Alderman Arnold Period (Nov. 1748–March 1750)." *Apollo* (London) 71, no. 420 (February 1960a): 40–44. ("*Bow Porcelain, 1744–1776*. A special exhibition of documentary material to commemorate the bi-centenary of the retirement of Thomas Frye" was held in the King Edward VII Gallery at the British Museum in London, October 1959–April 1960.)

———. "Some Consequences of the Bow Porcelain Special Exhibition. Part II: The Thomas Frye Period (September 1750–April 1759)." *Apollo* (London) 71, no. 422 (April 1960b): 93–98.

Tapp, William H., M.C. *Jefferyes Hamett O'Neale, 1734–1801, Red Anchor Fable Painter, and Some Contemporaries*. London: University of London Press, 1938.

———. "Thomas Hughes, First Enameller of English China, of Clerkenwell." *English Ceramic Circle Transactions* 2, no. 6 (1939): 53–65.

Thom, Bill, and Philip Miller. *Machin Porcelains and Earthenwares*. Berwick-upon-Tweed: Castlehills Publishing, 2008.

Toppin, Aubrey J. "The Origin of Some Ceramic Designs." *English Ceramic Circle Transactions* 2, no. 10 (1948): 270–276.

———. "A Ceramic Miscellany: (1. Francis Place (1647–1728). 2. Holdship's Transfer-printing at Derby. 3. The Ranelagh Figures.)." *English Ceramic Circle Transactions* 3, no. 1 (1951): 65–70.

Towner, Donald. "Some Cream Ware Comparisons." *English Ceramic Circle Transactions* 4, no. 3 (1957): 9–16.

———. *The Leeds Pottery*. London: Cory, Adams & Mackay, 1963.

———. "Robinson and Rhodes: Enamellers at Leeds." *English Ceramic Circle Transactions* 9, no. 2 (1974): 134–139.

———. *Creamware*. London: Faber and Faber, 1978.

Toynbee, Paget, ed. *Strawberry Hill Accounts. A Record of Expenditure in Building Furnishing &c. Kept by Mr Horace Walpole From 1747 to 1795*. Oxford: Clarendon Press, 1927.

Trapnell Collection. *Catalogue of Bristol and Plymouth Porcelain, with Examples of Bristol Glass and Pottery, Forming the Collection Made by Mr. Alfred Trapnell*. Including a facsimile of the *Catalogue of a Valuable Collection of the Bristol Porcelane . . . Sold by Auction, By Mess. Christie and Ancell, At their Great Room, next Cumberland House, Pall Mall, On Monday, February 28, 1780, and 2 following Days*. Bristol: William George's Sons, 1905.

———. *Catalogue of Bristol and Plymouth Porcelain, with Examples of Bristol Glass and Pottery, Forming the Collection Made by Mr. Alfred Trapnell*. Catalogue of an exhibition held at Albert Amor, 31, St. James's Street, London. A reprint expanded and with illustrations of the identically titled exhibition catalogue published by William George's Sons, Bristol, 1905. London: Albert Amor, 1912.

Tuer, Andrew W. *Bartolozzi and His Works*. 2 vols. London: Field & Tuer, The Leadenhall Presse, 1881.

Turner, William. *The Ceramics of Swansea and Nantgarw: A History of the Factories*. London: Bemrose & Sons, 1897.

Twitchett, John. *Derby Porcelain*. London: Barrie & Jenkins, 1980.

———. *Derby Porcelain, 1748–1848*. Woodbridge, Suffolk, England: Antique Collectors' Club, 2002.

Valfré, Patrice. *Yixing: Des théières pour l'Europe* [Yixing: Teapots for Europe]. Poligny: Éditions Exotic Line, 2000.

Valpy, Nancy. "Charles Gouyn and the Girl-in-a-Swing Factory." *English Ceramic Circle Transactions* 15, no. 2 (1994): 317–326.

Vanke, Francesca. "The Islamic East and Englishness in Nineteenth Century Ceramics." *English Ceramic Circle Transactions* 19, no. 3 (2007): 533–558.

Walford, Tom, and Hilary Young, eds. *British Ceramic Design, 1600–2002*. London: English Ceramic Circle, 2003.

Walpole, Horace. *A Description of the Villa of Horace Walpole, Youngest Son of Sir Robert Walpole Earl of Orford, at Strawberry-Hill, near Twickenham. With an Inventory of the Furniture, Pictures, Curiosities, &c*. Strawberry-Hill [Twickenham, England]: Printed by Thomas Kirgate, 1774. The Appendix and List of Books, pp. 121–148, were printed in 1781; and further additions were printed, pp. 149–152 in 1784, and pp. 153–158 in 1786. Electronic reproduction of the original edition in the British Library, Farmington Hills, Michigan: Cengage Gale, 2009.

Walton, Peter. *Creamware and Other English Pottery at Temple Newsam House, Leeds: A Catalogue of the Leeds Collection*. London: Manningham Press, 1976.

Watney, Bernard. *Longton Hall Porcelain*. London: Faber and Faber, 1957a.

———. "The Proprietors of the Longton Hall Factory." *English Ceramic Circle Transactions* 4, no. 3 (1957b): 17–23.

———. "Excavations at the Longton Hall Porcelain Manufactory. Part III: The Porcelain and Other Ceramic Finds." With a Technical Appendix by Andrew P. Middleton and Michael R. Cornell. *Post-Medieval Archaeology* 27, no. 1 (January 1993): 57–109.

———. *Liverpool Porcelain of the Eighteenth Century*. Shepton Beauchamp, Somerset, England: Richard Dennis, 1997.

Watt, Sir George. *The Wild and Cultivated Cotton Plants of the World: A Revision of the Genus Gossypium*. London: Longmans, Green, 1907.

White, Peter. "Two Distinct Early Derby White Groups of Figures and Some Quandaries." *English Ceramic Circle Transactions* 25 (2014): 165–176.

Whiter, Leonard. *Spode: A History of the Family, Factory and Wares from 1733 to 1833*. London: Barrie & Jenkins, 1970. Reprinted with new color illustrations in 1989.

Wilkinson, Vega. *Spode-Copeland-Spode: The Works and Its People, 1770–1970*. Woodbridge, Suffolk, England: Antique Collectors' Club, 2002.

Williams, Haydn. *Turquerie: An Eighteenth-Century European Fantasy*. New York: Thames & Hudson, 2014.

Williams, Peter, and Pat Halfpenny. *A Passion for Pottery: Further Selections from The Henry H. Weldon Collection*. London: Sotheby's Publications, 2000.

Williamson, F[rederick]. *History and Classification of Derby Porcelain*. 2nd ed. Reprinted from the Derby Museum and Art Gallery's Journal, vol. 22, pp. 138–148, December 1922. Derby: Derby Museum and Art Gallery Committee, 1924.

Walter H. Willson Ltd. (Chicago, Illinois). Advertisement for the Annual May Sale. *The Magazine Antiques*, 59, no. 5 (May 1951): 355.

Winstone, H. V. F. (Victor). *Royal Copenhagen*. London: Stacey International, 1984.

Wittwer, Samuel. *A Royal Menagerie: Meissen Porcelain Animals*. Amsterdam: Rijksmuseum, and Los Angeles: J. Paul Getty Museum, 2000.

Yarbrough, Raymond C. *Bow Porcelain and the London Theatre*. Hancock, Michigan: Front and Center Publications, 1996.

Young, Hilary. *English Porcelain, 1745–95: Its Makers, Design, Marketing and Consumption*. Victoria and Albert Museum Studies in the History of Art and Design. London: V & A Publications, 1999.

———. "Pierre Stephan: The Career of a Derby Modeller Reviewed." In Valerie Baynton, ed., *Derby Porcelain International Society Journal* 4 (2000): 83–93.

Zappey, W. M., A. L. den Blaauwen, A. W. A. van der Goes, and A. C. Pronk. *Loosdrechts porselein, 1774–1784*. Catalogue of an exhibition at the Rijksmuseum, Amsterdam, February 27–March 15, 1988. Zwolle, the Netherlands: Uitgeverij Waanders and the Rijksmuseum, Amsterdam, 1988.

Zimmermann, Ernst. *Meissner Porzellan*. Leipzig: Verlag Karl W. Hiersemann, 1926.

Zühlsdorff, Dieter. *Keramik-Marken Lexicon: Porzellan und Keramik Report 1885–1935 Europa (Festland)*. Stuttgart: Arnoldsche, 1994.

INDEX

Illustrations are indicated by *italic* page numbers

Abraham, Birte, 44
Abston, Esther Cook, 26n101
acanthus-molded saucer, 40, *41*
Adams, Elizabeth, 33, 35, 40, 43, 104
Adams, William, & Sons, factory, earthenware teabowl and saucer, *116*
Adventures of Roderick Random, The (Smollett), 35
Aesop. See *Fables of Aesop's and Others*; *Lethe, or Aesop in the Shades*
Aesop's Fables (Dodsley), 73
Aesop's Fables, with his Life (Barlow), 40, 73, *73*
Afbildning af Normandsdalen, 130
'Africa' allegorical group, *128*
"Aga, eine Türckische Standes Person" (Weigel), 70
Alcock, Samuel, & Co. factory, 105, 133; teacup, coffee cup, and saucer, *101*; white stoneware jug, *119*
allegorical figures. See under figures
Allied English Potteries, 133
American Association of Tennessee Antiquities, 26n107
American Ceramic Circle, xiii, 16, 18
Amor, Albert, Ltd., 11, 12, 24n77
'Amor on Bolting Panther' (Rietschel), 86
'Amour, L'' pattern, Worcester factory, 64, *65*
Amstel factory, vase and cover, *129*
'Angoulême Sprig' pattern: custard cup and cover, *128*; plates, *47*, 48
animals, 73, 77. See also birds; 'Camel' pattern, John Rogers & Son factory; cows; dogs; 'Dragon in Compartments' pattern; dragons; goats; insects; lions; panther; rabbit tureen; 'Red Bull' pattern, Worcester factory; rhinoceros horn libation cup; serpents or snakes; sheep; silkworms; squirrels; tigers
Annual Antiques Forum, 26n107
Ansbach factory: salt cellar, 25n90; waste bowl, 25n90
Ansell, Mr., 38, 56
Antiquarians Inc., The, 12, 14, 15, 16, 21n23; handbook, 26n101; incorporation documentation, 24n75
Antiquarians of Memphis, The, xiii, 9, 10, 26n105; with Memphis Brooks Gallery exhibition, 24n69; Ralph H. Wark and, 23n52, 26n95
Antique Porcelain Digest (C.M. Scott and G.R. Scott), 13
Antiques (magazine), 7, 8, 21n18, 22n41, 24n68
Antique Shop, The, 23n45
Apollo, Wedgwood factory, earthenware, *117*
apricot-ground plates, *caillouté*-patterned, *82*

apron, 55, *130*
arbor figure of seated musician playing bagpipe, *53*
"Archer" (fictional character), 35
architecture, 8, 14, 19, 20, 86; architectural vignettes, *65*; Islamic, 115
archives. See Stout-Hooker Archives
Arita. See under Japan
armorial style: Chinese export waste bowl, *122*; Duke of Clarence service, 5, *78*; English 'Famille-Rose' armorial octagonal plate, *104*; plates, *81*; Sulkowski Service, 15
Arnold, George, 32
Art Deco, 3
Art Fund, 71n3
Art Institute of Chicago, 24n66
Artist's Vade Mecum, The, 65
Art Nouveau, 3
Arts and Crafts, 21n16, 117
Art-Union, 98
'Ascension, The,' 122
Ashton, Geoffrey, 35
Ashworth, G. L., & Bros. factory, ironstone pudding plate, *119*
'Asia' figure, Bow factory, 36, *37*
Askew, Richard, 46, 46n1, 110
'Astrologer, The' pattern, *18*
Atlanta History Center, 26n105
Atterbury, Paul, 95
Auchincloss, Louis, 95, 97
auction catalogues. See under catalogues
Augustus II (king of Poland), 38, 125
Austrian porcelain, 4
Aveline, Pierre Alexandre, 46, *46*
Avery, Louise, 24n68
Ayers, David, 122, 124, 131

bagpipes: boy playing, *126*; Chelsea factory bagpiper and his dog figure, 44; Derby factory bagpiper and his dog figures, *51*; musician playing bagpipes, *53*
Baker, Samuel, 33
baluster-form mugs, *31*, 64, *65*
'bamboo' pattern, Grainger, Lee & Co. Worcester factory, *85*
'Bang Up' pattern, Spode factory, *118*
Barlow, Francis, 40, 73, *73*
Barr, Flight and Barr Period. See under Worcester factory, Worcestershire
Barr, Martin, 49
barrel-shaped teapot and cover, *64*
Bartolozzi, Francesco, 83
Bartolozzi, Lucia Elizabeth (Madame Vestris) (granddaughter), 83
basalt teapot and cover, with mother-and-child knop, *118*

basin, Samson factory, *131*
baskets: basket-molded 'London' shape teacup, coffee cup, and saucer, *91*; 'basketwork' pattern, Staffordshire stonewares, 117; Grainger, Lee & Co. Worcester factory, *85*; "Old Paris basket," 21n22; Rockingham factory, 21n22; 'Snake in a Basket' pattern, *62*; Worcester factory, 21n2, *72*, *76*
bat prints: Miles Mason factory, 103; Minton factory, 95, *95*; Spode factory, *97*
Battam, Thomas, 98, *98*
Battersea, 64
Bavarian Girl's Song, The: Buy a Broom!, *83*
Baxter, J.D., factory, earthenware square dish, *116*
beakers: Chantilly factory, 9, 23n47; Chelsea factory, 6, 38, *39*; Meissen porcelain factory, 22n39
Beaux' Stratagem, The (Farquhar), 35
bees, 10, 12, 25n78, *37*, 38
Behn, Mrs. Aphra, 73
Bemrose, William, Jr., 44
Bentley, Thomas, 70
Bently Farm, 1, 2, 3, 21n17
bequests, xii, 5, 11, 13
Berlin cabinet, cups and saucers, 21n22
berried laurel swags, mugs painted with, *88*
Bevington, John, 108, *109*
Bevington, Timothy, 108, 109, *109*
biblical plate, *122*
Bicknell, Penny, 54
Billingsley, William, 49, 105, 106, 108, 109, 110
birds: 'Birds in Branches' pattern, Derby factory, 53, *53*; in cartouches, 40, *61*, *72*, *106*; Charles Gouyn factory figure, 12, *37*; Chelsea factory, *37*, *39*, *42*; Chelsea-style plate with 'Fancy Birds,' *132*; 'Chinese Lady and Bird in a Cartouche' pattern, *61*; on dishes, *42*; finch, *37*; hawks and falcons, 108; on jug, *113*; 'Lady with Bird in Hand' pattern, *114*; 'Lord Rodney Service' pattern of 'Fancy Birds,' 77; peacocks, *81*, *102*; plate painted with floral spray within bird-molded rim, *91*; on plates, 16, *17*, *39*, *42*, *72*, *74*, *77*, *110*, *114*, *132*; rooster pearlware figure, *112*, 113; teacup, coffee cup, and saucer painted with Meissen-style bird in rococo trellis, *93*; on vases, *45*. See also geese; parrots; 'Partridge' pattern, dishes; phoenix; 'Quail' pattern
Birmingham Museum of Art, 26n105
Bischoff, Ilse, 24n68
biscuit figures, 10, 12, 52, 131n7; Derby factory, *56*, 57; Minton factory, 70, 97, *97*
'Bishop Sumner' pattern, Worcester factory, *69*
Blaauwen, Den, 125n1
Black, Mrs. William T., Jr., 27n116
Blackburn, William W., 24n68

152

black-glazed stoneware milk jug, *117*
Blair's Brick House Antiques, 23n47
Blanc-de-Chine porcelain: Guanyin figure, 21n22, *121*; rhinoceros horn libation cup, *121*
Blatchford, George (Captain), 123–124
'Blind Earl' pattern, Worcester factory, *71*
Blohm, Magdalena, 25n84
Blohm, Otto, 25n84
blue. *See* powdered-blue; tin-glazed earthenware; underglaze blue
'Blue Bridge' pattern, Wedgwood Bone China factory, *99*
blue-ground: basket, 21n2; pale blue-ground 'Oxford Embossed' oval dessert dish, *95*; plates, 11; powdered-blue-ground coffee cup and saucer, *71*; royal-blue-ground oblong dessert dish, *85*; shell-shaped dessert dish, *ii*, *84*; teapot and cover reserved with cartouches of Kakiemon-style flowers, *58*; vase, 4; 'wet blue'-ground, *xviii*, *xix*, 11, *67*, *73*; Worcester-style blue-ground plate with panels of birds, *132*. *See also* blue-scale-ground
'Blue Onion' pattern. *See* 'Zwiebelmuster' pattern, Meissen porcelain factory
blue-scale-ground: basket, *72*; butter tub, cover, and stand, *72*; jug, *72*; plate reserved with cartouches of exotic birds and insects, *72*; teabowl and saucer, *68*; teacup and saucer, *68*
boats. *See* sailboat, sauceboat painted with; sauceboats; 'Sinking Boat Fisherman' pattern, Worcester factory
Bodenham Collection, 68
'Bodenham Service,' Worcester factory: teabowl and saucer, 13, *68*, 25n80
Boicourt, Jane, 104
Bone, Henry, 88
Bonhams, 17
Book of Small Figures from the Originals of Cochin junr, A (Vivares), 64
Boone's Antiques, 26n104
Borden Academy, 2
borders: British 'London' shape teacup and saucer with floral, *109*; British pink lustre milk jug molded and enameled with floral, *114*; comport from turquoise-bordered dessert service, *85*; English faceted coffee can and saucer with floral, *104*; 'Gold Star Border and Spangles Dessert Service,' *89*, *89*; lions on border pattern, *77*; Orders of the Garter and the Thistle, *78*; plate painted with 'Church Gresley' pattern border, *92*; spherical teapot and cover with guilloche, *104*; teacup and saucer with floral garlands above green shagreen, *76*; teapot and cover bordered by underglaze blue, *64*. *See also* pink-scale-bordered; rims
Boreman, Zachariah, 46, 47, *48*, 49, 110
Bossierer (repairer of components of pieces), 127
botanical decoration: Bow factory, 33, *34*; Chelsea factory, 33, *34*, *41*, *42*; Coalport factory, *93*; plate painted with 'Church Gresley' pattern border, *92*
Bott, Thomas, 86, *86*
Bott, Thomas John (son), 86
Bouchardon, Edmé, 43, 43n3
Boucher, François, 38, 46, 54, *54*
bow-and-arrow mark, 104
Bowcock, John, 32, 34
Bowers, George Frederick, & Co. factory, 133; sugar bowl and cover painted with flowers, *101*
Bow factory, London, 102, 133; busts, *x*, 11, *32*, *34*, *35*; dishes, *xii*, *9*, 23n47, 33, *33*, *34*; figures, 4, 12, 21n23, 24n70, *35*, *35*, *36*, *36*, *37*, 44, 50–51, 58; flatware handles, *9*; mugs, *31*, *32*, *33*; plates, 6, *31*, *32*, *32*, *33*; 'Quail' pattern, *9*, 23n47; sauceboat, *32*; teabowls, *31*, *34*; teacups and saucers, *34*, *35*
bowknotted floral garlands, 75
bowls: Marcolini Meissen factory, *125*; Meissen porcelain factory, *15*, 25n90; Wallendorf factory, *126*, 127. *See also* breakfast bowl, Worcester factory; compote, Derby factory; écuelles, Chelsea factory; finger bowls, Longton Hall Works factory; rice bowls, and cover; sugar bowls; teabowls; waste bowl
Boydell, J., 57
Boyle, Evelyn Johnston, 26n101
Boyle, Samuel, 52
'Boy with the Butterfly' pattern, New Hall factory, *90*
Bradshaw, Peter, 35, 52, 55, 56
Brameld & Co. *See* Rockingham factory
breakfast bowl, Worcester factory, *65*
breakfast cup, H. & R. Daniel factory, *100*
breakfast teabowls. *See* teabowls
bride. *See* 'Eloping Bride' pattern, Worcester factory
bridge. *See* 'Blue Bridge' pattern, Wedgwood Bone China factory; 'Tasker's Chinese Bridge' pattern, Chamberlain's Worcester factory
Bridgwood, Sampson, & Son factory, 133; teacup with gilt vermiculate decoration, *101*
'Bright Landscape' decoration, Caughley factory, 89, *89*
Bristol. *See* Champion, Richard, factory, Bristol; Lund, Benjamin, factory, Bristol
Britannia: Derby factory, 4, *52*, *53*; Minton factory, *95*
British earthenware: dates for Orient depicted on, 115; milk jug, *114*; tea wares, *114*
British 'London' shape teacup and saucer with floral borders, *109*
British Museum, 34, 54, 65
British porcelain factories, 133–134
British Treasures from Private Collections, 20, 30
'Brocade Imari' pattern: Chelsea factory, *40*; Derby factory, *49*
Brookside, 2
Brooks Memorial Art Gallery, 14, 16
'Broom-Girl, The,' theatrical figure, Chamberlain's Worcester factory, *83*
"Broom Girl, The" (Gunton), 83, *83*
'Broseley' pattern, Samuel & John Rathbone factory, *103*
Browne, Lord Grainger, 4
Brownlow Hill, 78
Bruhwiler, John A., 26n101
Buchanan, John E., Jr., 20
Buen Retiro, 128
Burnsall, David, 38
Burslem potteries, 109
busts: Bow factory, *x*, 11, *32*, *34*, *35*; Shakespeare, *103*; 'Two Bacchantes Adorning [a Bust of] Pan,' 57
'Bute' shape: Grainger's Worcester factory, *84*; Miles Mason factory, *103*; Minton factory, *94*; Spode factory, *97*; Wedgwood Bone China factory, *99*
Butler, Sidney Johnston, 26n101
butterflies: 'Boy with the Butterfly' pattern, New Hall factory, *90*; sauceboat painted with, *60*
butter tub, 26n95, *72*
"Buy a Broom" (Lane, R.J.), 83

cabbage leaf: 'Cabbage Leaf' pattern jug, *72*; cabbage leaf-shaped dish, Worcester factory, *71*; jug, *72*, *91*
cabinet cups: Berlin, 21n22; cabinet cup stand, *82*; Gotha, 25n90; J. &. M. Perston Bell, Ltd. factory, *111*
caillouté-pattern, Chamberlain's Worcester factory, *82*
cake dish, Hilditch & Sons factory, *102*
camaïeu: dish in turquoise *camaïeu* and white enamel, *86*; green *camaïeu* birds, *42*; potpourri 'frill' vase and cover painted in puce *camaïeu*, *46*; tan-ground plate printed and painted with sepia *camaïeu* flowers, *98*; teabowl and saucer in purple *camaïeu*, *129*; teacup and saucer in purple *camaïeu*, *99*
'Cambrian China' mark, 116
Cambrian Pottery, London Warehouse, 116
Cambrian Pottery factory, Swansea, 116
camellias, 3, 13, 20, 25n79
'Camel' pattern, John Rogers & Son factory, 115, *115*
Campagnola, Domenico, 38
candlesticks: Derby factory, *53*; "Redstart candlesticks," *53*; Vauxhall factory, *58*
canisters. *See* tea canisters
'Capo-di-Monte' vase, *132*
'Captain, The' ('Narcisin') figure, *43*, 44
Carborundum Company, 134
Carl (prince of Denmark), 131
Carlini, Agostino, 51
Carnegie, Andrew, 5
carpenter figure, Chelsea factory, *43*
Carpentier, Donald G., 52
Carpentier, François Joseph, 43
Carter, Frederick Walter, 21–22n25; collection of, 5, 21–22n25
Carter, Grieg & Company, 21n25
cartouches: birds, 40; butter tub, cover, and stand reserved with, 40; 'Chinese Lady and Bird in a Cartouche' pattern, *61*; jug with bearded mask spout and reserved floral, *72*; pierced circular basket reserved with, *72*; plate reserved with, *72*; teacup, coffee cup, and saucer painted with floral, *91*; teacup and saucer with, *68*; teapot and cover reserved with, *68*
Cascade, La (The Fountain) (Watteau), 45
Cascade—Aqua Saliens, La (Watteau), 45
Casey & Casey, Inc., 21n22
Caspar, Lewis (father), 1
Caspar, Mary Alice (1858–1941), 1, 2
'Castle Painter,' 59, 60, *60*
casts, plaster, 119
Catalogue (Part the First) of the last Year's Produce of the Derby and Chelsea Porcelaine Manufactories, Derby, 54, 55, 56
catalogues: auction catalogues, 4, 12, 19; Christie, Manson & Woods, 79, 79n4; clippings, xi; *Duesbury's Annual Catalogue of his Derby Porcelain*, 56; *A History of Eighteenth-Century German Porcelain: The Warda Stevens Stout Collection*, xii; J.P. Morgan property sale, 97; Lempertz, 128; *Mrs. C.B. Stout Collection of Early Meissen Porcelain, ca. 1708–1750*, 26n94; Parke-Bernet Galleries, Inc., 4; *Pictures in the Garrick Club*, 35; Sotheby's, 102
Catmur, Eric A., xii, 27n116
caudle cup, *45*
Caughley factory, Shropshire, 75, 133; kidney-shaped dish, *89*; saucer dish, *89*; sugar bowl and cover, *89*; teabowl, 88, 89
Cauldon Potteries, Ltd., 133
cauliflower-molded teapot and cover, earthenware, *116*, 117
Caylus, Anne Claude Philippe de Tubières-Grimoard de Pestels Levieux de Lévis, comte de, 43, 43n3
ceramics, 25n84, 26n112; societies, xiii, 12, 16, 18, 22n32, 24n71, 26n107
Ceres, 4
Chaffers, Richard, & Co. factory, 133
Chamberlain's Worcester factory, 89, 134; cabinet cup stand, *82*; dessert dish, *82*; figure, *83*; plates, *81*, *83*; saucer, *82*; sauce tureen, cover, and stand, *81*; teacup, *82*; teapot and cover, *81*. *See also* Worcester factory, Worcestershire
Champion, Judith (wife), 88
Champion, Richard, factory, Bristol, 70, 133; coffee cup and saucer, *87*; figure, *87*; Frye and, 35; with gold numeral system, 88; mug, *88*; with patents, 87; plate, *87*; teapot and cover, teacup and saucer, 88
Chantilly factory: beaker and saucer, *9*, 23n47; 'Quail' pattern, *9*, 23n47; teabowl, 38
'Chantilly Sprig' pattern: Derby factory, *47*, *47*; Worcester factory, *77*, *77*
'Charity' allegorical group, Bow factory, *36*
Charles B. Stout Laboratory for Neuroscience, The, 19, 27n114

INDEX 153

Charlotte (queen of England), 52
Charlotte Stout Hooker Collection: British porcelain factories in, 133–134; collecting years, 4–7; Deed of Gift and, xii, xiii, 5, 13–20; formation of, xi–xiii, 4; lectures, 27n122; Pygmalion effect, 7–13
Charlton, Mrs. Will H., 131
Charm House, The, 22n28
Chattanooga Little Theater, 26n107
Cheere, John, 53, 54, 55
Chelsea-Derby factory, London and Derby, 133; caudle cup, cover, and stand, 45; history of, 38; plate, 44; teabowl and saucer, 44
Chelsea factory, London, 34, 133; beakers and saucers, 6, 38, 39; Boreman and, 48; coffee cups, 42, 43; Continental porcelain Chelsea-style plate, 16, 17, 132; covers, 40, 41; dishes, 9, 39, 40, 41, 42; écuelles, 40, 41; figures, 12, 24n70, 37, 43, 44, 44, 51–52; history of, 38; influence of, 52; jugs, 10, 12, 25n78, 37, 38; plates, 11, 12, 13, 16, 17, 33, 39, 40, 41, 42; platters, 39, 40; 'Quail' pattern, 9, 23n47; saucers, 6, 38, 39, 40, 41, 42, 43; soup plates, 11, 12, 13, 39; tureen, 24n77
"Chelsea Figures, No. 2, 'Mistress Robinson'" (Wilkinson), 98
'Chelsea figures' of the 'Ranelagh Dancers,' 98, 99
Chelsea Physic Garden, 42
Chelsea Porcelain: The Gold Anchor Wares (Mackenna), 24n76
Chelsea Porcelain: The Red Anchor Wares (Mackenna), 24n76
Chelsea Porcelain: The Triangle and Raised Anchor Wares (Mackenna), 24n76
cherubs ("enfants de Boucher"), vase and cover with, 46
'Chesterfield Vase,' 54
chestnut basket, 76
chickens, 21n17
Child & Co., 115
children. *See* toys
Chilton, Meredith, 44, 52
China for the West (Howard and Ayers), 122
Chinese: 'Chinese Bridge on a Scroll' pattern, Wedgwood Bone China factory, 99; Chinese ceramics, 121–125; 'Chinese Family' pattern, Worcester factory, 66; 'Chinese Flower Show' pattern, Liverpool factory, 61; 'Chinese Lady and Bird in a Cartouche' pattern, Liverpool factory, 61; 'Eggshell' porcelain rice bowl and cover, 124, 125; 'Famille-Rose' pattern, Chinese garden scene, 62; leaf-shaped chamber candlestick with Chinese landscape, 58; lustre jug with clock face and roundel of Chinese figure in garden, 114; milk jug printed in black and painted with Chinese vessels of flowers, 105; stone China leaf-shaped small dishes with Chinese garden, 118; 'Tasker's Chinese Bridge' pattern, 81; teabowl and saucer painted with 'Les Garçons Chinois,' 65; teacup and saucer painted with Chinese flowers, 99
Chinese export, 21n19; custard cup and cover, 124; milk jug, 16; ovoid tea canister with domestic scene within squirrels on vines, 123; pearl-glazed earthenware plate, 115; plate for Near Eastern market, 124; plates, 8, 9, 122, 124; porcelain armorial waste bowl, 122; 'Quail' pattern, 9; reticulated plates, 123; rice bowl and cover, 122, 123; soup plate painted in 'Mandarin Palette,' 123; teabowl and saucer with figures in garden, 123; tea canister, 16
Chinese Qingbai porcelain, lobed small dish, 121
'Chinese Tigers' pattern, 99
Chinoiserie decoration, 25n80; cake dish with, 102; earthenware mug with, 112; ironstone green-ground pudding plate with, 119; jug, 113; printed plate, 32; saucebouats, 63, 86, 87; 'Tall Chelsea Ewer' pattern milk jug, 66; teabowl and saucer, 63; tea wares printed with 'Lady with Bird in Hand' pattern, 114
Christian, Philip, factory, 133

Christie, Manson & Woods (Christie's), 79, 79n4, 95, 128
Christie, Mr., 38, 56
'Chrysanthemum' pattern, Worcester factory, 64
'Church Gresley' pattern, Coalport factory, 92
cinquefoil: beaker and saucer, 38, 39; dish, 9, 23n47
circular: basket, 72; bowl and cover, 126; butter tub, cover, and stand, 72; comport, 85; dish painted with 'Hop Trellis' pattern, 76; écuelles, 40, 41; Imari inkstand, 49, 50; reticulated comport, 93; saucer, 9, 23n47; teapot and cover, 121
claret-ground panels, coffee cup and saucer with, 42, 43
Clark, Kenneth F., Jr., 27n116
Clark, Louise B., 24n75
Clarke, T. H., 25n84, 38–39
Clive, Kitty, figure, v, 50, 51, 51n3
'clobbered' cup, 77
clocks: lustre jug reserved with clock face, 114; Vienna clock-case, 21n22
Coalbrookdale factory, Shropshire, 107, 133; flower pot or vase, 94
Coalport factory, Shropshire, 106; Coalbrookdale factory, 94, 107, 133; Coalport China, Ltd., 133; coffee cups, 30, 93; comport, 93; dessert plate, 93; ice cup, 92; John Rose & Co., 92, 93, 133; plate, 92; potpourri vase, 4; potpourri vase and cover, 5; potpourri vase and pierced cover, 93; teacup, coffee cup, and saucer, 93; teacups, 92, 93; teapot, cover, and stand, 92; Thomas Rose, 133
Cochin, Charles-Nicolas, the Younger, 64
coffee cans: Doccia factory, 127; English faceted saucer and, 104; Marcolini Meissen factory, 21n22; Le Nove factory, 22n28, 128; Wedgwood Bone China factory, 99
coffee cups: Chelsea factory, 42, 43; Coalport factory, 30, 93; Derby factory, 47, 48, 49; Flight and Barr Worcester factory, 79; Grainger, Lee & Co. Worcester factory, 85; H. & R. Daniel factory, 100; Marcolini Meissen factory, 22n39; Meissen porcelain factory, 125, 126; Minton factory, 95, 96; New Hall factory, 91; Richard Champion's factory, 87; Samuel Alcock & Co. factory, 101; Swansea factory, 108; Worcester factory, 9, 12, 23n47, 62, 63, 66, 67, 69, 71, 74, 75
coffee service, Höchst porcelain, 25n84
Cohn, Bertrand W., 24n66, 24n75
Cohn, Rosalee S. (wife), 24n66, 24n75
Coke, Gerald, 68
"Collecting Old Meissen Porcelain" (Wark), 7–8
collections, 22n29. *See also* Charlotte Stout Hooker Collection; Constance I. and Ralph H. Wark Collection; Frederick Walter Carter Collection; Gilhespy Collection; J.P. Morgan Collection; Lady Ludlow Collection; Marcel H. Stieglitz Collection; Marshall Collection of Worcester Porcelain; Ole Olsen Collection; Sigmund J. Katz Collection; von Brüning Collection; Wallace Collection; Warda Stevens Stout Collection
Collector's Room, The. *See* Marshall Field & Company
Columbian Exposition (1893), 2
Columbus, Christopher, 4
Commercial Appeal, The, 6, 22n29
'Common Jassamine,' in iron-red script, 92
comports: Coalport factory, 93; Grainger, Lee & Co. Worcester factory, 85; Staffordshire comport, 106
compote, Derby factory, 21n22
Constance I. and Ralph H. Wark Collection, 15, 22n41, 25n93
Continental ceramics, 5, 25n84
Continental porcelain, 6, 7, 8, 10, 12, 22n27; "bisque figures," 21n19; 'Capo-di-Monte' campaniform vase, 132; Chelsea-style plates, 16, 17, 132; grand tour of, 26n98; other factories, 128–131

Cookworthy, William, 87, 88
Cooper, William, Jr., 48, 49
Cooper, William, Sr., 49
Copeland, Ronald, 98
Copeland, William Taylor, 52, 98
Copeland & Garrett factory, 109, 134; child's toy teacup and saucer, 98; jug, 98. *See also* Spode factory, Stoke-on-Trent, Staffordshire
Copeland mark, 124, 124n1, 124n2
copper lustre. *See* lustre
copper plates: 'pluck and dust' techniques, 94; transfer-prints and, 64
cormorant. *See under* fishermen
cornflowers, 98
correspondence. *See under* Hooker, Charlotte Stout; Katz, Sigmund J.; Lautz, William H.; Scott, George Ryland; Simmons, Erwin E.; Stout, Warda Stevens; Wark, Ralph H.; Williams, Robert
cos lettuce leaf-molded sauceboats: Meissen porcelain factory, 15, 125; Worcester factory, 15, 71
costumed man holding spear, 128, 129
Cotton Ball, 26n107
'Cotton Tree' specimen, xii, 33, 34
court painter (*Hofmaler*), 127
Covent Garden, 83
covers: Amstel factory, 129; Caughley factory, 89; Chamberlain's Worcester factory, 81; Charles Meigh factory, 119; Chelsea-Derby factory, 45; Chelsea factory, 40, 41; Chinese export, 124; Coalport factory, 5, 92, 93; Derby factory, xx, 45, 46; Derbyshire, 104; Flight, Barr and Barr Worcester factory, 81; George Frederick Bowers & Co. factory, 101; Glamorgan Pottery factory, 120; inkstand with, 107; John and William Turner factory, 118; John Yates factory, 118; Liverpool factory, 61; Meissen porcelain factory, 15, 122, 123, 124, 125; rice bowl and, 122, 123, 124, 125; Richard Champion's factory, 88; rococo, 15; Samson factory, 132; sauce tureen, stand, and, 78, 79; Spode factory, 97; Staffordshire earthenware, 112; teapots and, 90, 121; vase, 21n12; Vinovo factory, 128; Wallendorf factory, 126, 127; Wedgwood/Whieldon-style earthenware, 116, 117; West Pans factory, viii, 60, 61; Worcester factory, 64, 66, 67, 68, 69, 72, 76
cows, 65
Cox, Alwyn, 107
Cox, Angela, 107
Cox, James, 38
Coypel, Charles-Antoine, 43
Cozzi factory, teabowl and saucer, 127
Crane, Paul, 38, 102
cream pitcher, Limoges porcelain, 4
crests: on dessert dishes, 81, 82; on oval platters, 80, 108; on plates, 78, 80, 123
'Cris de Paris' figure, 43
Crow, T. Leonard, 8, 23n45
crown and trident mark, 10
Crowther, John, 32
Croxall, Samuel (Rev.), 40, 73, 73
'Crucifixion, The,' 122
Cummer Gallery of Art, 15, 25n93
Cummings, Martha Hooker, 14, 19, 20, 21n17, 26n104, 26n106, 26n108, 26n109
Cupid, 46, 46; dish with 'Cupid Reining the Panther,' 86, 86; plaster cast, 119
Cupid figures, 4, 51, 56; Meissen porcelain factory, 126; 'Two Virgins Awaking Cupid,' 56. *See also* cherubs
cups: cabinet cup stand, 82; Davenport factory, 16; Meissen porcelain factory, 10, 25n90; rhinoceros horn libation, 121; Worcester factory, 6, 77. *See also* beakers; breakfast cup, H. & R. Daniel factory; cabinet cups; caudle cup; 'clobbered' cup; coffee cups; custard cup, and covers; ice cup, Coalport factory; mugs; teabowls; teacups
Cushion, John, 26n103, 131
custard cup, and covers: Chinese export, 124; Vinovo factory, 128
Cutts, John, 99, 99

154   INDEX

cylindrical: earthenware mug with Chinoiserie decoration, *112*; mugs, *32, 33, 63, 88*; stoneware teapot and cover with mother-and-child knop, *118*; teapot and cover, *112*
'Cyrene' pattern, William Adams & Sons factory, 116, *116*

d'Ablaing van Giessenburg, Jan Cornelis, 122
daisy. *See* 'Knife Handle Formal Daisy' pattern, Worcester factory
Dance-Holland, Nathaniel, 57, *57*
dancers: Chelsea factory, 51–52; 'Chelsea figures' of the 'Ranelagh Dancers,' 98, *99*; Derby factory, *51*, 52, *98*
Daniel, H. & R., factory, Stoke-on-Trent, Staffordshire, 133; cups, plate, and saucers, *100*
Daniell, A.B., 79
Daniell, Thomas, 115
Daniell, William, 115
dates: Bow figure, 58; Chinese export porcelain plates for Near Eastern Market, 124; for Joseph Hill, 55; Orient depicted on British pottery, 115; for Pierre Stephan, 55; purchase dates, xi, 4; for 'Red Ribbon' pattern, New Hall factory, 90
dating, problematic: as incomplete or contradictory, xi; Royal Copenhagen porcelain, 130; scientific techniques influencing, xiii; Yixing stoneware, 121
Davenport, John, 115
Davenport factory, 133; cup and saucer, 16; with design plagiarism, 114; dish, *101*
Davenport factory, earthenware: pearl-glazed plate, *115*; stone China soup plate, *119*
David Wilson & Sons, Hanley, 91
Dawson, Aileen, 70
Dayes, Edward, 106, 106n7
de Beijer, Jan, 129
decagonal, coffee cup, *62*
Deed of Gift. *See under* Charlotte Stout Hooker Collection
"Deer and the Lion, The" (fable), *77*
de Haen, Abraham, 129
'Dejeune' shape teacup, Chamberlain's Worcester factory, *82*
Delftware. *See* tin-glazed earthenware
Delhom, Mellanay, 26n103
Delormel, Pierre, 52
Derby factory, Derbyshire: Allied English Potteries, 133; biscuit figures, *56, 57*; candlestick, *53*; coffee cup and saucer, *47, 48, 49*; compote, 21n22; Derby Crown Porcelain Company, 133; dishes, *48, 49*; figures, v, vi, 4, 6, 22n31, *50, 51, 51, 52, 52, 53, 53, 54, 54, 55, 56, 57, 58, 98*; French porcelain Derby-style allegorical figures, *132*; inkstand, *49*, 50; 'Isabella, Gallant, and Jester,' 11, 24n67; jug, *48*; The Old Crown Derby China Works, 133; pastille burner, *50*; plates, *47, 48, 48, 49, 49*; porcelain statuettes, 4; Royal Crown Derby Co., Ltd., 133; Royal Doulton Tableware, Ltd., 133; saucers, *46, 47, 47, 48, 49*; six-shell sweetmeat or pickle stand, *45*; teabowl and saucer, *46, 47*; vases, *xx, 45, 46*; wall pocket, *45*
Derby International, 134
Derbyshire teapot and cover, *104*
design plagiarism, 114
'Desirable Residence' pattern, Bow factory, *32*
dessert dishes: Chamberlain's Worcester factory, *82*; Flight, Barr and Barr Worcester factory, *81*; 'Gold Star Border and Spangles Dessert Service' dish, 89; Grainger, Lee & Co. Worcester factory, *ii, 84, 85*; Minton factory, *95*; Worcester factory, *69, 74, 76, 77*
dessert plates: Coalport factory, *93*; Grainger, Lee & Co. Worcester factory, *84*; John Ridgway & Co. factory, *103*; Limoges porcelain, *4*; Wedgwood white ware 'Leafage,' *115*
Deupree, Mary Evelyn, 26n101
Deupree, Mrs. William, 24n75
'*deutsche Blumen*' (German flowers), *125*
Dibden, Charles, 35

Dillwyn, Lewis Weston, 109
dishes: Bow factory, *xii, 9,* 23n47, *33, 33, 34*; Caughley factory, *89*; Chelsea factory, *9, 39, 40, 41, 42*; Chinese Qingbai porcelain, *121*; C.J. Mason factory, *118*; Davenport factory, *101*; Derby factory, *48, 49*; Fürstenberg factory, 22n22, 22n33, 23n47; Spode factory, *118*; Tournai factory, 128, 129; Worcester factory, 11, *69, 71, 74, 76*. *See also* compote, Derby factory; dessert dishes; hot water dish, 'New Stone'; pickles; saucer dishes; saucers
Dixie-Portland Flour Company, 2–3, 4, 7
Dixon, John, 57, *57*
Dixon, Thomas, 93, *93*
Dixon Gallery and Gardens, 3; Deed of Gift and, xii, xiii, 5, 15, 19, 20, 25n88, 25n89, 25n90, 27n115; Library of the Dixon Gallery and Gardens, 30; Trustees of the Dixon, xii, 27n116
Doccia factory: coffee can and saucer, *127*; teacup and saucer, *126, 127*
documentary photographs, xi
Dodd, Joseph, 55
dodecagonal: '*gros bleu*'–bordered oval dish, *76, 77*; oval platter in 'Double Peacock' pattern, *102*
Dodsley, Robert, 73
dogs, 87; bagpiper and his dog figures, *44, 44*, 51, *51*; English earthenware puzzle jug with begging dog spout, 113, *113*; girl with puppy figure, 87, *87*; Lady Gardener Seated Beside a Dog, 24n70, 58, *59*
'Doll's House' pattern, Lowestoft factory, *62*
domestic scene: figures at domestic pursuits, *122, 123*; tea canister with, *123*; woman clasping her apron figure, 130, *131*
Domit, Moussa M., xii
Don Pottery factory, earthenware plate, *116*
Dorrance, John T., Jr., 38n10
double-ogee-shaped teacup and saucer, Richard Champion's factory, *88*
Dow, Virginia, 26n101
Dragesco, Bernard, 37
'Dragon in Compartments' pattern: Chamberlain's Worcester factory, 82, *82*; Coalport factory, 92, *92*; Worcester factory, 69, *69*
dragons: small bowl painted with, 125, *125*
'Draw Well, The' pattern, Worcester factory, *65*
Dresden Art Gallery, 86
Dresden figures, 21n22
'Dresden Flowers' pattern, Caughley factory, *89*
'Dresden Shepherds,' Derby factory, 22n31, 55
'Dry-Edge' figures, Derby factory, *51*
"Dubarry rose pitcher," 21n22
Duesbury, William, 38, 46, 46n1, 47, 48, 49, 50, 51, 53, 54, 55, 56, 73
Duesbury, William (son), 46, 54, *56*
Duesbury's Annual Catalogue of his Derby Porcelain, 56
Duke of Clarence service, Worcester factory, 5, 78, *78, 79*
'Duke of Weissenfels Series,' 43, 44, 53
Duncomb, Lady Mary, 56
Dutch decorations, 129
Dutch East India Company (VOC), 122, 129
Dutch porcelain, 22n28
Duvaux, Lazare, 46
Duvivier, Fidelle, 46–47

'Earl Dalhousie Service'–type pattern, Worcester factory, *77*
'Earl Manvers' pattern, Worcester factory, *76*
Earlom, Richard, 90
earthenwares: teapot, *18, 112, 116, 117*; Yorkshire Quin figure, 58. *See also* British earthenware; Davenport factory, earthenware; English earthenware; Staffordshire earthenware; tin-glazed earthenware; Wedgwood factory, earthenware

East India Company, 102, 104, 122, 129
Eberlein, Harold Donaldson, 127
ecclesiastical figures, *119*
écuelles, Chelsea factory, *40, 41*
Edwards, Alice S. (Stout, Alice Adeline), xii, xiii, 5, 13, 14, 25n88; The Antiquarians of Memphis and, 16; early life, 5; family life, 19
Edwards, Diana, 113, *117*
Edwards, Hubert C. (husband of Alice), 4, 19
'Eggshell' porcelain rice bowl and cover, *124, 125*
Ehret, Georg Dionysius, 42
Elliott, William, 64, *65*
'Eloping Bride' pattern, Worcester factory, *64*
enamel, 18, 52; creamware teapot and cover, *112*; dish in turquoise *camaïeu* and white, *86*; earthenware milk jugs, *112*; earthenware mug, *112*; earthenware plate, *115*; pearlware Chinoiserie jug, *113*; Limoges enamel style, 86; 'New Stone' hot water dish, *118*; painting skills, 88; pearlware milk jug, *120*; pearlware reticulated small plates, *120*; pink lustre milk jug, *114*; plates, *31, 32*; prunus-molded teabowls, *31*; toy teabowl, *34*
"enfants de Boucher." *See* cherubs
English Ceramic Circle, xiii, 12, 24n71, 26n107
English Ceramics (McKeown), 26n112
English Delft plate, *111*
English earthenware: creamware milk jug, *112*; jug reserved with birds and flowers, *113*; pearlware mug, *112*; puzzle jug, 113, *113*; Wedgwood/Whieldon-style teapot and cover, 116, *117*
English faceted coffee can and saucer, *104*
English '*Famille-Rose*' plate, *104*
English inkstand, *107*
English jug, *106*, 107
English plate, *106*, 107
English porcelain, xiii, 6, 7, 8, 9, 13; "English Porcelain: The Hooker Collection," 20, 30; in Frederick Walter Carter Collection, 5; "Let's Talk About English Porcelain," 20; other nineteenth-century factories, 101–107; "A Survey of English Porcelain" lecture, 12. *See also individual factories by name*
English pottery: plaster, *119*; tin-glazed earthenware, 111–112; various earthenwares, 112–117; various stonewares, 117–119
English teacup and saucer, *107*
Enlightenment, 42, 89
'Etruscan' shape, Minton factory, 95, *96*
Evans, David, 105, *109*, 110
ewer, Samson factory, *131*

fables: fable decoration, 40, *77*; 'Fable' pattern, Worcester factory, xviii, *xix*, 11, *73, 77*
Fables (Guy), 40
Fables Choisies par J de la Fontaine, 73
Fables of Aesop's and Others (Croxall), 40, 73, *73*
faceted: coffee cup and saucer, *69*; English faceted coffee can and saucer with floral border, *104*; teabowl and saucer, *69*
faïence, 43, 46, 128, *132*
Fairbairn, James, 108
falcons. *See under* birds
Falstaff figure, 21n22; Bow factory, 4, 21n23; Derby factory, 22n31, *58*
'Fame' pattern, Worcester factory, 64, *65*
'*Famille-Rose*' floral decoration: coffee cup, *63*; platter, *102*; teabowl and saucer, *122*
'*Famille-Rose*' pattern: Bow factory, *31, 32*; Chamberlain's Worcester factory, *82*; Chelsea factory, 12, *13, 39*; Chinese garden scene, Lowestoft factory, *62*; English '*Famille-Rose*' armorial octagonal plate, *104*; West Pans factory, *60*; Worcester factory, 62, *63*
'*Famille-Verte*' style, Worcester factory, *62, 69*
fans. *See* 'Old Japan Fan' pattern, Worcester factory
Farnsworth, Mrs. Sidney W., 24n75
feet: saucer and teacup foot, *80*; stoneware milk jug with three paw, *117*
feldspathic stoneware teapot and cover, *118*
Ferdinand (king of Spain), 4

INDEX 155

Ferriol, Charles de, 70
Fibiger, F.B., 24n67
'Fiesta Ware,' 117
figures, 41, 42, 51n3, 64, 114; allegorical, 4, 12, 24n70, 36, 37, 52, 53, 58, 59, 95, 112, 113, 126, 128, 132; Blanc-de-Chine porcelain, 21n22, 121; Bow factory, 4, 12, 21n23, 24n70, 35, 35, 36, 36, 37, 44, 50–51, 58; Chamberlain's Worcester factory, 83; Charles Gouyn factory, 12, 37; Chelsea factory, 12, 24n70, 37, 43, 44, 44, 51–52; Chinese export teabowl and saucer with figures in garden, 123; Continental porcelain 'Capo-di-Monte' campaniform vase with classical, 132; Derby factory, v, vi, 4, 6, 22n31, 50, 51, 51, 52, 52, 53, 53, 54, 54, 55, 56, 57, 58, 98; at domestic pursuits, 122, 123, 130, 131; Dresden, 21n22; Fürstenberg factory, 21n22; Longton Hall Works factory, 12, 24n70, 58, 59; Meigh, Charles, factory, 119; Meissen porcelain factory, 55, 126; mythological, 4, 53, 126, 127; Richard Champion's factory, 87; rococo vase painted with Watteau-type figures and birds, 45; Royal Copenhagen factory, 130, 131; Spode factory, 98, 99; Staffordshire earthenware, 58; Staffordshire pearlware, 22n28, 112, 113; on terrace with soup plate painted in 'Mandarin Palette,' 123; Vienna clock-case, 21n22; Volkstedt factory, 22n31, 126, 127; Wedgwood factory, earthenware, 117; Worcester factory, 70; Yorkshire, 58. See also biscuit figures
Figures of the Most Beautiful, Useful and Uncommon Plants described in the Gardeners Dictionary (Miller), 41, 42
finch. See under birds
'Finger and Thumb' pattern, Coalport factory, 92
finger bowls, Longton Hall Works factory, 15, 59, 60
First Period. See Worcester factory, Worcestershire
fishermen: 'Fisherman and Cormorant' pattern, 64, 64; 'Fisherman on a Towering Rock' (interior) pattern, 63; 'Sinking Boat Fisherman' pattern, 63, 63
Fitzclarence, Lord Frederick, 79
517 Goodwyn Avenue, 3, 4, 8, 9, 13, 14, 19, 27
flatware handles, 9, 63
Flaxman, John, 119
Flight, Barr and Barr factory, 21n2, 134. See also Worcester factory, Worcester
Flight, Barr and Barr period. See under Worcester factory, Worcestershire
Flight, Barr and Barr Worcester factory: crested oval platter, 80; crested plate, 80; dessert dish, 81; plates, 80; saucer and teacup foot, 80; teacup and saucer, 80; vase and cover, 81. See also Worcester factory, Worcestershire
Flight, John, 79
Flight, Joseph, 79
Flight and Barr Period. See under Worcester factory, Worcestershire
Flight and Barr Worcester factory: coffee cup, 79. See also under Worcester factory, Worcestershire
Flight Period. See under Worcester factory, Worcestershire
flower pot, Coalbrookdale, 94
flowers: birds and, 110, 113; breakfast cup and saucer painted with, 100; camellias, 3, 13, 20, 25n79, 72, 91; Chinese, 99; 'Chinese Flower Show' pattern, 61; Chinese vessels of, 105; Chinoiserie decoration and, 119; 'Chrysanthemum'-molded teapot and cover, 64; with clusters of leaves, 125; 'Common Jassamine' in iron-red script, 92; cornflowers, 98; 'deutsche Blumen,' 125; 'Dresden Flowers,' 89; earthenware jugs with, 112, 116, 120; Evans and, 105, 110; in floral borders, 104, 109, 114; in floral bouquets, 48, 91, 103; in floral clusters, 116; in floral decoration, 50, 81, 108, 124, 132; in floral garlands, 75, 76, 83, 87, 126, 127, 127; in floral panels, 71; in floral roundel, 48, 49;

flower-seller biscuit figure, 97, 97; "French tulip design," 109; fruit and, 109, 110, 110, 111; Imari-style or pattern, 66, 67, 92, 118; inkstand with cover formed as lotus blossom, 107; Kakiemon-style, 66, 68, 86, 87; 'Knife Handle Formal Daisy' pattern, 63; 'Mayflower Shape' plate with floret-molded ground, 63; Oriental, 32, 33, 106, 107, 119; pearlware milk jug enameled with, 120; pearlware plates enameled with, 120; plate molded with budding rose branch, 71; plate printed and painted with sepia camaïeu, 98; plate with floret-patterned and trellis-molded ground, 92; Pollard and, 110; Royal Copenhagen factory plate painted with, 130; 'Royal Lily' pattern, 78, 89; 'Sèvres'-style floral decoration, 83, 106, 110; in sprays and/or sprigs, 40, 41, 91, 103, 106, 107, 109, 110, 128, 74, 93; sugar bowls with, 89, 97, 101; Swansea-type roses, 107; teabowl and saucer painted with, 46, 47; toy teabowl enameled with, 34; wall pocket painted with, 45; vases decorated with, viii, 45, 46, 60, 61, 93, 103, 105, 106. See also 'Famille-Rose' floral decoration; 'Famille-Rose' pattern; gardens; thistles
fluted: coffee cup and saucer, 9, 23n47; hexagonal teapot stand, 68; plate, 48, 49; saucer dish, 77; 'strap fluting,' 66; teacup and saucer, 76
fonds, 20, 27n120
forgeries, 127
Foster, Kate, 16, 26n98, 26n99
Fountain, The. See Cascade, La
fountains. See 'Pastoral Group by a Fountain,' Derby factory
'Four Continents': 'Africa' as part of series, 128, 128; auction of, 128; Bow factory, 36, 37; on dessert dish, 95, 95
'Four Elements, The' set, Bow factory, 36, 37
Fournier, Louis, 130
'Four Quarters of the Globe, The' ('The Four Continents') set, Bow factory, 36, 37
'Four Seasons, The' set, Longton Hall Works factory, 58, 59
'Four Times of the Day' (Rietschel), 86
fox, 73
Fredensborg Castle, 130
Frederick II (king of Prussia), 122
Frederick Walter Carter Collection, 5, 21n25
Frederik V (king of Denmark), 130
Free Trade, 95
'French Blue' floral garlands, plate painted with, 83
"French Influences at Chelsea" (Clarke), 38
French porcelain, xiii, 5, 22n27, 22n28, 25n88; as Deed of Gift, 25n90; Derby-style allegorical figures, 132
French taste: coffee cups and saucers painted in, 87, 126
"French tulip design," teacup, 109
French white allegorical group of 'Africa,' 128, 128
'frill' vase, with cover, 46
fruits: fruit patterns, New Hall factory, 91; fruit-seller biscuit figure, 97, 97; plates with fruit decoration, 42, 44, 109, 110, 110, 111; strawberry-molded plate, 59; sugar bowl and cover with flowers and fruit sprigs, 97. See also grapevines, on dish; lemon-form knop; pear-shaped jugs
Frye, Thomas, 32, 35
Fulda factory, tea canister, 25n90
Fürstenberg factory: dish, 22n39; figure, 21n22

Gabszewicz, Anton, 32, 35, 102
gadrooning, 84, 100
Gaillard, René, 54, 54
Gambon, Fergus, 108, 109
'Garçons Chinois, Les,' Worcester factory, 65
Gardeners Dictionary, The (Miller), 42
gardens, 3, 4, 19–20, 21n15, 41, 52n2, 62; Chelsea Physic Garden, 42; Chinese export teabowl and saucer with figures in, 123; copper lustre jug with clock face and roundel of Chinese figure in, 114; Covent Garden, 83; garden vignettes, 31; Lady Gardener Seated Beside a Dog, 24n70, 58, 59; Memphis Garden Club, 21n14; platter with garden scene, 39, 40; stone China leaf-shaped small dishes with Chinese garden, 118; teabowl and saucer painted with garden vignettes, 127; 'Walk in the Garden' pattern, 63. See also Dixon Gallery and Gardens; 'Famille-Rose' floral decoration; 'Famille-Rose' pattern
Gardner, H. Bellamy, 34
Garrick, David, 35, 35n2, 50, 50, 57, 57, 58
"Gate Leading to a Mosque, Chunargarh, Uttar Pradesh, The," 115
geese, 73
gentleman playing recorder figure, 126
George Grainger & Co., 134
George II (king of England), 34
George III (king of England), 52, 88
George IV (king of England), 88
German flowers. See 'deutsche Blumen'
German porcelain, xii, 6, 9, 19, 20, 22n28; as Deed of Gift, 25n90; in Warda Stevens Stout Collection, 5. See also Meissen, Marcolini, factory; Meissen porcelain factory; Saxony; Thuringian porcelain; Volkstedt factory; Wallendorf factory, bowl and cover
Gilbody, Samuel, factory, 133
Giles, James, 25n80, 68, 74, 74, 75, 132
Gilhespy, F. Brayshaw, 102
Gilhespy Collection, 102
gilt, 52; botanical dessert plate, 93; caillouté-patterned apricot-ground plates, 82; coffee cups and saucers, 47, 87; inkstand, 107; oblong center dish, 101; plate with gilt-hatched blue lines, 110; sugar bowl and cover with gilt 'Dresden Flowers,' 89; teacup and saucer with gilt 'Seaweed' decoration, 80; teacup with gilt vermiculate decoration, 101; teapot and cover, teacup and saucer, 88; tripod vase and cover with gilt winged mermen supports, 81
'Girl in a Swing' factory. See Gouyn, Charles, factory
girl with puppy figure, Richard Champion's factory, 87, 87
Glamorgan Pottery factory: pearlware milk jug, 120; pearlware reticulated small plates, 120; pearlware teapot and cover, 120; plates, 28–29
glaze: Chinese Qingbai porcelain lobed small dish with pale green, 121; green-glazed earthenware plate, 16; manganese underglaze oxide decoration, 112; salt-glazed stoneware sauceboat, 117. See also black-glazed stoneware milk jug; smear-glazed; tin-glazed earthenware; underglaze blue; underglaze Pratt-type palette, rooster pearlware figure
Glendenning, O., 37
goats: 'Goat and Bee' jug, 10, 10, 12, 25n78, 37, 37–38; goat's-head handles, 38; *Two Goats at the Foot of a Tree* woodcut, 38
Godden, Geoffrey, 70, 90, 91, 93, 95, 97, 106, 107, 115
Goddess of Mercy (Guanyin) figure, 21n22, 121
Godfrey, James, 132
gold anchor mark, 38, 47
gold numeral system, 88
'Gold Star Border and Spangles Dessert Service,' Caughley factory, 89, 89
'Golfer and Caddy' ('Image') pattern, Bow factory, 6, 32
Gooch, Mrs. C.M., 26n101
Goodspeed's Bookshop, 5
Goodwyn Avenue. See 517 Goodwyn Avenue
Gotha factory, 25n90, 127
Gouyn, Charles, factory ('Girl in a Swing' factory): bird figure, 12, 37; St. James, 12, 50, 133
Graff, Johann Andreas, 33
Graham, John, 26n103, 131
Grainger, Lee & Co. Worcester factory, 134; basket, 85; coffee cup and saucer, 85; comport, 85; dessert dishes, ii, 84, 85; dessert plate, 84; plate, 84

Grainger's Worcester factory, 105; George Grainger & Co., 134; Grainger, Lee & Co. Worcester factory, ii, 84, 85, 134; Grainger, Wood & Co., 134; Grainger & Co., 84, 134; teacup and saucer, 84; Thomas Grainger & Co., 84, 134. See also Worcester factory, Worcestershire
'Grand Turk' biscuit figure, Minton factory, 70
grapevines, on dish, 33
Gray, Jonathan, 109, 116
Greatbatch, William, 18
Great Depression, 2
Great Exhibition of the Works of Industry of All Nations, 86, 86n1
Griffiths, Edwin, 93, 93
Grignion, Charles, the Elder, 58, 58
grisaille: coffee cup and saucer, 48; plate, 122; sauce tureen, cover, and stand, 78, 79
Gristina, Mary Campbell, 25n93
'gros bleu' dodecagonal dish, 76, 77
Grund, Johann Gottfried, 130
Grund statues, 131, 131n7
Guanyin (Goddess of Mercy) figure, 21n22, 121
Guest, Charlotte Elizabeth Bertie (wife), 54
Guest, Sir John, 54
Guest, Mary Enid Evelyn (daughter), 54
guilloche: Minton factory saucer dish, i, 94; spherical teapot and cover, 104
Gunton, W., 83, 83
Gustav III (king of Sweden), 131
Guy, John, 40
'Gypsy Encampment' white stoneware jug, 119

"Habit d'Arlequin Moderne" (Joullain), 52, 52
"Habit de Captain Italien" (Joullain), 44
"Habit de Narcisin de Malalbergo" (Joullain), 43
Hackenbroch, Yvonne A., 12, 24n68, 24n72
Hackwood, William, 119
Hague, The, 46, 51, 128, 129
Hald, Andreas, 130
Hamilton, Lady, 79
Hampson, Rodney, 117
Hampton, Charlotte, 79
Hancock, Robert, 64, 65
handles: double-handled caudle cup, cover, and stand, 45; flatware, 9, 63; goat's-head, 38; mugs, 32, 33; serpent, 105, 106; two-handled dish, 86. See also knops
Hanscombe, Stephen, 40, 68, 73
Hansen, Carl Martin, 131
'Hans Sloane' botanical plates, 33, 41
harlequin figures, Derby factory, 52
Haslem, John, 48–49, 52, 56, 110–111
Hastings, Warren, 40
hawks. See under birds
Hayden, Arthur, 75
Hayfield, John, 59, 60, 60
Hayman, Francis, 58, 58
Henry IV (Shakespeare), 58, 58
Henrywood, R.K., 98
Herculaneum factory, 133
Heuser, Paula, 23n47, 23n63
hexagonal: pearl-glazed earthenware jug, 116; teapot stand, 68
Heylyn, Edward, 32
Hicks & Meigh factory, 115; stone China leaf-shaped small dishes, 118
Hilditch, William, factory: Hilditch, William & John, 133; Hilditch & Hopwood, 133; Hilditch & Martin, 133; Hilditch & Sons, 102, 133
Hilditch & Sons factory, cake dish, 102
Hill, Joseph, 55
Hill, Mrs. Napoleon, 24n75
Hills, Maurice, 102
Hindman, Mrs. Frank T., 26n95
Histoire du Théâtre Italien (Riccoboni), 43, 43, 52, 52
History of Eighteenth-Century German Porcelain: The Warda Stevens Stout Collection, A, xii
Höchst porcelain, 8, 9; tea and coffee service, 25n84
Hodgson, Zorka, 38

Hofmaler (court painter), 127
Hogarth, William, 52n2
Holdship, Josiah (brother), 64
Holdship, Richard, 64, 65
'Holländisches Service,' 129; Meissen porcelain factory, 22n33
Holloway, Chris, 89
hollyhock leaf-molded dish, 59
Homer Laughlin China Company, 117
Honey, William B., 2
Hooker, Charlotte Stout, 13, 15; collecting years, 17–19; correspondence, 18–19, 23n47, 23n49, 25n89; family life, xiii, 3, 14, 19, 27n123; legacy, xi, xiii, 20; notebooks of, xi, 84, 91, 107, 131; shopping strategy, xiii, 17; with travel, xiii, 17; on Warda Stevens Stout, 21n14; on Warder W. Stevens, 21n6. See also Charlotte Stout Hooker Collection; Stout-Hooker Archives
Hooker, Martha (daughter), 14, 19. See also Cummings, Martha Hooker
Hooker, Mimi (daughter), 14, 19, 20, 21n17, 26n107
Hooker, Thomas Benjamin, III (husband), 4, 14, 19, 20, 27n124
Hooker, Tim (son), 14, 19, 21n17
'Hope Service,' Worcester factory, 78, 79, 79
'Hop Trellis' pattern, Worcester factory, 76
Horace, 57
hot water dish, 'New Stone,' 118
Houkjær, Ulla, 130–131
Houston, Richard, 64, 65
Houston Museum, 20, 26n105
Howard, David S., 104, 122, 123, 124, 131
Hudson, Thomas, 52
Huet, Christophe, 43
Hughes, Thomas, 40
Huis ten Bosch (House in the Woods), 51
Hullmandel, C., 83
Hunter Museum of American Art, 26n107
Hutton, A. de Saye, 90
'Huys Nederhorst by het Dorp den Berg, Het,' 129

ice cup, Coalport factory, 92
Ilmenau factory, saucer, 25n90
'Image' ('Golfer and Caddy') pattern, Bow factory, 6, 32
Imari: armorial plate, 81; Chinese ewer and basin, 131; circular inkstand, 49, 50; floral panels, 66, 67; 'King's' or 'Old Japan' pattern plate, 95, 97, 97; 'King's' pattern, Derby factory, 49; ironstone oval dish, 118; milk jug, 90; 'New Stone' hot water dish, 118; plate, Flight, Barr and Barr Worcester factory, 80; stone China soup plate, 119; teacup with 'Finger and Thumb' pattern, 92; teapot, cover, and stand, 92. See also 'Brocade Imari' pattern
imitators, 131–132
Imperial Russian state coat of arms, 130
Indiana State Board of Agriculture, 1
Indiana University, 2
information: for documentation, xi; as incomplete or contradictory, xi; records, xiii, 22n30, 27n113
initials, 127. See also monograms
inkstand: Derby factory, 49, 50; English, 107
inscriptions, 30, 33, 34, 95
insects, 33, 34; butter tub, cover, and stand reserved with cartouches of exotic birds and, 72; decagonal coffee cup painted with, 62; plate reserved with cartouches of exotic birds and, 72; sweetmeat or pickle stand painted with, 45; wall pocket painted with, 45. See also bees; butterflies
invoices, xi, 127; from Lautz, 6; Memphis Antique Shop, 4, 21n19
iron-red: coffee cup and saucer printed in, 85; 'Common Jassamine' in iron-red script, 92; English earthenware milk jugs enameled with, 112; sauceboat painted in, 86, 87; teacup and saucer printed in, 94
Isabella (queen of Spain), 4

'Isabella, Gallant, and Jester,' 11, 24n67
Islamic architecture, 115
'Island House' pattern, Bow factory, 31
Isleworth factory, 32, 133
Italian comedy figure, 43, 44, 52, 53
Italian porcelain, 22n28, 127–128. See also Cozzi factory, teabowl and saucer; Doccia factory; Nove, Le, factory, coffee can and saucer; Vinovo factory, custard cup and cover

'Jabberwocky' pattern, Worcester factory, 69
Jacob-Hanson, Charlotte, 46
James A. Lewis & Son, Inc., 7, 10, 22n39
'James Quin as Falstaff,' Derby factory, 22n31. See also Quin, James
Japan: Imari 'King's' or 'Old Japan' pattern plate, 95, 97, 97; Japanese Arita, 8, 9, 125n1; Japanese Palace Inventory mark, 22n33, 125, 125n1; 'Old Japan Fan' pattern, 67; 'Old Japan Lady' pattern, 39; 'Old Japan' pattern, 49, 95, 97, 97; 'Old Japan Star' pattern, 67; 'Old Mosaick Japan' pattern, Worcester factory, 8, 68; 'Scarlet Japan' pattern, 22n28, 69; teacup painted with 'Japan' pattern, 82. See also Imari
jasper. See white jasper oval medallions
Jazz Age, 3
Jellicoe, Roderick, 102
jewelry, 7, 24n72, 24n77
Jewitt, Llewellynn, 54
Jewitt, William, 49
John, W.D., 105, 109
John Cutts & Sons, 99
John Hay Center, 26n100
Jones, A.E., 105
Jones, Margaret Rowe, 24n75
Jörg, Christiaan, 122
Joseph, Sir Leslie, 105, 114, 116
Joullain, François, 43, 44, 52, 52
J.P. Morgan Collection, 95, 97
jugs: 'cabbage leaf,' 72, 91; Chelsea factory, 10, 12, 25n78, 37, 38; Copeland & Garrett factory, 98; Derby factory, 48; English earthenware, 113; English jug applied with floral sprays, 106, 107; lustreware, 21n22; Minton factory, 107; puzzle jug, 112, 113; Rockingham factory, 22n31, 107; Samuel Alcock & Co. factory white stoneware, 119; South Wales pottery, 120; Staffordshire earthenware, 112, 113, 114, 116; Worcester factory, 64, 65, 72. See also milk jugs
Jukes, Francis, 106, 106n7
'Jumping Boy' pattern, Liverpool factory, 61
Junior League, 26n107

Kakiemon style: Chelsea factory, 39, 40; Derby factory, 48, 49; flowers, 66; Japanese Arita, 8, 9, 125n1; Meissen porcelain factory, 15, 125; Plymouth factory, 86, 87; teacup and saucer with cartouches, 68; teapot and cover reserved with cartouches, 68
Kändler, Johann Joachim, 24n67, 34, 38, 38n10, 43, 51
Kangxi Period (1661–1772), 31
Katz, Jessie (wife), 12, 23n57
Katz, Sigmund J., 10, 12, 13; collection of, 23n57; correspondence, 24n74, 24n77, 25n78; purchases from, 24n70, 24n73
Kauffman, Angelica, 56, 56, 57, 57
Kean, Edmund, 57, 58
Kemble, John Philip, 57, 58
Kerr & Binns Worcester factory, dishes, 86, 134. See also Worcester factory, Worcestershire
Kevill-Davies, Sally, 33, 42
Keys, Edward (brother), 97
Keys, Samuel, Jr., 83, 97
Kiddell, A.J.B. "Jim," 102
kidney shapes: dessert dishes, 69, 74; dishes, 42, 89
'King of Prussia' pattern, Worcester factory, 64, 65
Kirk, James, 40
Kleinman, Bella, 70

INDEX 157

Klepser, Kenneth, 23n45
Kloster-Veilsdorf factory, 127
'Knife Handle Formal Daisy' pattern, Worcester factory, 63
knops, 118, 121, 126
Kotta, Franz, 127
Kramarsky, Lola, 24n68
Kramarsky, Siegfried, 24n68
'Kremlin Service,' plate from, 130

Labadists, 33
ladies, 50; 'Chinese Lady and Bird in a Cartouche' pattern, 61; Continental porcelain, 21n19; Lady Gardener Seated Beside a Dog, 24n70, 58, 59; 'Lady in a Pavilion' pattern, 39; lady playing xylophone figure, 126; 'Lady with Bird in Hand' pattern, British earthenware, 114; 'Old Japan Lady' pattern, 39; sweetmeat figure of lady, 44
Ladies Amusement, The (Sayer), 65, 73
ladle, Meissen porcelain factory, 125
Lady Ludlow Collection, 75
Lancake, R., 42
Lancret, Nicholas, 70
landscapes: 'Bright Landscape' decoration, 89, 89; candlestick with Chinese, 58; Minton factory teacups, coffee cups, and saucers with rural, 95, 96; sauceboat with Chinoiserie, 86, 87; teabowl and saucer in purple *camaïeu*, 129; teacup and saucer in purple *camaïeu*, 99; vases painted with rural landscape scenes, 101, 129
Lane, Arthur, 43, 59
Lane, Richard James, 83
Langeloh, Elfriede, 25n91
lass figure, Bow factory, 12
Lausanne School, 3
Lautz, William H., 8, 22n27, 104; correspondence, 6–7, 10, 22n34, 22n35, 22n40, 23n56, 23n57, 24n69; influence, 10; purchases from, 23n47, 127; with "Seattle Scheme," 22n32
Layard, Austen Henry (Sir), 54
leaves: cos lettuce leaf-molded sauceboats, 15, 71, 125; inkstand with cover as lotus blossom and leaves, 107; 'Leafage' dessert plate, 115; leaf-molded dish, 59; leaf-molded ladle, 125; leaf-molded oval dish, 60; leaf-molded sauceboat, 60; leaf-shaped chamber candlestick, 58; leaf-shaped dish, 60; leaf-shaped finger bowl and stand, 59; leaf-shaped pickle dish, 86, 87; stone China leaf-shaped small dishes, 118; white coffee cup and saucer with clusters of flowers and, 125. *See also* cabbage leaf
Ledger, Andrew, 46, 47, 48, 56
Leeds Pottery, 113
Lemaire, Rodolphe, 125
lemon-form knop, 126
Lempertz catalogue, 128
Le Noble, Richard, 22n28, 131
leopards, 77
Lethe, or Aesop in the Shades (Garrick), 50, 50
"Let's Talk About English Porcelain," 20
lettuce. *See* cos lettuce leaf–molded sauceboats
Library of the Dixon Gallery and Gardens. *See under* Dixon Gallery and Gardens
Limbach factory, tea canister, 25n90
Limehouse factory, London, 133
Limoges porcelain, 4, 21n16, 86
lions: on border pattern, 77; Britannia with her lion, 52, 53; lion knop, 118
Little, Lilian B., 5, 21n24, 22n28, 23n47
Littler, Jane Shaw (wife), 59
Littler, William, 59, 60
Liverpool factory, Lancashire, 133; part tea service, 61; teabowl and saucer, 61; teacup and saucer, 61; teapot and cover, 61
Livre de Vases (Boucher), 38
Loan Exhibition of Chelsea China, The, 23n47
lobed: small dish, 121; circular teapot and cover, 121; oval dessert dish, 82; sauceboat, 32
Lockett, Terence, 26n109, 115
London Delft, blue and white plate with Chinese River view, 111, 112

London Pleasure Gardens, The (Wroth), 52n2
'London' shape: British teacup and saucer, 109; coffee cup, 91; Staffordshire milk jug, 105; teacup, coffee cup, and saucer, 108; teacup and saucer, 91; toy teacup and saucer, 98
'Long Eliza' pattern, Worcester factory, 63
Longton Hall Works factory, Staffordshire, 134; allegorical figures, 12, 24n70; dishes, 59, 60; excavations at, 24n71; figures, 12, 24n70, 58, 59; finger bowls, 15, 59, 60; influence of, 34; plate, 59; 'Quail' pattern, 23n47; teacup and saucer, 23n47
Loosdrecht factory, teabowl and saucer, 129
'Lord Henry Thynne' pattern, Worcester factory, 11, 77
'Lord Rodney Service' pattern of 'Fancy Birds,' Worcester factory, 77
Lorraine, Claude, 90
lotus blossom, inkstand with cover formed as, 107
"Lowdin's Bristol," 6
Löwenfinck, Adam Friedrich von, 12
Lowestoft factory, Suffolk, 134; teabowl and saucer, 62
lozenge-shape: dessert dish, 77; dish decorated at The Hague with floral sprays, 128; 'Gold Star Border and Spangles Dessert Service' dish, 89
Ludlow Collection. *See* Lady Ludlow Collection
Ludwig Friedrich II (prince of Schwarzburg-Rudolstadt), 127
Ludwigsburg factory, plate, 22n39
Lund, Benjamin, factory, Bristol, 134
Luplau, Anton Carl, 130
lustre: copper and pink lustre jug, 113; copper lustre-ground pearlware Chinoiserie jug, 113; copper lustre jug, 114; lustreware jugs, 21n22; tea wares with Chinoiserie 'Lady with Bird in Hand' pattern within pink lustre edges, 114
lutes: lutanist with sheep figure, 51; musicians playing, 53
Lutheran *Nederduytse Bijbel*, 122
Luyken, Jan, 122, 122
Lyceum, 83
Lygo, Joseph, 56

Macalester, Sheelah, 23n47
MacAllister, Mrs. Donald, 37
Macbeth (Shakespeare), 35, 35n2
Mackenna, F. Severne, 13, 24n76, 24n77, 25n78, 87–88
Madame Vestris. *See* Bartolozzi, Lucia Elizabeth
Madeley porcelain works, Shropshire, 106
Malcolm Franklin, Inc., 71
Mallet, John, 40, 51
Malowney, Megan-Anne, 59
'Mandarin Palette,' soup plate painted in, 123
Manheim, B., 4, 21n22
Manheim, David (brother), 106
Manheim, D. M. & P., 7, 104, 106
Manheim, Millie, 106
Manheim, Peter (brother), 106
Manners, Errol, 40
'Mansfield' pattern, Caughley factory, 88, 89
Marcel H. Stieglitz Collection, 11, 24n66
'Marchioness of Huntly' pattern, Worcester factory, 75
Marion, Louis J., 4
marks: Battam, 98; bow-and-arrow mark, 104; 'Cambrian China,' 116; Copeland, 124, 124n1, 124n2; crown and trident, 10; discrepancies, 70, 107, 116, 125, 126; gold anchor, 38, 47; Japanese Palace Inventory, 22n33, 125, 125n1; red anchor, 107; Soar, 44; Sprimont, 38; triangle, 55; triple-wave, 130; ubiquitous, 21, 35; Yixing stoneware, 121
Marno, Felicity, 58, 70, 89
Marshall, Henry Rissik, 71, 71n3, 73
Marshall, Mrs. Henry Rissik, 71
Marshall Collection of Worcester Porcelain, 71n3
Marshall Field & Company, 2, 79; The Collector's Room, 5, 21n24; purchases from, 22n28, 23n47, 91, 95
Mary, Duchess of Ancaster and Kesteven, 52

mask-molded wall pocket, 45
Mason, C.J., factory, 115, 134; ironstone shaped and molded oval dish, 118
Mason, Miles, factory, 102, 102, 103, 134
Mason factory: Charles James Mason, 134; C.J. Mason factory, 115, 118, 134; George M. and Charles James Mason, 134; Miles Mason factory, 102, 102, 103, 134
Massey, Roger, 32
master modeler (*Modellmeister*), 127
Matthews, Charles James, 83
'Mayflower Shape,' H. & R. Daniel factory, 100
McArdell, James, 52, 58
McCarnell, Adeline, 2
McKeown, Julie, 26n112
McNair, Anne, 75
Mead, Richard, 33–34
medallions. *See* white jasper oval medallions
Meehl, Hans, 130
Meigh, Charles, factory, drab stoneware teapot and cover with ecclesiastical figures, 119
Meissen, Marcolini, factory, 21n22, 22n39, 125
Meissen porcelain factory, Saxony, xi, xii, 6, 13, 25n93, 25n94; beaker, 22n39; bowls, 15, 25n90; coffee cup and saucer, 125, 126; "Collecting Old Meissen Porcelain," 7–8; cups, 10, 25n90; dishes, 9, 21n22, 23n33, 23n47; 'Duke of Weissenfels Series,' 43, 44, 53; figures, 55, 126; influence of, 40, 44, 55; ladle, 125; Marcolini Meissen factory, 21n22, 22n39; 'The Mockery of Age,' 11, 24n67; musical group, 4; plate, 22n33; porcelain groups, 11; 'Quail' pattern, 9, 23n47; sauceboats, 15, 125; saucers, 10, 22n39, 125, 126; sugar bowl, 21n2; sugar caster, 126; Sulkowski Service, 15, 25n92, 26n96; teacup, coffee cup, and saucer with Meissen-style bird in rococo trellis, 93; tureens, 15, 25n92; VOC and, 129
Meissonnier, Juste-Aurèle, 38
Memorandum Book (Bowcock), 32, 34
Memphis Antique Shop, 4, 21n19
Memphis Brooks Gallery, 12, 14; exhibition, 24n69; with "A Survey of English Porcelain" lecture, 12
Memphis Country Club, 3, 21n17
Memphis Garden Club, 21n14
Mennecy factory, 38
Merian, Maria Sibylla, 33–34, 34
mermen, 81
Messenger, Michael, 93
Metamorphosis insectorum Surinamensium (Merian), 33, 34
Metropolitan Museum of Art, 24n72, 97
Meyrick, John, 106n7
Midland Counties Exhibition, 44n1
Miles Mason factory. *See* Mason factory
military trophies on baluster-form mug, 64, 65
milk jugs: British earthenware, 114; Chinese export, 16; English earthenware enameled with iron-red flowers, 112; Glamorgan Pottery factory, 120; Limoges porcelain, 4; New Hall factory, 90; Nymphenburg factory, 25n90; Staffordshire 'London' shape, 105; Staffordshire stonewares, 117; Worcester factory, 66, 69
'Milkmaids, The' pattern, Worcester factory, 65
'Mill, The' pattern, Glamorgan Pottery factory, 120
Miller, John (brother-in-law), 42
Miller, Philip, 41, 41–42
Milton, John, figure, 52, 54, 55
Minerva: Derby factory, 4, 52, 53; Volkstedt factory, 22n31, 126, 127
Mint Museum, 26n105
Minton, Herbert, 95
Minton factory, Stoke-on-Trent, Staffordshire, 107; biscuit figures, 70, 97, 97; coffee cups, 95, 96; dessert dish, 95; Herbert Minton & Co., 134; jug, 107; Minton & Boyle, 134; Minton Design Book of 1839, 97, 97; Mintons, 134; *Ornamental Design Books*, 107; plates, 95, 96, 97, 97; 'pluck and dust' technique of printing,

158　INDEX

94; saucer dishes, *i*, *94*; saucers, *94*, *95*, *96*; teacups, *94*, *95*, *96*; Thomas Minton, 134
'Mockery of Age, The,' 11, 24n67
Modellmeister (master modeler), 127
Monconseil, Marquise de, 39
Mongolian bust, *x*, 11, 32, 34, *35*
monk, Bow factory, *36*
monograms: jug, *48*; plates, *78*, *123*. See also initials
Montague, Guitel, 22n39
Morgan, John Pierpont, collections of, 95, 97
Morgan, John Pierpont, Jr., 95, 97
Morgan, Junius Spencer (father), 95
Morning Herald (newspaper), 102
Morris, Henry, 105, 109, *109*
Morrison, Alasdair, 47
Morrow, Louisa, 16
Morrow, Louise Rogerson, 26n101
Mortlock, John, 108, 110, 111
'Mosaic' pattern, Staffordshire stonewares, *117*
Mosely, Charles, *50*
mother-and-child knop, *118*
Mr. Garrick in Richard III (Dixon), *57*
Mrs. C.B. Stout Collection of Early Meissen Porcelain, ca. 1708–1750, 26n94
Mrs. Clive in the Character of the Fine Lady in Lethe (Mosley), *50*
mugs: Bow factory, *31*, *32*, *33*; English pearlware, *112*; Richard Champion's factory, *88*; Worcester factory, *63*, *64*, *65*
Mulder, J., *34*
Müller, Frantz-Heinrich, 130
Müller, Johann Sebastian, 70
'Muses Modeller,' *36*; Bow factory, 24n70, *35*
musical instruments. See bagpipes; lutes; recorder; xylophone
musician figures: Chelsea factory, *44*; Derby factory, 22n31, *51*, *53*
mythological figures. See under figures

Nance, E. Morton, 105, 108–109, 110, 114
Nantgarw China Works factory, Mid-Glamorgan, South Wales, 49, 105, 108, 134; plates, 22n39, *109*, 110, *110*, 111
'Narcisin' ('The Captain') figure, *43*, 44
'Narcissus' pattern, Plymouth factory, 86, *87*
National Gallery of Victoria, 54n7
'Nativity, The,' 122
'Nautilus' pattern, South Wales pottery, *120*
Neale & Co., 75, 113
Near Eastern market, *124*
Nelson, Christina H., 22n33, 23n44
neoclassical: basalt teapot and cover, *118*; part tea service, *61*; pastille burner, *50*; plate, *44*; teabowl and saucer, *44*; teapot and cover, *44*; teacup and saucer, *88*; yellow-ground vase and cover, *129*
Neptune, 4; Bow factory, *36*, *37*
New China Works. See under Worcester factory, Worcestershire
New Hall factory, Staffordshire, 134; milk jugs, *90*; plate, *91*; saucer, *90*; teacup, coffee cup, and saucer, *91*; teacup and saucer, *91*; tea wares, *90*
'New Stone' hot water dish, *118*
New York Stock Market, 2
Nicholas I (czar of Russia), *130*
Nine Muses figures, Wedgwood factory, earthenware, *117*
'No. 6' pattern, Davenport factory, earthenware, *115*
Norcross, Helen Eakin, 26n101
Norfleet, Mrs. Vance, 24n75
"North East View of the Cotsea Bhaug, on the River Jumna," 115
Northrop, Guy, 23n52
Norway Spruce (Miller), *41*
Noss, Aagot, 131, 131n7
notebooks. See under Hooker, Charlotte Stout; "Stout Notebooks"
Nove, Le, factory, coffee can and saucer, 22n28, *128*

numeral system, in gold, 88
nun, Bow factory, *36*
Nymphenburg factory, milk jug, 25n90
Nyon factory, 'seaux à liqueurs,' 21n22, *129*

oblong: center dish, *101*; dessert dish, *85*; milk jug, *120*; teapot, cover, and stand, *92*
octagonal: beakers, *9*, 23n47; plates, *32*, *32*, *33*, *39*; soup plates, 11, 12, *13*, *39*; teacup and saucer, *9*, *61*
octofoil: plate, *87*; saucer, *40*, *41*
'Oeil-de Perdrix' pattern, Flight, Barr and Barr Worcester factory, *80*
ogee. See double-ogee-shaped teacup and saucer
Old Crown Derby China Works, The. See under Derby factory, Derbyshire
'Old India' pattern, Grainger, Lee & Co. factory, *84*
'Old Japan Fan' pattern, Worcester factory, *67*
'Old Japan Lady' pattern, Chelsea factory, *39*
'Old Japan' pattern: Derby factory, *49*; Minton factory, 95, *97*, *97*
'Old Japan Star' pattern, Worcester factory, *67*
'Old Mosaick Japan' pattern, Worcester factory, 8, *68*
"Old Paris basket," 21n22
'Old Worcester Parrot' pattern, Worcester factory, *66*
Ole Olsen Collection, 24n67
"Olim truncus eram ficulnus inutile lignum" (Ryland), *57*, 57
Olsen, Ole, 131; collection of, 24n67
O'Neale, Jefferyes Hamett, 11, 40, 41, 73, *73*, *77*
'Opaque China' pattern, 115
Orchard Street Theatre Company, 50
Orders of the Garter and the Thistle, 78
Oriental: 'Bute' shape teacup and saucer printed in Oriental shrubbery, *94*; dates for Orient depicted on British earthenware, 115; flowering plants, *32*, *33*; ironstone oval dish painted in Imari style with Oriental flowers, *118*; plate painted with Oriental-type floral decoration and rocaillerie, *106*, *107*; stone China soup plate with Oriental flowers, *119*
Oriental Scenery (Daniell and Daniell), 115
Ornamental Design Books (Minton factory), 107
Oude Loosdrecht factory, 46
Oudry, J.B., 73
ovals: basket, *85*; dessert dishes, *76*, *95*, *82*; dishes, *9*, *33*; ironstone dish, *118*; leaf-molded stand, *85*; medallions, *117*; platters, *39*, *40*, *102*, *80*, *108*; sugar bowl and cover, *97*; teapot and cover, *81*, *90*
ovoid, tea canister, *123*
'Oxford Embossed' oval dessert dish, Minton factory, *95*

Panama Canal, 2
"Panier Misterieux, Le" (Boucher), *54*, 54
panther, 86, *86*
Paradise Lost (Milton), *54*, 55
parian: bust of Shakespeare, *103*; parianware jug, *98*
Parke-Bernet Galleries, Inc., 5, 6, *106*; catalogues, 4; with J.P. Morgan and property sale, 97; with Marcel H. Stieglitz Collection, 11, 24n66; purchases from, 22n28, 22n31
Park Lane, 78
parrots, *66*, 108
'Partridge' pattern, dishes, *48*, 49
pastille burner, Derby factory, *50*
'Pastoral Group by a Fountain,' Derby factory, 54
'Patent Ironstone' pattern, C.J. Mason, 115
patents, 87
Patterson, Malcolm R., 27n124
peach-shaped dish, *39*
peacocks, *81*, *102*
pearlware: Chinoiserie jug, *113*; English earthenware mug, *112*; Glamorgan Pottery factory, *28–29*; milk jug enameled with flowers, *120*; pearl-glazed earthenware hexagonal jug, *116*;

pearl-glazed earthenware plates, *115*; pearl-glazed earthenware teabowl and saucer, *116*; reticulated small plates, *120*; Staffordshire figures, 22n28
pear-shaped jugs, *65*, *66*
'Penciled' pattern, Worcester factory, *63*
Pennington, James, 78
Pennington, James, factory, 134
Pennington, John (son), 78–79
Pennington, John, factory, 46, 134
Pennington, Robert (son), 79
Pennington, Seth, factory, 134
perfume burners, 21n22
Perston Bell, J. & M., Ltd. factory, Glasgow, 133; cabinet cup, *111*
Peru, 7, 33
Pesne, Antoine, 64, *65*
Peterinck, François-Joseph, 43
Petiver, James, 33
Petrovich, Pavel (grand duke), service made for, *130*
Pflueger, Edward, 24n68
Pflueger, Kiyi, 24n68
Phillips, London, 88
phoenix, *39*, *125*
photographs, documentary, xi
pickles: pickle dish, Plymouth factory, South Devon, 86, *87*; pickle stand, Derby factory, *45*
Pictures in the Garrick Club (Ashton), 35
'Picturesque Movement,' 89
Pillement, Jean-Baptiste, 65
pine-cone-molded: caudle cup, cover, and stand, *45*; cups and saucers, 34, *35*, *42*, *43*
pink lustre. See lustre
pink-scale-bordered: dessert dish, *74*; waste bowl, *74*, 75
Pinxton Porcelain Works factory, 49, 99, 134
pistol-shaped flatware handle, *63*
pitchers, 21n19, 21n22
plagiarism, with designs, 114
Planché, Andrew, 50, *50*, 51
Planché, Catherine (wife), 50
plants: acanthus-molded saucer, *40*, *41*; teacup and saucer printed in Oriental shrubbery, *94*; scolopendrium-molded cinquefoil beaker and saucer, *38*, *39*. See also berried laurel swags, mugs painted with; botanical decoration; cabbage leaf; cauliflower-molded teapot and cover; flowers; fruits; gardens; grapevines, on dish; leaves; seaweed; shamrocks; vegetable decoration, plates; vines
plaster, English pottery, *119*
plates: biblical, *122*; Bow factory, 6, *31*, *32*, *32*, *33*; Chamberlain's Worcester factory, *81*, *82*, *83*; Chelsea-Derby factory, *44*; Chelsea factory, 11, 12, *13*, *16*, *17*, *33*, *39*, *40*, *41*, *42*; Chinese export, 8, *9*, *122*, *124*; Coalport factory, *92*; Davenport factory, earthenware, *115*; Derby factory, *47*, *48*, *48*, *49*, *49*; Don Pottery factory, *116*; English 'Famille-Rose' armorial octagonal, *104*; Flight, Barr and Barr Worcester factory, *80*; Glamorgan Pottery factory, *28–29*, *120*; 'Gold Star Border and Spangles Dessert Service,' *89*; Grainger, Lee & Co. Worcester factory, *84*; H. & R. Daniel factory, *100*; John Rogers & Son factory, *115*; Longton Hall Works factory, *59*; Ludwigsburg factory, 22n39; Meissen porcelain factory, 22n33; Minton factory, *95*, *96*, *97*, *97*; Nantgarw China Works factory, 22n39, *109*, 110, *110*, 111; for Near Eastern market, *124*; New Hall factory, *91*; with Oriental-type floral decoration and rocaillerie, *106*, *107*; pudding, *119*; reticulated, with swan crest, *123*; Richard Champion's factory, *87*; Royal Copenhagen factory, *130*; St. Petersburg factory, *130*; Samson factory, *132*; Samuel & John Rathbone factory, *103*; soup, 11, 12, *13*, *39*, *119*, *123*, *130*; Spode factory, *98*; Strasbourg factory, *128*, *129*; Swansea factory, *109*; tin-glazed earthenware, *111*, *112*; Wedgwood Bone China factory, *99*; Worcester factory, *xviii*, *xix*, 8, 11, *67*, *68*, *71*, *72*, *73*, *74*,

75, 77, 78. *See also* comports; dessert plates; dishes; platters; scalloped plates
platters: Chelsea factory, *39*, *40*; in 'Double Peacock' pattern, *102*; Flight, Barr and Barr Worcester factory, *80*; Swansea factory, *108*
'pleated' pattern: Plymouth factory, 86, *87*; Worcester factory, *66*
'pluck and dust' technique, 94, *94*
Plymouth factory, South Devon, 134; Frye and, 35; pickle dish, 86, *87*; sauceboats, 86, *87*
"Poet's Corner," 55
Pollard, William, 105, *109*, 110
porcelain, xi, xii, *4*. *See also* Austrian porcelain; Continental porcelain; English porcelain; French porcelain; German porcelain; Höchst porcelain; Italian porcelain; Limoges porcelain; Samson porcelain; soft paste porcelain; Welsh porcelain
Porcelain and Fine China Companies, Ltd., The, 134
Portmeirion Group, PLC, 52, 134
potpourri vases: Coalport factory, *4*, *5*, *93*; Staffordshire, *105*, *106*; flower-encrusted rococo 'frill,' *46*
pottery. *See* English pottery; Glamorgan Pottery factory; Welsh pottery
Pottery and Porcelain of Derbyshire, The (Wallis and Bemrose), 44
powdered-blue: plates, *32*, *33*; powdered-blue-ground coffee cup and saucer, *71*
Practical Book of Chinaware, The (Eberlein and Ramsdell), 127
Preller, Patricia, 91
Premier Livre de Groupes d'Enfans, 46, *46*
"Price List of Groups and Single Figures Enamelled and Gilt, and in Biscuit" (Haslem), 52
priest reading his breviary figure, Bow factory, *36*
prints: cake dish, *102*; on Chinoiserie plate, *32*; coffee cup and saucer, *85*; Minton factory bat prints, 95, *95*; plate with sepia *camaïeu* flowers, *98*; 'pluck and dust' technique, 94; tea ware, *90*. *See also* bat prints; transfer-prints
Priore, Alicia, 38
Pritchard, Hannah, 35n2
Pronk, Cornelis, 129
prunus: coffee cup painted with insects above rockwork and, *62*; prunus-molded plates, *31*; prunus-molded teabowls, *31*; saucer painted with prunus tree, *48*, *49*; small bowl painted with, *125*
pudding plates, G.L. Ashworth & Bros. factory, *119*
puissance, symbols of, *52*
Pulver, Martin, 91
purchase dates, xi, 4
Putto soldier figure, *126*
puzzle jugs, *112*, *113*

'Quail' pattern, 8, *9*, 23n47
quatrefoil: chestnut basket, *76*; oval platter, *40*; sauce tureen, cover, and stand, *81*
queen. *See* 'Rich Queen's' pattern, Worcester factory
'Queen Charlotte' pattern, Worcester factory, *68*, *69*
Questers, The, 26n107
Quin, James, 22n31, 58, *58*

rabbit tureen, 24n77
Rackham, Bernard, 71
Ramsdell, Roger Wearne, 127
Randall, John (nephew), 106
Randall, Thomas Martin, 106, 110, 111
'Ranelagh Dancers' figures: Derby factory, *51*, *52*, *98*; Spode factory, *98*, *99*
'Ranelagh Figures, The,' 98
'Ranelagh Masqueraders' figures, Chelsea factory, 51–52
Ranson, Robert, 43
Rape of Proserpina, The. See Ratto di Proserpina, Il

Rathbone, Samuel & John, factory, *103*, 134
Ratto di Proserpina, Il (The Rape of Proserpina), 83
"Recollections of Mrs. Warda Stevens Stout" (Stout), 1, 2
recorder, *126*
records. *See* information; invoices
rectangular pearlware teapot and cover, *120*
Recueil de Cent Estampes Représentant Différentes Nations du Levant (Ferriol), 70
red. *See* iron-red
red anchor mark, 107
'Red Bull' pattern, Worcester factory, 22n34, 65, *65*
'Redgrave'-style 'Doll's House' pattern, Lowestoft factory, *62*
'Red Ribbon' pattern, New Hall factory, 90
"Redstart candlesticks," 53
Redstone, David, 33, 35, 104
'Reeded Teaware Centre' pattern, Worcester factory, *63*
Reformed Church, 33
Reid, William, & Co. factory, 134
Reilly, Robin, 99
Reinicke, Peter, 43
repairer of components of pieces (*Bossierer*), 127
Restell (buyer), 79
'Resurrection, The,' on Chinese export plate, *122*
"Resurrection, The" (Luyken), *122*
reticulated: circular comport, *93*; plates, *120*, *123*; teapot and cover, *118*, *132*;
Reynolds, Joshua. *See* 'Sir Joshua Reynolds' pattern, Worcester factory
Rhead, Frederick Alfred, 117
Rhead, Frederick Hurten (son), 117
Rhead, G. Woolliscroft (brother), 117
rhinoceros horn libation cup, *121*
Rhode Island School of Design Museum, 24n66
Riccoboni, Luigi, 43, *43*, 52, *52*
rice bowls, and cover, *122*, *123*, *124*, *125*
Richard III (Shakespeare), 57, *57*
Richardson's Glass Works, 86
'Rich Queen's' pattern, Worcester factory, *67*
Ridgway, Job, & Sons factory: John and William Ridgway, 134; John Ridgway & Co. factory, *103*, 134
Ridgway, John, & Co. factory, 134; dessert plates, *103*
Rietschel, Ernst Friedrich August, 86, 86n1
Riley, Noël, 114
rims: crested oval small platter with C-scroll-molded, *108*; plate painted with floral spray within bird-molded, *91*
rivers, 106, 106n7; Delft plates with river views, *111*, *112*
Roberts, Gaye Blake, 89
Roberts, Letitia, 22n33, 23n44
Robins, Richard, 106, 110, 111
Robinson & Leadbeater, Ltd. factory, 134; Parian porcelain bust of Shakespeare, *103*
rocaillerie: ewer, *131*; plates, *42*, *106*, *107*; sugar caster, *126*
Rockingham factory (Brameld & Co.), 134; basket, 21n22; jug, 22n31, 107; spill vase, *103*
'Rockingham-glazed' red earthenware puzzle jug, *113*
rockwork, painted, *32*, *33*, *62*
rococo style: sauceboat, 86, *87*; teacup, coffee cup, and saucer, *93*; wall brackets, 34; vases, *viii*, 15, *45*, *46*, *60*, *61*
Rogers, John & Son, factory, *115*
Rollins College, 4
roosters. *See under* birds
Rose, John, 49
Rose, John, & Co. *See under* Coalport factory, Shropshire
Rose, Thomas. *See under* Coalport factory, Shropshire
roses. *See under* flowers
roundels: 'Kremlin Service' plate with Imperial Russian state coat of arms, *130*; lustre jug with clock face and roundel of Chinese figure in

gardens, *114*; plate with floral roundel, *48*, *49*; vase and cover with topographical landscape, *129*
Rovensky, Mrs. John E., 24n77
Royal Academy, 51, 88
Royal Academy of Arts, 83
royal-blue-ground. *See under* blue-ground
Royal Company, 21n22
Royal Copenhagen factory: figures, *130*, *131*; plate, *130*
Royal Copenhagen Manufactory, 130
Royal Crown Derby Co., Ltd. *See* Derby factory, Derbyshire
Royal Doulton, PLC, 134
Royal Doulton Tableware, Ltd., 133
'Royal Lily' pattern, *78*, *89*
Royal Scottish Academy, 21n25
Royal Worcester. *See under* Worcester factory, Worcestershire
Royal Worcester Spode, Ltd., 134
Russell, Carroll J., 26n101
Ryland, William Wynne, 56, *56*, 57, *57*
Rysbrack, John Michael, 55

Sack, Michael, 115
sailboat, sauceboat painted with, *63*
sailors: sailor figure, Bow factory, 12, 35, *36*; sailor's lass figure, *36*
Saint-Cloud factory, 38; flatware handle, *63*
St. James. *See* Gouyn, Charles, factory
St. John, Frederick, 3rd Viscount St. John and Viscount Bolingbroke, 46
St. Petersburg factory: plate, *130*; soup plate, *130*
Salem Democrat (newspaper), 1
salt: salt cellar, Ansbach factory, 25n90; white salt-glazed stoneware sauceboat, *117*
Samson, Edmé, 57, 58
Samson factory: Chinese 'Imari'-style ewer and basin, *131*; teapot and cover, *132*; Worcester-style plate, *132*
Samson porcelain, 21n19, 26n103
Sandby, Paul, 89, *89*
Sandon, Henry, 26n109, 35, 79, 84
Sandon, John (son), 68, 84
Sansom, Mrs. W.W., 26n101
Sargent, William, 122
Satires (Horace), 57
sauceboats: Bow factory, *32*; Meissen porcelain factory, *15*, *125*; Plymouth factory, South Devon, 86, *87*; role of, 66; Staffordshire stonewares, *117*; stands, 41; West Pans factory, *60*; Worcester factory, 11, *15*, *62*, *63*, *66*, *71*
saucer dishes: fluted, *77*; Minton factory, *i*, *94*; with 'Royal Lily' pattern, *89*
saucers: Berlin cabinet, 21n22; Bow factory, *34*, *35*; Chamberlain's Worcester factory, *82*; Chantilly factory, *9*, 23n47; Chelsea-Derby factory, *44*; Chelsea factory, 6, 38, *39*, *40*, *41*, *42*, *43*; Chinese export, *122*, *123*; Coalport factory, *93*; Copeland & Garrett factory child's toy teacup and, *98*; Cozzi factory, *127*; Davenport factory, 16; Derby factory, *46*, *47*, *47*, *48*, *49*; Doccia factory, *126*, *127*, *127*; English faceted coffee can and, *104*; Flight, Barr and Barr Worcester factory, *80*; Grainger, Lee & Co. Worcester factory, *85*; Grainger's Worcester factory, *84*; H. & R. Daniel factory, *100*; Ilmenau factory, 25n90; Liverpool factory, *61*; Longton Hall Works factory, 23n47; Loosdrecht factory, *129*; Lowestoft factory, *62*; Marcolini Meissen factory, 21n22, 22n39; Meissen porcelain factory, 10, 22n39, *125*, *126*; Miles Mason factory, *103*; Minton factory, *94*, *95*, *96*; New Hall factory, *90*, *91*; Le Nove factory, 22n28, *128*; Richard Champion's factory, *87*, 88; Samuel Alcock & Co. factory, *101*; Swansea factory, *108*, *109*; with teacup painted with Swansea-type roses, *107*; Wedgwood Bone China factory, *99*; West Pans factory, *9*; William Adams & Sons factory, *116*; Worcester factory, *9*, 13, 22n34, 23n47, *63*, *64*, *65*, *66*, *67*, *68*, *69*, *69*, *71*, *74*, *75*, *76*, *77*

sauce tureen. *See* tureens
Savage, George, 99
Sayer, Robert, 40, 58, 64, 65, 73, *73*
scalloped plates, 40, 42, 47, 48
'Scarlet Japan' pattern, Worcester factory, 22n28, *69*
Scheemakers, Peter, 55
Schloss Jägerhof, 23n63
Schloss Lustheim, 23n63
Schneider, Ernst, 23n63
Scholten, Constance, 129
Schreiber, Charles, 54
Schreiber, Lady Charlotte, 50, 51n3
Schrezheim factory, 128
scientific techniques, xiii
scolopendrium-molded cinquefoil beaker and saucer, 38, *39*
Scotin, Gerard Jean-Baptiste, II, 45, *45*
Scott, Cleo (wife), 6, 9, 12, 13, 25n83
Scott, George Ryland, 6, 12, 13, *14*, 23n51, 25n83; on The Antiquarians of Memphis, 23n52; collection of, 22n29; correspondence, 9, 24n68
Scott, Sir Joseph, 81–82
Scott, Margaret, 81
Scottish porcelain, 60, 111. *See also* Perston Bell, J. & M., Ltd. factory, Glasgow; West Pans factory, near Musselburgh, Scotland
scrolls: 'Chinese Bridge on a Scroll' pattern, Wedgwood Bone China factory, *99*; coffee cup and saucer with floral garlands and gilt, *87*; crested oval small platter with C-scroll-molded rim, *108*; 'Earl Manvers' pattern of hops, swags and s-scrolls, *76*; oblong center dish with gilt scroll and dot decoration, *101*; scroll-molded wall pocket, *45*
seasons. *See* 'Four Seasons, The' set; 'Summer' figure; 'Winter' figure
Seattle Ceramic Society, 22n32
"Seattle Scheme," 22n32
'seaux à liqueurs' (small wine bottle coolers), Nyon factory, 21n22, *129*
seaweed: inkstand with cover as lotus blossom and gilt seaweed-patterned dish, *107*; 'Seaweed' decoration, 80; six-shell sweetmeat or pickle stand encrusted with, *45*
'Second Bell Shape,' H. & R. Daniel factory, *100*
'Second Gadroon Shape' pattern, H. & R. Daniel factory, *100*
"Serene Beauty, Elegance In the Meissen Exhibit" (Hindman), 26n95
serpents or snakes, 62, *105*, 106
'Sèvres'-style, 102; blue-ground vase, *4*; plate painted in London with 'Sèvres'-style flower sprays and gilt-hatched blue lines, *110*; plate painted with 'French Blue' floral garlands, *83*; Staffordshire comport with 'Sèvres'-style floral decoration, *106*; *tasse à glace* shape, *92*
shagreen border, on teacup and saucer, *76*
Shakespeare, William, 35, 35n2, 55, 57, *57*, 58, *58*, *103*
shamrocks, *116*
shapes: baluster-form mug, 64, *65*; barrel-shaped teapot and cover, *64*; double-ogee-shaped teacup and saucer, *88*; leaf-shaped dish, *60*; leaf-shaped finger bowl and stand, *59*, 60; peach-shaped dish, *39*; pear-shaped jugs, *65*, 66; pistol-shaped flatware handle, *63*; 'Second Bell Shape' teacup, coffee cup, and saucer, *100*; 'Sèvres'-style *tasse à glace* shape, *92*; shaped oval basket, *85*; strawberry-molded plate, *59*; trumpet-shaped spill vase painted with floral sprigs, *103*. *See also* circular; cylindrical; decagonal; fluted; hexagonal; kidney shapes; lobed; 'London' shape; lozenge-shape; oblong; octagonal; ovals; scalloped plates; silver; spherical; squares
Sharpe, Elisabeth, 16
Sharpe, Matthew, 16
Sheafer, Emma, 24n68
Sheafer, Leslie, 24n68
sheep, *51*
Sheffield, Mrs., 34

shells: shell-shaped dishes, ii, *48*, 49, *84*; earthenware jug with flowers in 'Nautilus' pattern, *120*; shell-form basin, *131*; shell-molded wall pocket, *45*; six-shell stand, *45*
shepherds: 'Dresden Shepherds,' 22n31, *55*; shepherd bagpiper and his dog, 51, *51*
shields, *123*
Sigmund J. Katz Collection, 23n57
silkworms, 33
silver: English silver resist lustre jug reserved with birds and flowers, *113*; flatware handle mounted with silver collar, *63*; silver-shape dish, *40*, 41; silver-shape saucebot, 62, *63*, 86, *87*
Simmons, Erwin E., 22n34; correspondence of, 23n59
Sims, John, 49, 110–111
'Sinking Boat Fisherman' pattern, Worcester factory, 63, *63*
'Sir Joshua Reynolds' pattern, Worcester factory: plate, *67*; teacup and saucer, *67*
sky-blue-ground oval basket, *85*
slip molds, plaster, *119*
Sloane, Hans (Sir), 34, 41, 42
Sluyter, P., *34*
small wine bottle coolers. *See* 'seaux à liqueurs'
smear-glazed: white biscuit group of 'Two Bacchantes Adorning [a Bust of] *Pan*,' *57*; white stoneware jug, *119*
'Smith's Blue' pattern: coffee cup and saucer, *48*; jug, *48*
Smollett, Tobias George, 35
'Snake in a Basket' pattern, Worcester factory, 62
Snowden, Grace M., 24n75
'Snowman Family' pattern, Longton Hall Works factory, 12, 24n70, 58, *59*
Soar, Thomas, 44
Society for the Encouragement of the Arts, 73
Society of Apothecaries, 41
soft paste porcelain, 6, 8, 50, 130
Sotheby's, 13, 24n77, 102, 128
soup plates. *See* plates
South America, 7, 33
South Wales pottery, pearl-glazed earthenware jug, *120*
Spängler, Jean-Jacques, 56
spear. *See* costumed man holding spear
Spero, Simon, 37, 40, 68
spherical: teapot and cover, *61*, *64*, *104*
spill vases, *101*, *103*
spirally writhen octofoil saucer, *40*, 41
Spode, Josiah, 98
Spode, Ltd., 134
Spode factory, Stoke-on-Trent, Staffordshire: accident at, 52; Copeland & Garrett, *98*, 134; figures, *98*, *99*; Josiah Spode I and II, 134; Josiah Spode II and William Taylor Copeland, 134; 'New Stone' hot water dish, *118*; plate, *98*; 'pluck and dust' technique of printing, 94; sugar bowl and cover, *97*; teacup, *97*; W.T. Copeland, 134; W.T. Copeland & Sons, 134; W.T. Copeland & Sons, Ltd., 134
spouts: English earthenware puzzle jug with begging dog spout, 113, *113*; jug with bearded mask spout and reserved floral cartouches, *72*
Sprimont, Nicholas, 37–38, 40, 41, 43, 47n1
'Spring' figure, French porcelain Derby-style allegorical, *132*
squares: dessert dish, *76*; earthenware dish painted with floral clusters, *116*; stoneware square teapot and reticulated cover with lion knop, *118*
squirrels: on tea canister, *123*; vase modeled as, *107*
Staffordshire earthenware: jugs, *112*, *113*, *114*, *116*; pearlware figures, *112*, 113; Quin figure, 58; in "Stout Notebooks," 113; teapot and cover, *112*
Staffordshire porcelain: comport with 'Sèvres'-style floral decoration, *106*; figures, 22n28; 'London' shape milk jug, *105*; vases *105*, 106, *107*

Staffordshire Pots and Potters (Rhead and Rhead), 117
Staffordshire stonewares: milk jug with three paw feet, *117*; sauceboat, *117*
Stag Looking into the Water, The, 73, *73*
stands: cabinet cup, *82*; Chamberlain's Worcester factory sauce tureen, cover, and, *81*; Chelsea-Derby factory caudle cup, cover, and, *45*; Coalport factory teapot, cover, and, *92*; finger bowl, *15*; Limoges porcelain milk jug and, *4*; sauceboat, 41; sauce tureen, covers, and, *78*, *79*; sweetmeat or pickle, *45*; underglaze blue leaf-molded oval, *60*; Worcester factory, *76*; Worcester factory basket, pierced cover, and pierced, *76*; Worcester factory butter tub, cover, and, *72*; Worcester factory teapot stand, 68. *See also* feet
Stanhope, Philip Dormer (earl of Chesterfield), 38–39
statues, 70. *See also* Grund statues
statuettes, 'Derby,' *4*
Stephan, Pierre, 54, *54*, 56, *56*, 57, *132*
Stephens, Amy Metford (wife), 88
Stephens, Ann Dawe (wife), 88
Stephens, Peter, 88
Stephens, William, 87
Stern, Henry, 10, 22n28, 24n70
Stevens, Ray Caspar (brother), 1–2
Stevens, Warder W. (father), 1, 2, 21n6
Stevens Memorial Museum, 26n100
Stieglitz, Marcel H., collection of, 11, 24n66
Stoner & Evans, 75
stonewares: English pottery and various, 117–119; stone china wares, 115; Yixing red stoneware, 121, *121*
Stoopendaal, D., *34*
Stout, Alice Adeline. *See* Edwards, Alice S.
Stout, Charles Banks (1881–1965) (husband), 2–3, 5, 8, 12; health of, 14, 15, 27n114; legacy, 19; travel, 4, *7*
Stout, John T. (father-in-law), 2
Stout, John T. (nephew), 27n116
Stout, Warda Stevens: with bequests, xii; with chickens, 21n17; collecting years, 4–7; correspondence, 6–7, 8, 10, 11, 14, 16, 18–19, 22n34, 22n35, 22n40, 23n47, 23n49, 23n51, 23n56, 23n57, 24n69, 24n74, 24n77, 25n78, 25n81, 25n85, 26n99, 27n116, 27n117; death of, xii, 20; early years, 1–4; family life, xiii, 1–2, *19*; gardens and, 21n14, 21n15; influences on, 6–13; legacy, xi–xiii, 16, 20; shopping strategy, xiii; travel and, 4, *7*; at Wellesley College, 2, 21n12. *See also* Warda Stevens Stout Collection
Stout Archives. *See* Stout-Hooker Archives
Stout-Hooker Archives, 13; contents of, xi, 15
"Stout Notebooks," 107, 131; Chinoiserie Decor, 25n80; discrepancies in, xi; on Doccia teacup and saucer, 127; historic merit, xi; purchases, 25n91; Staffordshire earthenware in, 113; on 'Zwiebelmuster' pattern, 126
'strap fluting,' 66
Strasbourg factory, plates, 128, *129*
strawberry-molded plate, *59*
"study pieces," 15
sugar bowls, *47*; Caughley factory cover and, *89*; George Frederick Bowers & Co. factory cover and, *101*; Limoges porcelain, *4*; Meissen porcelain factory, 21n2; Spode factory cover and, *97*; Worcester factory cover and, *67*
sugar caster, Meissen porcelain factory, *126*
Sulkowski Service, Meissen porcelain factory, 15, 25n92, 26n96
'Summer' figure: French porcelain Derby-style allegorical, *132*; Longton Hall Works factory, 12, 24n70, 58, *59*; Staffordshire pearlware, *112*, 113
Suriname, 33, *34*
swan crest, *123*
Swansea factory, Swansea, South Wales, 105, 106, 110, 134; English teacup and saucer painted with Swansea-type roses, *107*; history of, 108;

INDEX 161

plate, *109*; platter, *108*; teacup, coffee cup, and saucer, *108*; teacup and saucer, *109*
Swarthmore College, 3
sweetmeats: figure of lady, Chelsea factory, *44*; stand, Derby factory, *45*
Syz, Hans, 24n68

Taggart, Ross, 131
Taiping Rebellion, 124
Tait, Hugh, 50
Takey's, 23n47
'Tall Chelsea Ewer' pattern, Worcester factory, *66*
tan-ground, plate with sepia *camaïeu* flowers, *98*
Tapp, William H., 40, 45
'Tasker's Chinese Bridge' pattern, Chamberlain's Worcester factory, *81*
tasse à glace shape, 'Sèvres'-style, *92*
tax deductions, 12, 24n74
teabowls: Bow factory, *31*, *34*; breakfast teabowl and saucer, *64*; Caughley factory, *88*, *89*; Chantilly factory, *38*; Chelsea-Derby factory, *44*; Chinese export, *122*, *123*; Cozzi factory, *127*; Derby factory, *46*, *47*; Liverpool factory, *61*; Loosdrecht factory, *129*; Lowestoft factory, *62*; New Hall factory, *90*; William Adams & Sons factory, *116*; Worcester factory, 13, 22n34, *63*, *64*, *65*, *68*, *69*, *69*, *75*
tea canisters: Chinese export, 16; domestic scene within squirrels on vines, *123*; Fulda factory, 25n90; Limbach factory, 25n90
teacups: Bow factory, *34*, *35*; Chamberlain's Worcester factory, *82*; Coalport factory, *92*, *93*; Copeland & Garrett factory child's toy saucer and, *98*; Doccia factory, *126*, *127*; Flight, Barr and Barr Worcester factory, *80*; "French tulip design," *109*; Grainger's Worcester factory, *84*; H. & R. Daniel factory, *100*; Liverpool factory, *61*; Longton Hall Works factory, 23n47; Miles Mason factory, *103*; Minton factory, *94*, *95*, *96*; New Hall factory, *91*; Richard Champion's factory, *88*; Sampson Bridgwood & Son factory, *101*; Samuel Alcock & Co. factory, *101*; with saucer painted with Swansea-type roses, *107*; Spode factory, *97*; Swansea factory, *108*, *109*; teacup foot, Flight, Barr and Barr Worcester factory, *80*; Wedgwood Bone China factory, *99*; West Pans factory, *9*; Worcester factory, *66*, *67*, *68*, *76*
'Tea Party, The, No. 2' pattern, Worcester factory, *64*, *65*
teapots: Chamberlain's Worcester factory, *81*; Charles Meigh factory drab stoneware cover and, *119*; Coalport factory cover, stand, and, *92*; Derbyshire squat spherical cover and, *104*; earthenware, *18*, *112*, *116*, *117*; Glamorgan Pottery factory pearlware cover and, *120*; gold-ground, 26n96; John and William Turner factory stoneware covers and, *118*; John Yates factory stoneware cover and, *118*; Limoges porcelain, *4*; Liverpool factory cover and, *61*; Richard Champion's factory cover and, *88*; Samson factory, *132*; Staffordshire earthenware cover and, *116*; Wedgwood/Whieldon-style earthenware cover and, *116*, *117*; Worcester factory, 22n28, *64*, *66*, *68*; Worcester factory cover and, *64*, *66*, *68*, *69*; Worcester factory teapot stand, *68*
tea service: Höchst porcelain, 25n84; Liverpool factory part, *61*
tea wares: British earthenware, *114*; New Hall factory, *90*
Tebo (Mr.), 70
Teniers, David the Younger, 74
Terwilliger, Carola, 24n68
theatrical figure. *See* 'Broom-Girl, The,' theatrical figure
thistles: on earthenware plate, *16*; Orders of the Garter and the Thistle, *78*; 'Thistle Pattern,' Don Pottery factory, *116*
Thomas, Francis, 38
Thomas Grainger & Co., *84*, 134

Thomas Sidney Antiques, 21n22
Three Cupids of which one holds an arrow. *See* *Trois Amours dont un tient une flèche*
Thuringian porcelain, *127*
tigers, 11, 22n33, *39*, *99*
Tilley, Frank, 24n77
Tilley, Kathleen, 24n77
Tilley & Co., 12
tin-glazed earthenware (Delftware): English Delft plate, *111*; London Delft plate, *111*, *112*
Tintern Abbey, Monmouthshire, 106, 106n7
Tintern Abbey from across the Wye (Dayes), 106
'Tom Bowling,' 35, *36*
topographical: coffee cup and saucer, *48*; royal-blue-ground oblong dessert dish, *85*; sky-blue-ground shaped oval basket, *85*; vase and cover with topographical landscape roundel, *129*
Toppin, Aubrey J., 52n2, 64
Torré, Andreina, 16, 26n98, 26n99
Toullous, Charles, 35
Toulouse, John, 35, 70, *70*, 87
Tournai factory, dish, *128*, *129*
Towner, Donald, 12
toys: teabowl enameled with flower, *34*; teacup and saucer, *98*
transfer-prints: of baluster-form mug in black with 'King of Prussia,' 'Fame,' and military trophies, *64*, *65*; of breakfast bowl in black with 'The Draw Well' and two other architectural vignettes, *65*; of earthenware and enamel teapot with 'The XII Houses of Heaven' and 'The Astrologer,' *18*; on earthenware mug and enameled with Chinoiserie decoration, *112*; on enameled documentary cylindrical teapot and cover, *112*; invention of, 64; of 'New Stone' hot water dish, *118*; on pearl-glazed earthenware jug with shells and flowers, *120*; on pearl-glazed earthenware plate and enameled, *115*; on pearl-glazed earthenware plate in underglaze blue, *115*; on pearlware Chinoiserie jug, *113*; on pearlware teapot and cover in underglaze blue, *120*; of pear-shaped mask jug in black with 'L'Amour,' and 'The Tea Party, No. 2,' *64*, *65*; of plate in underglaze blue with 'Broseley' pattern, *103*; on plate with Oriental-type floral decoration and rocaillerie, *106*, *107*; on saucer in black and painted with 'Chinese Family' pattern, *66*; on stone China leaf-shaped small dishes in underglaze blue, *118*; of teabowl in black and painted with 'Les Garçons Chinois,' *65*, *65*; of teabowl and saucer in black and painted with 'Red Bull' pattern, *65*, *65*; of teabowl and saucer in black with 'The Milkmaids,' *65*, *65*; of teabowl and saucer in underglaze blue with 'Chinese Lady and Bird in a Cartouche' pattern, *61*; of teabowl in underglaze blue with 'Mansfield' pattern, *88*, *89*; of teapot and cover in underglaze blue with 'Fisherman and Cormorant' pattern, *64*, *64*
Transferware Collectors Club, 115
Treasure House, 24n67
Treaty of Nanking, 95
trees, *57*, *57*; bird on tree peony soup plate, *39*; 'Cotton Tree' specimen, *xii*, 33, *34*; *Norway Spruce*, *41*; prunus, *31*, *48*, *49*, *62*, *125*; *Two Goats at the Foot of a Tree* woodcut, 38. *See also* arbor figure of seated musician playing bagpipe
trellis, *92*, *93*
'Trembly Rose Painter,' 59
triangle mark, 55
triple-wave mark, 130
tripod vase and cover, *81*
Trois Amours dont un tient une flèche (Three Cupids of which one holds an arrow) (Aveline), *46*, *46*
Truchy, Louis, 58, *58*
trumpet-shaped, spill vase painted with floral sprigs, *103*
Trustees of the Dixon. *See under* Dixon Gallery and Gardens

"*Turc Amoureux, Le*" (Lancret), 70
tureens: Chelsea factory, 24n77; Meissen porcelain factory, 15, 25n92; sauce tureen, Chamberlain's Worcester factory, *81*; sauce tureen, Worcester factory, *78*, *79*; Volkstedt factory, 25n90
Turk, leaning on scimitar, *70*
Turner, John and William, factory, stoneware teapot and cover, *118*
Turner, Joseph Mallord William, 106
turquoise: Coalbrookdale factory turquoise-ground vase, *94*; comport from turquoise-bordered dessert service, *85*; turquoise-ground cabinet cup, *111*; turquoise-ground two-handled dish, *86*
Tvede, Claus, 130
'XII Houses of Heaven, The' pattern, *18*
XII Views in North and South Wales (Sandby), 89
XII Views in North Wales (Sandby), 89
XII Views in Wales (Sandby), 89
XII Views of South Wales (Sandby), 89
Twitchett, John, 46, 48, 49, 110
'Two Bacchantes Adorning [a Bust of] *Pan*,' *57*
Two Goats at the Foot of a Tree woodcut (Campagnola), 38
'Two Virgins Awaking Cupid' biscuit figure, *56*

ultraviolet light, 10, 23n56
underglaze blue: breakfast teabowl and saucer, *64*; candlestick, *58*; 'clobbered' cup and saucer, *77*; coffee cans and saucer, *99*; coffee cup and saucer with version of 'Zwiebelmuster' pattern, *126*; coffee cup painted in, *63*; dessert plate and painted with 'Old India' pattern, *84*; dishes, *33*, *89*; leaf-molded oval stand, *60*; mugs, *32*, *33*, *63*; pearl-glazed earthenware plate transfer-printed in, *115*; pearlware teapot and cover transfer-printed in, *120*; pickle dish, *86*, *87*; pistol-shaped flatware handle painted in, *63*; plate and painted with 'Old India' pattern, *84*; plates, *32*, *99*; plate transfer-printed in underglaze blue with 'Broseley' pattern, *103*; plate with 'Royal Lily' pattern, *78*; rococo base and cover, *45*; sauceboat, *32*, *63*, *87*; saucer dish with 'Royal Lily' pattern, *89*; stone China leaf-shaped small dishes transfer-printed in underglaze blue, *118*; sugar bowl and cover, *89*; teabowl, *88*, *89*; teabowl and saucer, *61*, *62*, *64*; teacup and saucer, *61*; teapot and cover bordered by, *64*; teapot and cover transfer-printed in, *64*
underglaze Pratt-type palette, rooster pearlware figure, *112*, *113*
'Union' design, Chamberlain's Worcester factory, *82*
University of Indiana at Bloomington, 21n6
University of Tennessee, 27n114
Untermyer, Irwin, 12, 24n68, 24n72
urn, 21n19, 38

Valfré, Patrice, 121
Vanke, Francesca, 115
Van Vleet, McKay, 26n101
vases, 38; Amstel factory, *129*; 'Chesterfield Vase,' *54*; Coalbrookdale factory, *94*; Continental porcelain 'Capo-di-Monte' campaniform, *132*; Derby factory, *45*; Derby factory cover and, *xx*, *45*, *46*; Flight, Barr and Barr factory, 21n2; Flight, Barr and Barr Worcester factory, *81*; rococo, 15; Staffordshire vase modeled as squirrel holding nut, *107*; West Pans factory, *viii*, *60*, *61*. *See also* potpourri vases; spill vases
Vauxhall factory, London, 134; candlestick, *58*
vegetable decoration, plates, *42*
Venus figure, *4*, *51*
Verheerlijkt Nederland of Kabinet van Hedendaagse Gezichten, Het (The Exalted Netherlands or a Cabinet of Present-day Views), 129
vermiculate decoration, *101*
Vetris, Auguste Armand, 83

Victoria and Albert Museum, 32, 44, 54
'Victory' allegorical figure, *126*
Vienna clock-case figure, 21n22
"View of Tintern Abbey on the River Wye" (Dayes), 106n7
Views on the River Wye (Dayes), 106
Vincennes factory, 38
vines, *33, 74, 123*
Vinovo factory, custard cup and cover, *128*
'Vintage, The' pattern of Bacchic Putti, Copeland & Garrett factory, *98*
violet ray lamp. *See* ultraviolet light
Virtuosi's Museum, The: Containing Select Views, in England, Scotland, and Ireland (Sandby), 89
Vivares, Francis, 64
VOC. *See* Dutch East India Company
Volkstedt factory: figure, 22n31, *126, 127*; tureen, 25n90
von Brüning Collection, 8, 9

Wadsworth Atheneum, 97
Waldhorn Company, 21n22
Wale, Samuel, 70
Walker, Samuel, 49
'Walk in the Garden' pattern, Worcester factory, *63*
"Walk of Triumphal Arches and the Statue of Mr. Handle [*sic*] in Vauxhall Garden, The" (Müller, J. S.), 70
Wallace Collection, 45
wall brackets, rococo style, *34*
Wallendorf factory, bowl and cover, *126, 127*
Wallis, Alfred, 44
wall pocket, Derby factory, *45*
Walpole, Horace, 50
Warda Stevens Stout Collection: collecting years, 4–7; Deed of Gift, 13–20; Pygmalion effect, 7–13
Warda Stevens Stout Gallery, 20
Ware, George W., 23n51
Wark, Constance (sister), 8, 15, 22n41, 25n93
Wark, Florence (mother), 23n43
Wark, Ralph H., 7, 13, 23n43, 23n63, 25n83; with The Antiquarians of Memphis, 23n52, 26n95; collection of, 15, 22n41, 25n93; correspondence, 8, 9, 10, 11, 14, 16, 19, 23n51, 24n68, 25n81, 27n116, 27n117; influence, 11. *See also* Constance I. and Ralph H. Wark Collection
Wark Collection, The: Early Meissen Porcelain (Gristina and Wark), 25n93
'Warren Hastings' type pattern, Chelsea factory, 40, 41
Washington County Historical Society, John Hay Center, 26n100
Wasserman, Otto M., 22n34, 23n46
waste bowl: Ansbach factory, 25n90; Chinese export porcelain armorial style, *122*; Worcester factory, *74, 75*
'Water' figure, Bow factory, *36, 37*
Waterford Wedgwood Group, 134
Watney, Bernard M., 12, 24n71, 59, 60, 71
Watteau, Antoine, 45, *45*
Weatherby, John, 32

Weber, Fritz, 8
Webster, Moses, 110
Wedgwood, Aaron, 59
Wedgwood, Josiah, 54, 70, 73, 79, 87, 99, *119*
Wedgwood Bone China factory, Etruria, Staffordshire, Porcelain Period, *98*; coffee can and saucer, *99*; plate, *99*; saucer, *99*; teacup, *99*
Wedgwood factory, 134
Wedgwood factory, earthenware: figures, *117*; Wedgwood/Whieldon-style earthenware teapots and, *116, 117*; white ware 'Leafage' dessert plate, *115*
Wedgwood factory, stonewares, medallions relief-molded with figures, *117*
Wedgwood Group, 133
Weigel, Christoph the Elder, 70
Wellesley, Arthur (Duke of Wellington), 44
Wellesley College, 2, 21n12
Wellford, John L., 26n101
Welsh porcelain, 8, 18. *See also* Nantgarw China Works factory, Mid-Glamorgan, South Wales; Swansea factory, Swansea, South Wales
Welsh pottery, 116, 120
"Western Entrance of Shere Shah's Fort, Delhi, The," 115
West Pans factory, near Musselburgh, Scotland, 134; 'Quail' pattern, 9, 23n47; sauceboat, *60*; stand, *60*; teacup and saucer, 9; vase and cover, *viii*, *60*, 61
'wet blue'-ground. *See* blue-ground
Whitby, Edward, *81*
White, Peter, 51
white feldspathic stoneware teapot and cover, *118*
white jasper oval medallions, *117*
Wilkinson, Vega, 98
Willems, Pierre-Joseph, 43, 44
Willem V (Prince of Orange and Nassau), *129*
William (Lord Cheyne), 41
William Henry (Prince), 78, 79
William IV (king of England), 79, 88
William IV (prince of Orange and Nassau), 51
Williams, John, 56
Williams, Robert, 14, 15, 16, 25n84, 25n85, 26n99
Williams, Winifred, 102
Williams, Winifred (mother), 23n47, 25n84, 25n92
Wilson, R. Thornton, 24n68
Winchester, Alice, 8, 24n68
Winifred Williams Antiques, 11, 15
Winkel & Magnussen, 24n67, *131*
Winstone, H. V. F., 130, *131*
Winter, Peter, 83
'Winter' figure: Fürstenberg factory, 21n22; Longton Hall Works factory, 12, 24n70, 58, *59*; Staffordshire pearlware, *112*, 113
Wirksworth factory, 78, 134
wisdom, 52, 53
'Witches' pattern, Derby factory, 49, 50
Wolf, Bess Millen, 21n23, 26n101
Wolf, John Quincey, 21n23, 24n75
Wolfe, James (General), 51
Wolfe, Thomas, 102
woman clasping her apron figure, 130, *131*
Wood, Aaron, *117*

Wood, Edward, 37
Wood, John, 84
woodcut, *Two Goats at the Foot of a Tree*, 38
Wood family, 113
Woodward, Henry, 51n3
Worcester factory, Worcestershire, 134; Barr, Flight and Barr Period, 134; basket, 21n2, *72, 76*; basket, pierced cover, and pierced stand, *76*; 'Bodenham Service,' 13, 25n80, *68*; breakfast bowl, *65*; breakfast teabowl and saucer, *64*; butter tub, cover, and stand, *72*; Chamberlain's Worcester factory, *81, 82, 83, 89*, 134; coffee cups, 9, 12, 23n47, *62, 63, 66, 67, 69, 71, 74, 75*; cups, *77*; dessert dish, *69, 74, 76, 77*; dishes, 11, *67, 69, 71, 74, 76*; Duke of Clarence service, 5, *78, 78, 79*; figures, *70*; First Period, 21n25, 134; flatware handle, *63*; Flight, Barr and Barr factory, 21n2, 134; Flight, Barr and Barr period, 79; Flight, Barr and Barr Worcester factory, *80, 81*; Flight and Barr Period, 134; Flight and Barr Worcester factory, 79; Flight Period, 134; Frye and, 35; Grainger's Worcester factory, *ii, 84, 85*, 105, 134; jugs, *64, 65, 72*; Kerr & Binns factory, *86*, 134; "Lowdin's Bristol," 6; milk jugs, *66, 69*; mugs, *63, 64, 65*; New China Works, 105, 134; 'Old Mosaick Japan' pattern, 8, *68*; pine cone-molded teacup and saucer after, *34, 35*; plates, *xviii, xix*, 8, 11, *67, 68, 71, 72, 73, 74, 75, 77, 78*; 'Quail' pattern, 9, 23n47; Royal Worcester, 52, 134; sauceboats, 11, *15, 62, 63, 66, 71*; saucer dish, *77*; saucers, 9, 13, 22n34, 23n47, *63, 64, 65, 66, 67, 68, 69, 71, 74, 75, 76, 77*; sauce tureen, cover, and stand, *78, 79*; sugar bowl and cover, *67*; teabowls, 13, 22n34, *63, 64, 65, 68, 69, 69, 75*; teacups, *66, 67, 68, 76*; teapot and cover, *64, 66, 68, 69*; teapots, 22n28, *64, 66, 68, 69*; teapot stand, *68*; waste bowl, *74, 75*; Worcester-style plate, *132v*
Worcester Royal Porcelain Company, 134
Wordsworth, William, 106
Worlidge, Thomas, 50, *50*
Worshipful Company of Goldsmiths, The, 50
Wroth, Warwick, 52n2
WWRD Holdings, Ltd., 134

xylophone, *126*

Yarbrough, Raymond, 35, 58
Yates, John, 44
Yates, John, factory, *118*
yellow-ground: crested dessert dishes, *81*; neo-classical vase and cover, *129*; plates, *48*, 49; sauceboat, 11, *66*
'Yellow Tiger' pattern: Chelsea factory, 11, *39*; Meissen porcelain factory, 22n33
Yixing red stoneware: dating as problematic, 121; lobed circular teapot and cover with recumbent kylin knop, *121*
Yorkshire earthenware, Quin figure, *58*
Young, Hilary, 50, 54, 70

Zoffany, Johan, 35, 35n2
'Zwiebelmuster' ('Blue Onion') pattern, Meissen porcelain factory, *126*

ELEGANT ENGLISH
*The Charlotte Stout Hooker Collection
of British Porcelain and Related Ceramics*
was produced under the auspices of the
Dixon Gallery and Gardens, Memphis
Julie N. Pierotti, Curator

PRODUCED BY WILSTED & TAYLOR
Project manager Christine Taylor
Production assistant LeRoy Wilsted
Copy editors Nancy Evans and Melody Lacina
Designer and compositor Yvonne Tsang
Indexer Robert Swanson
Printer's devils Maisie Tsang Choi,
Miles Tsang Choi, and Lillian Marie Wilsted

Elegant English was composed in Walbaum.
The book was printed and bound by
EM Printing in Bartlett, Tennessee.